THE LANGUAGE OF LITERATURE
General Editor: N. F. Blake
Professor of English Language and Linguistics
University of Sheffield

THE LANGUAGE OF LITERATURE
General Editor: N. F. Blake
Professor of English Language and Linguistics
University of Sheffield

Published titles

An Introduction to the Language of Literature	N. F. Blake
The Language of Shakespeare	N. F. Blake
The Language of Chaucer	David Burnley
The Language of Wordsworth and Coleridge	Frances Austin
The Language of Irish Literature	Loreto Todd
The Language of D. H. Lawrence	Allan Ingram
The Language of Thomas Hardy	Raymond Chapman
The Language of James Joyce	Katie Wales
The Language of Drama	David Birch
The Language of Jane Austen	Myra Stokes
The Language of George Orwell	Roger Fowler

Series Standing Order

If you would like to receive future titles in this series as they are published, you can make use of our standing order facility. To place a standing order please contact your bookseller or, in case of difficulty, write to us at the address below with your name and address and the name of the series. Please state with which title you wish to begin your standing order. (If you live outside the United Kingdom we may not have the rights for your area, in which case we will forward your order to the published concerned.)

Customer Services Department, Macmillan Distribution Ltd, Houndmills, Basingstoke, Hampshire, RG21 2XS, England.

The Language of
George Orwell

ROGER FOWLER

First published 1995 by
MACMILLAN PRESS LTD
Houndmills, Basingstoke, Hampshire RG21 2XS
and London
Companies and representatives
throughout the world

ISBN 0-333-54907-4 hardcover
ISBN 0-333-54908-2 paperback

A catalogue record for this book is available
from the British Library.

10   9   8   7   6   5   4   3   2   1
04   03   02   01   00   99   98   97   96   95

Printed in Malaysia

Contents

Preface   vii

Acknowledgements and Editions Used   ix

1 **Orwell's Life and Career**   1

2 **Preliminaries**   7
   The Styles of George Orwell   7
   Linguistic Criticism   11

3 **Orwell's Views on Language**   19
   Language and Class   20
   'That horrible plummy voice from the radio'   22
   Demotic Speech   24
   Spoken and Written Language, and Standard English   25
   'A catalogue of swindles and perversions'   28
   Language and Thought   31
   'An instrument which we shape for our own purposes'   33

4 **A Personal Voice**   35
   Linguistic Varieties   37
   Examples of the Personal Style   41
   Linguistic Markers of Orwell's Idiolect   53
   Orwell Over the Top   55

5 **Versions of Realism**   60
   The Three 'Realisms': Brief Characterisation   63
   Descriptive Realism and the Sense of 'place'   65
   Naturalism and Surrealism in *Down and Out
      in Paris and London*   70
   Naturalism in *Homage to Catalonia*   79
   Realism, Judgement and Symbolism in *The Road
      to Wigan Pier*   81

6   Voices of the Other   **87**
Heteroglossia   88
Literary Representation of Speech   90
English Dialects and Accents in the Early Fiction   93
Experiment in Polyphony: the Trafalgar Square
    Chapter in *A Clergyman's Daughter*   109

7   Further Aspects of Style   **119**
The Picturesque   119
Heteroglossia in *Burmese Days*   129

8   Point of View in Orwell's Fiction   **136**
The Mind-style of Gordon Comstock   140
Self-narration: *Coming Up for Air*   148

9   *Animal Farm*   **159**
Narrative Style in *Animal Farm*   164
Focalisation, Empathy and Distance   170
The Rhetoric of Dominance and the Perversion
    of Language   174

10   *Nineteen Eighty-Four*   **181**
Focalisation: The Hyperconscious Anti-hero   184
Memory, Dream and Hallucination   191
The Golden Country   193
Sordid Realism   195
Violence   199
Heteroglossia and the Grotesque   203
Newspeak and the Language of the Party   211

Notes   228

Bibliography   241

Index   246

Preface

When I was invited to write a study of the language of a writer of particular interest to me, I thought a lot about the choice of a possible subject, and George Orwell suddenly 'clicked'. He is a writer and a political thinker whom I have admired since my student days; he is a tremendously versatile stylist; he not only practises the arts of language, but the central theme in much of his work is language itself; and his interest in language centres on topics which have been my own preoccupations in linguistics: language as a political instrument, as an expression of or an inhibitor of thought, and as a practice which is central to all the workings of society: the media, the formation of history, literature, the ideas and the play of people.

Orwell's political and social analyses have had a profound influence on the way we think, largely thanks to the power and the memorable phrasing of his last two books, *Animal Farm* and *Nineteen Eighty-Four*. But the language in which he expressed his vision has been largely neglected. While James Joyce and Virginia Woolf, for example, are recognised as having created distinctive and influential linguistic structures for the representation of consciousness, and D. H. Lawrence is seen as having forged a powerful modern romantic style, Orwell is not seen as a stylist, but as a source of political ideas, strikingly worded. In this book I have tried to show, through detailed analysis of his language, how he evolved the distinctive 'Orwellian voice' (which some critics have mentioned, but not analysed). Beyond the personal voice, there is in fact a great diversity of stylistic technique: precise description, striking figurative expression, pastoral, naturalism, surrealism, representation of thought, powerful evocations of violence, a keen eye for the grotesque and an ear for what I have called 'voices of the other', trenchant parody of political styles; finally, quite different from these heightened modes of writing, the purest simplicity of style in the satires of *Animal Farm* and the Newspeak Appendix to *Nineteen Eighty-Four*.

Although I have not consciously attempted to write a history of Orwell's stylistic development, this book follows roughly the sequence of his writing career. I was determined to take his early

vii

fiction and non-fictional writings seriously, not least because the early books, particularly the novels, tend to get short shrift. Most of the techniques of style of his last writings are deployed in lively and effective ways early in his career. It could be argued – though I have not pressed this argument – that there is a fundamental unity to his lifetime's writings, despite their apparent diversity.

This study uses, broadly speaking, the theory and the analytic concepts of the method of 'linguistic criticism' as it has been developed over the past fifteen years or so. That is to say, I not only describe the patterns of language which form Orwell's various styles of writing, but also discuss their functions within the composition of the books and in relation to aspects of the historical context (space permits far less of this than I would have liked). Not only linguistic concepts are used, but also ideas drawn from French and Russian studies of literature and language: particularly in the areas of 'point of view' (focalisation) and 'voices of the other'. I have found the notion of 'heteroglossia', and a cluster of related ideas, originating in the work of Mikhail Bakhtin, particularly relevant to Orwell. Being conscious that 'jargon' can be off-putting to the student of literature, I have kept technical terminology to a minimum, and explained such terms as we do need as we go along.

ROGER FOWLER

Acknowledgements and Editions Used

The author and publishers wish to thank the following for permission to use copyright material:

A. M. Heath & Company Ltd on behalf of the Estate of the late Sonia Brownell Orwell and Martin Secker & Warburg, and Harcourt Brace & Company, for excerpts from George Orwell, 'Shooting an Elephant' from *Shooting an Elephant and Other Essays*, Copyright © 1950 by Sonia Brownell Orwell and renewed 1978 by Sonia Pitt-Rivers; George Orwell, 'Politics and the English Language' from *Shooting an Elephant and Other Essays*, Copyright © 1946 by Sonia Brownell Orwell and renewed 1974 by Sonia Orwell; George Orwell, *Burmese Days*, Copyright © 1934 by George Orwell and renewed 1962 by Sonia Pitt-Rivers; George Orwell, *Coming Up For Air* and George Orwell, *Down and Out in Paris and London*, Copyright © 1933 by George Orwell and renewed 1961 by Sonia Pitt-Rivers; George Orwell, *A Clergyman's Daughter* and George Orwell, *Animal Farm*, Copyright © 1946 by Harcourt Brace & Company and renewed 1974 by Sonia Orwell; George Orwell, *Nineteen Eighty-Four*, Copyright © 1949 by Harcourt Brace & Company and renewed 1977 by Sonia Brownell Orwell; George Orwell, 'Why I Write', from *Such, Such Were the Joys*, Copyright © 1953 by Sonia Brownell Orwell and renewed 1981 by Mrs George K. Perutz, Mrs Miriam Gross and Dr Michael Dickson, executors of the estate of Sonia Brownell Orwell; George Orwell, *Homage to Catalonia*, Copyright © 1952 and renewed 1980 by Sonia Brownell Orwell; George Orwell, *Keep the Aspidistra Flying*, George Orwell, *The Road to Wigan Pier*, George Orwell, *The Collected Essays, Journalism and Letters of George Orwell, Volume I: An Age Like This 1920–1940, Volume II: My Country Right or Left 1940–1943, Volume III: As I Please 1943–1945, Volume IV: In Front of Your Nose 1945–1950*, edited by Sonia Orwell and Ian Angus, Copyright © 1968 by Sonia Brownell Orwell.

Every effort has been made to trace all the copyright-holders, but if any have been inadvertently overlooked the publishers will be pleased to make the necessary arrangement at the first opportunity.

For quotations and references to Orwell's works, I have tried to use accessible editions, as follows:

Animal Farm, Penguin, 1973; *Burmese Days*, Penguin, 1967; *A Clergyman's Daughter*, Penguin, 1964; *The Collected Essays, Journalism and Letters*, ed. Sonia Orwell and Ian Angus, 4 volumes, Penguin, 1968; *Coming Up for Air*, Penguin, undated reprint of 1962 edition; *Down and Out in Paris and London*, Secker and Warburg, 1986; *Homage to Catalonia*, Penguin, 1984; *Keep the Aspidistra Flying*, Penguin, 1975; *Nineteen Eighty-Four*, Penguin, 1984; *The Road to Wigan Pier*, Penguin, 1984.

1 Orwell's Life and Career

The life of George Orwell was packed with activities and experiences. Because many of them are consciously used, and reflected, in his works, literary critics make much reference to his life and opinions. Yet his life history is very complex, even to contradiction, and often obscure: so if some of his writings are to some extent autobiographical, or if they seem to voice his own views on politics and on art, any criticism which relates his works to his life must proceed with care.

It is not the purpose of the present book to detail his life.[1] But in the case of Orwell, some sense of his personal history is relevant to an understanding of his language. From early adulthood, Orwell seems to have experienced his life primarily as the life of a professional writer, a life to be established and developed by the continuous production of texts, by daily practice of the crafts of language, taking precedence over family life and all else. In a sense his life was constructed of words. Through language Eric Blair became George Orwell.

'George Orwell' was a pseudonym adopted with the publication of his first book, *Down and Out in Paris and London*, in 1933. Orwell was born Eric Arthur Blair on 25 June 1903 at Motihari, Bengal. His father, Richard Walmsley Blair, was an official in the Indian Government's Opium Department; his mother was Ida Mabel Blair, *née* Limouzin. In 1904 Mrs Blair returned to England with Eric and his older sister, Marjorie.[2] A second sister, Avril, who cared for Orwell in his last years, was born in 1908. After attending a local school, Eric was sent to St Cyprian's preparatory boarding school near Eastbourne in 1911, then went to Eton as a scholar in May 1917 after a term at Wellington College; he left Eton in 1921. He seems to have done little work at Eton, but helped to organise, and wrote for, college magazines. He did not go to university, but served as an Assistant Superintendent of Police with the Indian Imperial Police in Burma (1922–7), resigning his position

1

while on leave. In 1940 he wrote 'I gave it up partly because the climate had ruined my health, partly because I already had vague ideas of writing books, but mainly because I could not go on any longer serving an imperialism which I had come to regard as a racket' (*CEJL*, II, 38). The exact state of Blair's health after Burma is unclear, but he was dogged all his life by serious chest conditions, from the pneumonia which hospitalised him in Paris in 1929, bronchitis and pleurisy, to the recurrent tuberculosis which finally killed him in 1950.

From the autumn of 1927 to the winter of 1929 Blair opened himself to ways of life which were not normally accessible to someone of middle-class colonial upbringing: he voluntarily tramped and lived rough, first in London and then in Paris. On his return to England he based himself at his parents' home in Southwold, Suffolk, and taught, tramped and went hop-picking. His low-life experiences are recorded in his first book, *Down and Out in Paris and London*, published in January 1933 by Gollancz under the Orwell pseudonym. *Down and Out* initiates a form of writing which typifies much of Orwell's work, a mixture of documentary, fictionalised autobiography, and general comment. His essays carry this technique remarkably well, and some of the best of them had already been published in 1931. In the period 1931–3 he worked on his 'colonial' novel, *Burmese Days*. This book's evident hatred of colonialism, and its vitriolic portrayal of English and native characters whose originals in Blair's own Burmese days might have been identified, posed problems which were to become familiar: English publishers, nervous of causing political offence, and of libel, refused to take it. But the American publishers Harper published *Burmese Days* in October 1934.

Despite illness (pneumonia had hospitalised him and ended his teaching career in December, 1933), he had been working incredibly hard. By October 1934 he had finished a second novel, *A Clergyman's Daughter* (published in 1935); and in October, 1934, he moved from his parents' house in Southwold, where he had stayed after the episode of pneumonia, to London, working in a bookshop until January 1936, reviewing books and writing *Keep the Aspidistra Flying* (published April, 1936). Orwell regarded *A Clergyman's Daughter* and *Keep the Aspidistra Flying* as his least successful books. The former is a poorly constructed and implausible novel containing such diverse undigested ingredients as a surrealist sequence parodied from

Joyce's *Ulysses* and a section of 'naturalistic' narrative
on his hop-picking experiences. *Keep the Aspidistra Flying*
influenced by *Ulysses*, a copy of which Orwell had acquired in
1933. Bernard Crick helpfully comments that the brief *Ulysses* period shows an appreciation for 'the formal structure of *Ulysses*' (the
formal structure of extended narrative was always a problem for
Orwell) and 'his growing absorption in the mechanics and craft of
fiction'.[3] Furthermore, both these 'experimental' novels herald the
development of the frustrated, alienated anti-hero, a type of character
which had first appeared with John Flory in *Burmese Days* and was
to be taken further in the character of George Bowling in *Coming
Up for Air* and finally manifested in Winston Smith in *Nineteen
Eighty-Four*.

In January 1936 Gollancz commissioned Orwell (presumably on
the strength of his earlier achievement in *Down and Out*) to write a
book about conditions in the industrial North of England; from the
end of January to the end of March he travelled in Wigan, Barnsley
and Sheffield, living with families and observing working conditions; in Barnsley he made two trips down coal-mines, an acutely
uncomfortable experience for someone so tall. From April 1936 to
1940 he lived at The Stores, Wallington, Hertfordshire, a primitive
cottage and shop; on 9 June 1936 he married Eileen O'Shaughnessey.
He wrote *The Road to Wigan Pier*, based on his northern travels, in
1936 and it was published in March 1937. The first part of *The
Road to Wigan Pier* is an excellent example of Orwell's concrete,
socially realistic, presentation; the second part is an extended political and autobiographical essay which provoked the hostility of
the Left. Orwell did not hesitate to mix genres in the same book.

Another adventure began in December 1936 when Orwell went
to fight in the Spanish Civil War, and to observe and write on the
war as a journalist; he enlisted in the POUM (United Marxist Workers'
Party). Eileen joined him in Spain. Disillusioned with marxism, he
transferred to the Independent Labour Party contingent, and in a
second spell of active service, he was shot through the throat on 20
May 1937. After his convalescence the Blairs left Spain and returned to Wallington, arriving in early July. The remainder of 1937
was spent in writing his Spanish record, *Homage to Catalonia*, in
journalism, and in conflict with the British Left. His publisher,
Gollancz, refused *Homage to Catalonia*, but it was published by
Warburg in April 1938.

Orwell was now writing and publishing one book per year; this schedule seems to have become a target; if he did not fulfil it, he was anxious. But in 1938 his work was seriously set back by tuberculosis. From March to September he was at a sanatorium in Kent, forbidden to write; then a gift enabled him and Eileen to spend some months in the drier, warmer climate of Morocco, where, working with his customary speed, he drafted *Coming Up for Air*. They returned to England at the end of March 1939, and were at Wallington the next month. *Coming Up for Air* was published in June, and Orwell was working on a book of essays that were to be published in March 1940 as *Inside the Whale*. Orwell had published little else in 1938–9. His two masterpieces were still to come, and they have overshadowed *Coming Up for Air*, in which the Joyce influence was more successfully assimilated than it had been in *A Clergyman's Daughter* and *Keep the Aspidistra Flying*. Orwell's hero's thoughts, cast in a stylistically consistent and impressive first-person monologue, convey a politically complex statement about the relationship of the present to the past, highly relevant to Orwell's last and more famous book *Nineteen Eighty-Four*.

The Second World War broke out on 3 September 1939. The patriot Orwell made several attempts to enlist but was medically unfit. He and Eileen moved to London in May 1940. A few essays and reviews appeared in 1940 and 1941, as well as his book *The Lion and the Unicorn*. Orwell had little income, but Eileen worked for the Censorship Department, and later, the Ministry of Food. From August 1941 to November 1943 Orwell had a salaried post as a talks producer in the Indian section of the Eastern service of the British Broadcasting Corporation (an experience which provided seeds for the treatment of propaganda in *Nineteen Eighty-Four*). Essays and reviewing continued, for an increasing range of periodicals. Orwell also found a way to play a part in the war effort, working enthusiastically in the Home Guard until his poor health forced him to give it up in late 1943. Also in November 1943, Orwell left the BBC and became literary editor of the magazine *Tribune*, a post he held until February, 1945. His weekly column 'As I Please' for *Tribune* provided an ideal medium for short essays on diverse topics. From 1943 he also reviewed regularly for *The Observer* and for the *Manchester Evening News*. He was now firmly established as a literary journalist and political and social essayist.

In the winter of 1943–44 he wrote his most accomplished book yet, which was to establish his reputation and, with vast sales, secure his finances at last: the allegorical political satire, *Animal Farm*. English publishers – Gollancz, Cape and Faber – found its attack on Soviet Russia and Stalinism too hot to handle in the context of the war. Not until October, 1944 did Orwell find a publisher, Secker & Warburg. *Animal Farm* was finally published on 17 August 1945: a first impression of 4500 copies was rapidly sold, followed by a second printing of 10 000 copies, in November.[4] Orwell became instantly famous. The book was applauded by reviewers and reviled by the Left. In August 1946 it was published in the USA and, as the choice of the American Book of the Month Club, sold over half a million copies.

Meanwhile, Orwell's domestic circumstances changed, at first happily and then tragically. In June 1944 Orwell and Eileen adopted a baby boy, Richard. Eileen gave up work to look after Richard. They remained in London, and Orwell continued with writing and journalism. In February 1945 Orwell was sent to France by *The Observer*. Eileen took Richard to her sister-in-law's house in Stockton-on-Tees in March. She had been ill for several years, and entered hospital in Newcastle for surgery, apparently for a hysterectomy necessitated by fibroids, but there is speculation that she had cancer; she died as she was going under anaesthetic on 29 March 1945, aged 39.

Orwell returned to Europe for about six weeks after the funeral. *Animal Farm* was, as we have seen, published in August 1945. In September he visited Jura, in the Hebrides. On 23 May 1946, he moved to Barnhill, a remote farmhouse on Jura where he was joined by his sister Avril, and by Richard with Orwell's housekeeper, Susan Watson, who had been looking after the boy. Orwell moved between Barnhill and his flat in Canonbury Square in London in 1946 and 1947. In the second half of 1946, as well as writing reviews and essays, he was working on his last novel *Nineteen Eighty-Four*, for which a plan exists dating from late 1943. The first draft was completed by October 1947, but Orwell was increasingly unwell; just before Christmas 1947 he was admitted to hospital near Glasgow with tuberculosis of the left lung. He was in hospital for seven months, but managed to do some writing in the first half of 1948, including redrafting *Nineteen Eighty-Four*, after initially successful treatment with streptomycin. He left hospital in late July 1948, and returned to Barnhill. In the autumn of 1948 he completed his revision of the novel and, though very weak, retyped it in the second half of November. He realised he was very unwell and was seeking a sanatorium: on 6 January, 1949, he was admitted to a sanatorium at Cranham, in the Cotswold Hills in Gloucestershire.

Orwell was unable to do much more writing, but he corrected the proofs of *Nineteen Eighty-Four* in March, and had plans for a new novel. He was highly anxious about the loss of writing time (see *CEJL*, IV, p. 573). His last article, a review of Winston Churchill's *Their Finest Hour*, was published on 14 May 1949. *Nineteen Eighty-Four* was published in June 1949. Orwell became very seriously ill that summer, and was transferred to University College Hospital, London, on 3 September. On 13 October he married Sonia Brownell, whom he had known since 1945. Orwell died on 21 January 1950, aged 46.

2 Preliminaries

THE STYLES OF GEORGE ORWELL

The language of George Orwell makes an intensely distinctive contribution to the character of modern writing in English. Having said that, his reputation perhaps has him in the shadow of some slightly earlier, more obviously 'experimental' modernist writers such as James Joyce, Virginia Woolf, T. S. Eliot, D. H. Lawrence, who are all known for specific stylistic techniques which have helped to shape modern literature. Joyce and Woolf, for example, developed styles for representing the thoughts and preoccupations of their characters; Joyce is known for inventive word-play and for juxtaposing different styles and even scraps of foreign languages in a linguistic collage, a feature also of some of Eliot's poetry. Lawrence developed a very recognisable, syntactically and metaphorically elaborate language for exploring and commenting on his characters' psyches. In the 1930s, Orwell made his experiments with *avant-garde* techniques, and was not comfortable with them (see Chapters 6 and 8). His goal was truth rather than stylistic impact, and to attain his artistic ambitions he used a variety of ways of writing. But his best work is as individually recognisable and as original in style as that of any of the modernists.

What are the qualities of Orwell's language? We must generalise from a voluminous output in a literary career of only about twenty years, roughly from 1930 until his early death in 1950. Orwell is known popularly for two works of fiction published late in his short life: *Animal Farm* (1945) and *Nineteen Eighty-Four* (1949); these are very different from one another stylistically. Previously he had published seven books, from *Down and Out in Paris and London* (1933) to *Coming up for Air* (1939): some of them fiction, some documentary, and some a mixture of novel, reportage and essay. There are also reviews, essays, journalistic pieces and letters totalling 2200 pages in the collected (but not complete) edition. The four-volume *Collected Essays, Journalism and Letters* contains many pieces of accomplished and justly popular writing spanning his career, from

'A Hanging' (1931) to 'Politics and the English Language' (1946). As might be expected, we find a range of styles in such a diverse body of writings, but there is one major quality which we experience throughout: the voice of a person, and an unmistakeable voice:

> The *Ami du Peuple* is a Paris newspaper . . . sold at ten centimes . . . Nothing is abnormal about it except its price.
>
> Nor is there any need to be surprised at this last phenomenon, because the proprietors of the *Ami du Peuple* have just explained all about it, in a huge manifesto which is pasted on the walls of Paris wherever bill-sticking is not *défendu*. On reading this manifesto one learns with pleased surprise that the *Ami du Peuple* is not like other newspapers; it was the purest public spirit, uncontaminated by any base thoughts of gain, which brought it to birth. The proprietors, who hide their blushes in anonymity, are emptying their pockets for the mere pleasure of doing good by stealth. Their objects, we learn, are to make war on the great trusts, to fight for a lower cost of living, and above all to combat the powerful newspapers which are strangling free speech in France. In spite of the sinister attempts of these other newspapers to put the *Ami du Peuple* out of action, it will fight on to the last. In short, it is all that its name implies. ('A Farthing Newspaper', Orwell's first published essay in English, 1928: *CEJL* I, 34–5)

> Because of the general revulsion against Allied war propaganda, there has been – indeed there was, even before the war was over – a tendency to claim that [Ezra] Pound was 'not really' a Fascist and an antisemite, that he opposed the war on pacifist grounds, and that in any case his activities only belonged to the war years. Some time ago I saw it stated in an American periodical that Pound only broadcast on the Rome radio when 'the balance of his mind was upset', and later (I think in the same periodical) that the Italian Government had blackmailed him into broadcasting by threats to relatives. All this is plain falsehood. Pound was an ardent follower of Mussolini as far back as the nineteen-twenties, and now concealed it. He was a contributor to Mosley's review, the *British Union Quarterly,* and accepted a professorship from the Rome Government before the war started. . . . His broadcasts were disgusting . . .

He *may* be a good writer (I must admit that I personally have always regarded him as an entirely spurious writer), but the opinions that he has tried to disseminate by means of his works are evil ones, and I think that the judges should have said so more firmly when awarding him the prize. ('The Question of the Pound Award,' published in May, 1949, a few months before Orwell's death: *CEJL,* IV, 551–2)

Orwell always said what he thought, and he did so with an individual wit and irony which will repay analysis. We will see that the Orwellian personal voice is a particular linguistic artifice (this is not negative): linguistic techniques give his written prose a spoken and colloquial, at times vernacular, quality, and consistent stylistic markers provide a sense of individuality, an 'idiolect'. This linguistically constructed effect of a personal voice is not only a feature of the essays; it is also an important part of a broad narrative strategy that Orwell employs, particularly in the earlier, quasi-documentary writings. He offers a prominent characterisation of himself as an on-the-scene observer, as if to lend validity to his observations. This narrator-cum-reporter is also very ready to pronounce judgements in the 'plain, blunt' manner, a style which is more likely to be artfully contrived than to be a result of writing at speed.

Orwell required prose to be 'like a window pane', and his own writings have been praised for this quality.[1] As a matter of fact, transparency does not come naturally to language: the structure of the linguistic medium tends to shape our apprehension of what is being communicated.[2] Orwell works hard and effectively at the illusion, and is often cited as an example of the clear or realistic style. We will look carefully at the techniques which accomplish this impression of clarity, particularly in the 'documentary realism' of sections of the earlier writings, and also at the somewhat different style of low-key simplicity in *Animal Farm.* We will find in fact that, outside such special contexts, Orwell's style tends not to be a spotless window – it is often flecked with literary rhetoric or with personal polemic.

To put it more positively, though *Animal Farm* is a triumph of consistency, Orwell's style is overall not uniform or monotonous. His books are enlivened by many types of stylistic variation. There are frequent changes of pace and complexity; alternations of plain and metaphorical language; transitions from personal commentary to realistic presentations, even lists of facts. Narrative is interspersed with essay-like analyses which the reader is invited to skip. Because Orwell's writings are not highly decorative or 'poetic', they can without shock accommodate quotations from non-literary texts, and representations of various kinds of speech style. Orwell had a keen sense of the words of the 'other': tramps, foreigners, intellectuals, politicians. He was adept at parody, either sympathetic or hostile. From his earliest book, *Down and Out in Paris and London* (1933) to his last, *Nineteen Eighty-Four* (1949), the juxtaposition of different styles is a basic narrative technique; these styles are usually framed by the distinctive Orwellian narrative voice, especially in the first-person books.

By contrast with the essayistic and other non-literary modes of writing encountered in his novels, we also find 'high styles' echoing modern experimental and romantic writers: the Joycean techniques in parts of *A Clergyman's Daughter* (1935) and *Keep the Aspidistra Flying* (1936), for instance, and the landscape descriptions in *Burmese Days* (1934) and *Homage to Catalonia* (1938) which recall Lawrence's highly coloured descriptive writing. Critics sometimes regard these attempts as flaws, blemishes in apprentice writing, preferring his own blunt vernacular manner; and this may be a merited critical judgement on the diverse earlier work. However, the assays at modernist styles are one aspect of a ranging virtuosity in techniques of writing, into which Orwell put great professional effort throughout his career. Writing for Orwell was difficult and deliberate: even the plain style is, as I have said, a result of craftsmanship.

In his masterpiece *Nineteen Eighty-Four,* Orwell shows a fine ear for the styles of the 'other', underpinning a variety of devastating and memorable parodies. Various kinds of offiicial and demagogic discourse (analysed and condemned in the essays) are parodically represented; for further discussion, see Chapter 10. His rhetorical purposes in these parodies and elsewhere can be understood against the background of his stated views on language, politics, and representational truth; his views on language are presented and discussed in Chapter 3.

I would not want the above paragraphs to give an impression of unqualified praise of Orwell as a stylist excelling in a variety of modes of writing; a lot of it *is* parody. It is significant that he had a broad sensitivity to the kinds of writing and speaking which were important in his age, and that his works make connections with a plurality of texts. His linguistic importance is narrower, however. The striking personal voice, with complex roots in not only the vernacular but also in review-writing and fictional narration (particularly the manner of Dickens) is one legacy. The quite specific linguistic achievements of *Animal Farm* and *Nineteen Eighty-Four* have had a profound influence on the way in which totalitarian ideology is popularly perceived.

As has been noted, Orwell was a prolific writer of texts of many different kinds. He is best known for his novels (and a handful of essays), and indeed principally for the two last novels. The fact is that his strongest linguistic quality *as a writer* – what I have called the personal voice – was until his last years a source of difficulty to him *as a novelist*. Some of his earlier narrative works are semi-autobiographical and quasi-documentary. The personal voice, presumably developed as a way of vouching for authenticity, has its own life: a highly dramatic persona is created. This Orwell-figure is concerned to voice opinions, hence the intrusive essays within some of the books: they distract from the narrative. In places (see for example pp. 80–2 of *Homage to Catalonia*, where finite verbs are avoided, presumably for an effect of narrative immediacy) Orwell has to encourage his narrative into running by deploying special stylistic techniques which jar against the ongoing oral mode. And there are problems of point of view. The first-person narrator in the early books has such a strong presence, and such sharply focused powers of observation, that the other characters are seen from the outside, a point of view that leads to flatness and lack of inner motivation.[3] The linguistic indications of these compositional problems, and the linguistics of the attempted and then the triumphant resolution, make Orwell's language a fascinating study in the techniques of modern fiction.[4]

LINGUISTIC CRITICISM

This study of the language of George Orwell is grounded in a particular critical approach established in the late 1970s and early 1980s, known generally as *linguistic criticism*. The study of literature through its language has in fact a much longer history, stretching back to the Russian Formalists in the early years of this century, and achieving great distinction in the work of the Prague Linguistic Circle through the 1930s. Building on this Russian and Czech work, the French structuralists of the 1960s devised methods of analysing literature which were strongly inspired by linguistics.[5] The Russian Formalist Roman Jakobson emigrated to the USA, and disseminated crucial linguistic ideas from Moscow and Prague, perhaps his most useful contribution to debate being a series of polemical claims culminating in the assertion, in 1958, that:

> Poetics deals with problems of verbal structure, just as the analysis of painting is concerned with pictorial structure. Since linguistics is the global science of verbal structure, poetics may be regarded as an integral part of linguistics.

He added the important qualification:

> Insistence on keeping poetics apart from linguistics is warranted only when the field of linguistics appears to be illicitly restricted . . .[6]

Since literary critics are notoriously suspicious of any 'scientific' treatment of the literary work, it is not surprising that the linguistic study of literature has been a controversial topic! But the controversy has been invigorating rather than destructive.

From the 1960s, this interface between linguistics and literature was greatly developed by a number of articulate enthusiasts in the USA and in Great Britain: journals, anthologies and introductory textbooks began appearing in some quantity.[7] At the time, this interdisciplinary activity was commonly known as 'stylistics', not necessarily a helpful designation, since the idea of 'style' was of little importance to the activities of many of the 'linguistic stylisticians', and the term 'style' is very hard to define anyway. (Roughly it means 'a characteristic manner of writing'; but the basis of such a definition is difficult to pin down formally.) In practice, stylistics was concerned with many different kinds of literary phenomena (e.g. metre, metaphor, rhetorical figures), used different linguistic models (generative grammar, systemic linguistics, traditional grammar, etc.), and was directed to a range of applications (practical criticism of individual texts, authorship studies, language teaching, theorising about literature, etc.). The common properties of stylistics were the systematic approach and the use of technical apparatus from linguistics; as the British linguist Michael Halliday puts it:

In talking therefore about the linguistic study of literary texts we mean not merely the study of the language, but rather the study of such texts by the methods of linguistics. There is a difference between *ad hoc*, personal and arbitrarily selective statements such as are sometimes offered, perhaps in support of a preformulated literary thesis, as textual or linguistic statements about literature, and a description of a text based on general linguistic theory. It is the latter that contributes to what has sometimes been called 'linguistic stylistics'.[8]

Linguistics is sometimes known as 'the science of language'; whether or not it is a science (and it is irrelevant to our discussion whether it is or not), it does share some of the characteristics of scientific activity: it is very aware of the need for theory, and it tries to use an explicit and defined methodology and terminology in analysis. These are qualities that are present when we apply linguistics to literature in the spirit that Halliday requires. Basic concepts like 'text', 'narration', 'meaning', 'cohesion', usually taken for granted unexamined in literary studies, are defined with respect to some general theory of how language works; and more detailed and specialised descriptive terms such as 'phoneme', 'register', 'transitivity', 'modality' are again defined as precisely as possible within the chosen theoretical model. The effect of describing literature according to these principles is to make available a considerable range of analytic tools that are not available in literary criticism, allowing much more detail, and finer distinctions; and it is difficult to use these tools sloppily or impressionistically. Moreover, since the terms are generally current in the community of linguists, it is possible for different practitioners to use them with consistent meanings. This may sound like a mechanical art to the literature student, but all literary analysis *does* require a descriptive method, and linguistics simply extends and sharpens the critic's apparatus.

Linguistics is not a *discovery procedure*. Describing a text using linguistic means will not tell us something that is inaccessible without linguistics; linguistics basically provides a better way of giving an account of the verbal structuring that is already there. Let us develop the argument by linking the 'verbal structuring that is already there' to the writer's and the reader's *knowledge* of verbal structure. Let us think about the abilities of someone who reads a poem competently – who can for instance share a reading with others, can comment according to the conventions for talking about poetry which prevail in the culture, who is saying something recognisably consistent with what we know about the poet's literary achievement, style and usual themes. That person is manifesting command of a whole battery of types of knowledge: this allows him/her to register the structure of words and sentences in the text because s/he has acquired the English language; to reconstruct their meanings, through knowledge of language and of the world; to recognise and respond to a genre of text (sonnet, short story, etc.) through the experience of reading and literary education; to perceive the style of an author or a period, again a kind of secondary linguistic knowledge. And so on. It is not the business of this book to spell out all that is involved in a person possessing 'literary competence',[9] but it is a fundamental principle of linguistic criticism that reading and literary experience involve the use of literary knowledge that is 'in' readers even before they sit down with the book.

The point to be made, then, is that a linguistic description of a literary text is not simply a mechanical account of textual structure; it is an account of the linguistic part of what readers know when they successfully realise a literary text in their minds and in talking to others. The advantage of linguistics is that it provides a way of vastly improving talk and writing about this dimension of literature.

I stated earlier that this book uses one particular model of 'stylistics', a linguistic approach to literature (and indeed non-literary texts such as the media) known as *linguistic criticism*.[10] Linguistic criticism attempts to give an account of a text, or an author, according to exactly the principles just mentioned. That is to say, linguistic criticism approaches a text as a potential structure of meanings which can be realised by appropriate readers. It goes beyond the purely semantic meanings of words and sentences, the 'literal' meanings which one could reconstruct using a dictionary and a grammar. Linguistic criticism relates texts to writers and readers who exist within a culture and a history, and who can thus achieve access to the social significances of texts – the additional semiotic layers that emerge in informed critical interpretation and in discussion among readers. This model is interpretive, setting the structures of language found in the text in the context of the cultural meanings that writers and readers bring to it.

Linguistic criticism, then, does not simply use linguistics to talk about what is objectively present at the surface of the text (its diction, its syntactic arrangements, pronouns, syllable structures, etc.), but it sees these objective structures as always having some further meaning in a given social context. In order to carry out this interpretive aim, linguistic criticism needs a particular kind of grammatical model as its basis: one that can do more than just spot, say, passive structures, or learned words, rhyme, metaphor, onomatopoeia or whatever, describe them, and just leave it at that without explanation. The model chosen is in fact that developed by M. A. K. Halliday, which is a *functional* grammar and a *semiotic* grammar.[11] The functional approach was summed up in an early, popular, essay of Halliday's:

> The particular form taken by the grammatical system of language is closely related to the social and personal needs that language is required to serve.[12]

We assume that the words and structures chosen by a writer are *motivated*: that is, they have a rationale, possibly unconscious, in terms not only of the statements the writer consciously wishes to make, but more fundamentally in terms of his/her communicative purposes, social background, preferred reading, views and beliefs, and assumptions about readership. These considerations give rise to the *social semiotic* dimension of language. Linguistic criticism proposes that characteristic arrangements of language, in given settings, communicate a cultural semiotic in addition to the literal meanings of the words and sentences. Let us relate this principle to Orwell. As we have seen, Orwell writes in a variety of styles. He can write like this:

1. In our time, political speech and writing are largely the defence of the indefensible. Things like the continuance of British rule in India, the Russian purges and deportations, the dropping of the atom bombs on Japan, can indeed be defended, but only by arguments which are too brutal for most people to face, and which do not square with the professed aims of political parties. Thus political language has to consist largely of euphemism, question-begging and sheer cloudy vagueness. ('Politics and the English Language,' 1946: *CEJL*, IV, 166)

Or this:

2. After two miles the road ended at the ford of a shallow stream. The jungle grew greener here, because of the water, and the trees were taller. At the edge of the stream there was a huge dead pyinkado tree festooned with spidery orchids, and there were some wild lime bushes with white waxen flowers. They had a sharp scent like bergamot ... [A track] led to a pool fifty yards upstream. Here a peepul tree grew, a great buttressed thing six feet thick, woven of innumerable strands of wood, like a wooden cable twisted by a giant. The roots of the tree made a natural cavern, under which the clear greenish light bubbled. Above and all around dense foliage shut off the light, turning the place into a green grotto walled with leaves ...

There was a stirring high up the the peepul tree, and a bubbling noise like pots boiling. A flock of green pigeons were up there, eating the berries. Flory gazed up into the great dome of the tree, trying to distinguish the birds; they were invisible, they matched the leaves so perfectly, and yet the whole tree was alive with them, shimmering, as though the ghosts of birds were shaking it. (*Burmese Days*, 1935: Penguin, pp. 105–6)

Or this:

3. 'That's the mulligatawny! Coming on fine, she is. Well, kid, 'z I was saying, here's us three going down hopping, and got a job promised us and all – Blessington's farm, Lower Molesworth. Only we're just a bit in the mulligatawny, see? Because we ain't got a brown between us, and we got to do it on the toby – thirty-five miles it is – and got to tap for our tommy and skipper at night as well. And that's a bit of a mulligatawny, with ladies in the party. But now s'pose f'rinstance you was to come along with us, see? We c'd take the twopenny tram as far as Bromley, and that's fifteen miles done, and we won't need skipper more'n one night on the way. And you can chum in at our bin – four to a bin's the best picking – and if Blessington's paying twopence a bushel you'll turn your ten bob a week easy.' (*A Clergyman's Daughter*, 1935: Penguin, p. 86)

Or this:

4. 'Comrades!' cried an eager, youthful voice. 'Attention, comrades! We have glorious news for you. We have won the battle for production! Returns now completed of the output of all classes of consumption goods show that the standard of living has risen by no less than 20 per cent over the past year. All over Oceania this morning there were irrepressible spontaneous demonstrations when workers marched out of factories and offices and paraded through the streets with banners voicing their gratitude to Big Brother for the new, happy life which his wise leadership has bestowed upon us. Here are some of the completed figures. Foodstuffs . . .' (*Nineteen Eighty-Four*, 1949: Penguin, p. 54)

The distinctive wording of each style draws on established semiotic resources in English writing. Extract 1, a version of what I call Orwell's 'personal voice', taps the stylistic resources of an older English essay tradition, and those of the 'omniscient author' who comes over so strongly in most novelists of the nineteenth century. The style connotes authority, confidence, and passionate rectitude, but it only does so because experienced readers are aware of the rhetorical traditions that underpin it, and can supply the social meanings which have accreted to it. For readers who have read a certain amount of Orwell's writing, this style connotes 'Orwell', his manner of self-presentation against that traditional authoritarian background. The style of extract 2., quite different, draws its meanings from descriptive writings in fiction and in travel literature: linguistic items such as plant names, colours, the exotic, a tone of lyricism, quickly cue a conventional style for a reader with some prior experience of it. Extract 3 renders a dialect, in this case Cockney, and again there are conventional ways of doing this in writing, and these conventions embody attitudes toward the dialect materials and the communities from which they come, and associate social meanings with them (Cockney means something like a rough, open vigour, the survival instinct, loyalty to one's kind). Extract 4 is a pastiche of a genre of political speaking, the rhetoric of totalitarian lying. Here it should be noted that, for the modern reader, Orwell's two last novels have had the greatest influence in the establishment of this parodic style.

All these styles will be discussed in more detail in their appropriate places below. The theoretical point I want them to make here is that none can be analysed critically just in terms of the surface linguistic features of style, but only when the styles are put in the context of the social and historical meanings that are available for the reader. Thus we need a linguistics with a built-in social dimension, and Halliday's socio-functional model is the best for the purpose.

Whatever technical linguistic apparatus needs to be drawn from functional linguistics in this book – powerful concepts like *register, transitivity, modality* – will be introduced piece by piece as different linguistic ideas are needed.

3 Orwell's Views on Language

In 1946, toward the end of his career but with one great novel still to be written, Orwell published an essay called 'Why I Write', reflecting on his aims and motives. This paper is helpfully reprinted right at the beginning of the otherwise chronologically arranged four volumes of *Collected Essays, Journalism and Letters* (*CEJL*, I, pp. 23–30), and it gives valuable insights into Orwell's artistic and linguistic goals. At its climax we find the often-quoted comment that 'Good prose is like a window pane.' Clarity is the prime requirement in prose writing. 'Of later years,' he writes, 'I have tried to write less picturesquely and more exactly.' And again in this essay: 'So long as I remain alive and well I shall continue to feel strongly about prose style, to love the surface of the earth, and to take pleasure in solid objects and scraps of useless information.' Prose is to be clear, exact, precise. Orwell's essays contain many other references to precision and clarity, and in the later years, repeated analyses of what he felt to be abuses of language which worked against this quality of transparency.

There is a tradition, still very much alive, of complaint against jargon, Americanisms, dead metaphors and obscure grammar, all usages which militate against Plain English.[1] Orwell's sentiments put him squarely within that tradition. But his thoughts on the implications of such practices take him far beyond the average guardian of good English who writes indignantly to the newspapers. Orwell's statements in this area are part of a complex and deeply felt intellectual and moral argument, which we find most passionately voiced in 'Politics and the English Language' (1946; *CEJL*, IV, pp. 156–70). The window pane on reality can be achieved only when the writer has a sharp and urgently experienced purpose. When Orwell himself lacked this, he confesses, 'I wrote lifeless books and was betrayed into purple passages, sentences without meaning, decorative adjectives and humbug generally'. Good prose comes from honesty and sincerity; and in turn, it promotes these qualities. Bad prose has the opposite causes and effects. The process is reciprocal: 'if thought corrupts language, language can also corrupt thought' ('Politics and the English Language', *CEJL*, IV, 167).

Orwell's view of what we may for the moment call 'public' uses of the English language was deeply disapproving. (But not finally pessimistic; as we will see, he believed that the situation could be remedied.) He refers to the ills of language with a variety of strongly emotive negative expressions: not only 'corrupt' but 'decadence' (*CEJL*, III, p. 43; IV, p. 167), 'vices' (III, p. 45), 'perversions' (III, p. 133), 'degradation' (III, p. 171), 'in a bad way' (IV, p. 156), 'bad habits' (IV, p. 157). These seem strong words for the linguistic habits Orwell is talking about: dead metaphors, abstract terms, foreign words, etc., the ordinary targets of the complaints tradition. But Orwell was firmly convinced at this time (roughly 1940–46) that such usages have evil mental and moral consequences. He makes a plausible, if over-stated and over-emotional, case, which we will review in more detail below. To illustrate for one moment how far Orwell takes his argument, the ultimate evil effect of the 'corruption' of language is totalitarianism (see *CEJL*, IV, pp. 167, 188, 543), an effect dramatically presented in his last works *Animal Farm* and *Nineteen Eighty-Four* (see Chapters 9 and 10). To understand how Orwell gets this far, we must first examine some more elementary aspects of his interest in and response to uses of the English language.

LANGUAGE AND CLASS

Throughout his career, Orwell was intensely aware of the wide range of different varieties of English, and the way they related to different social positions; thus, to the ways of life and the attitudes of people in those positions. Now the social meanings of accents, ways of address and naming, specialised and technical usages, etc., are well understood and documented today;[2] but there was no academic discipline of sociolinguistics in Orwell's day, and it is doubtful that he would have had any respect for such a study anyway! Orwell approaches the subject of language and social class as an amateur, but as an involved amateur, curious and intelligently speculative, yet moved, embarrassed, and often angry. The early essay 'Hop-Picking' (1931; *CEJL*, I pp. 75–97) includes notes on slang in the East End of London; a fuller annotated list, with speculations on the history of 'London Slang and Dialect' and notes on the history of swearing, appears in the semi-autobiographical *Down and Out in Paris and London* (1933) Ch 32. The essay 'Clink' (1932), his account of a deliberately contrived spell in police cells, has fairly extensive representations of the London vernacular, obscenities and all (*CEJL*, I, pp. 109–9). Conventional literary representations of Cockney appear in *Down and Out in Paris and London* (1933):

> In front of the fire a fully dressed man and a stark-naked man were bargaining. They were newspaper-sellers. The dressed man was selling his clothes to the naked man. He said:
> 'Ere y'are, the best rig-out you ever 'ad. A tosheroon [half a crown] for the coat, two 'ogs for the trousers, one and a tanner for the boots, and a 'og for the cap and scarf. That's seven bob.'
> 'You got a 'ope! I'll give yer one and a tanner for the coat, a 'og for the trousers, and two 'ogs for the rest. That's four and a tanner.'
> 'Take the 'ole lot for five and a tanner, chum.'
> 'Right y'are, off with 'em. I got to get out to sell my late edition.'
> (*Down and Out*, pp. 159–60)

Such conventions are deployed very extensively in *A Clergyman's Daughter,* Orwell's most ragged and unconvincing, and stylistically pretentious, novel. On the whole, Orwell's attempts at Cockney produce a kind of Dickensian caricature, often incongruous because not in a comic context. The use of Cockney is discussed further in Chapter 6; for its use as the language of the 'proles' in *Nineteen Eighty-Four*, see Chapter 10.

We will see that, in more theoretical discussions, Orwell proposes that working-class speech is the opposite of the 'anaemic' upper-class accent which he came to so despise. We are bound to ask, in this context, what *positive* qualities working-class speech is taken to symbolise. There is a literary tradition, going back to Mrs Gaskell in the early nineteenth century and still vigorous in Lawrence in the generation just before Orwell, which suggests that the varieties of working-class speech express various admirable qualities: robustness, vitality, directness, for example, or honest sincerity, simplicity, tenderness, solidarity.[3] We might instance the simple honesty and pathos carried in the representation of Stephen Blackpool's speech in Dickens's *Hard Times* (1854), or the bluff manliness connoted by Mellors's dialect in Lawrence's *Lady Chatterley's Lover* (1928). Although Orwell was clearly aware of the unifying function of dialect, there is little evidence that he intended his renderings of regional accents to symbolise specific desirable human qualities. He recognised in fact that dialect speech had negative connotations for the English, whatever their class:

> Nearly every Englishman, whatever his origins, feels the working-class manner of speech, and even working-class idioms, to be inferior. Cockney, the most widespread dialect, is the most despised of all. Any word or usage that is supposedly cockney is looked on as vulgar, even when, as is sometimes the case, it is merely an archaism. ('The English People', 1943, *CEJL*, III, 44)

Adopting a phrase attributed to Wyndham Lewis, Orwell says that 'the English working class' are '"branded on the tongue"' (*CEJL*, III, p. 19), and in the same essay he proposes 'to remove the class labels from the English language' through a 'national accent' based on a modification of one of the local accents – but not on BBC English which is 'a copy of the mannerisms of the upper classes' (ibid, p. 51).

And yet elsewhere he acknowledges the effectiveness of dialect speakers such as J. B. Priestley in addressing a large audience for which the '"educated", upper-class accent' is 'deadly' ('Propaganda and Demotic Speech', 1944, *CEJL*, III, 167). There is an apparent inconsistency here which can be understood if we disentangle a number of separate dichotomies which govern Orwell's thinking.

'THAT HORRIBLE PLUMMY VOICE FROM THE RADIO' (1940, CEJL, II, 404)

Orwell was acutely conscious of the distance between working-class speech of whatever region and the upper-class accent which we now (rather tendentiously!) call 'Received Pronunciation'. When he was preparing to go roughing it in the early 1930s, Orwell was apprehensive that his upper-class accent would betray him as not genuine in the company of tramps and hop-pickers (see his reminiscence in *Wigan Pier* (1937) p.132). He could dissimulate his class with dirty old clothes, but not hide his accent. Throughout his writings, this accent of the class from which he sought to dissociate himself was a topic on which he frequently expressed his loathing: he saw it as symbolising undeserving and callous power and prestige – a conscious separation from working-class values. An entry written in a notebook in hospital some months before he died gives a poignant and violent expression to his feelings:

> Curious effect, here in the sanatorium, on Easter Sunday, when the people in this (the most expensive) block of 'chalets' mostly have visitors, of hearing large numbers of upper-class English voices. I have been almost out of the sound of them for two years, hearing them at most one or two at a time, my ears growing more & more used to working-class or lower-middle-class Scottish voices. In the hospital at Hairmyres, for instance, I literally never heard a 'cultivated' accent except when I had a visitor. It is as though I were hearing these voices for the first time. And what voices! A sort of over-fedness, a fatuous self-confidence, a constant bah-bahing of laughter abt nothing, above all a sort of heaviness & richness combined with a fundamental ill-will – people who, one instinctively feels, without even being able to see them, are the enemies of anything intelligent or sensitive or beautiful. No wonder everyone hates us so. (*CEJL*, IV, 578)

Orwell's hatred for the values symbolised in the upper-class accent, for the way it perpetuates class-division and makes the working class invisible to foreigners (*CEJL*, III, 15), is only part of his sociolinguistic vision. As the 1940s progressed, he was less concerned with accent and class in general, concentrating specifically on the faults of a cluster of language varieties all at the 'top' of the high/low linguistic polarity: Standard English, official English ('Stripetrouser', 1944, III, p. 133), propaganda, political speech, the written style of intellectuals, especially Marxist intellectuals. It was less the plummy voice at Ascot or garden parties that appalled him, but the plummy voice *on the radio*: that is to say, a high-class voice, symbol of privilege, mediating an official position for a mass audience including the working-class majority. What he felt to be the inadequacy and offensiveness of this official voice was of course an issue of particular concern in the years of the Second World War, when radio broadcasting was full of official voices while Orwell's mature position on language was shaping.

DEMOTIC SPEECH

As far as I am aware, the concept of 'demotic speech' is first so-named in a war-time diary entry of 24 June 1940. Regarding Government leaflets and broadcasts, 'there is still nothing in really demotic speech, nothing that will move the poorer working class or even be quite certainly intelligible' (*CEJL*, II, p. 403). Looking forward to 'the disappearance of that horrible plummy voice from the radio', Orwell recounts how, 'watching in public bars, I have noticed that working men only pay attention to the broadcasts when some bit of demotic speech creeps in' (ibid, p. 404). The anecdote of the pub is repeated, with more detail, in the essay 'Propaganda and Demotic Speech' of 1944, which explores further the opposition between demotic and official language (*CEJL*, III, pp. 161–8). Demotic speech is 'simple, concrete language', 'clear, popular, everyday language', 'spoken English', 'ordinary language', 'ordinary, slipshod, colloquial English'; not the 'bloodless dialect', the 'stilted bookish language' of broadcast speeches and news bulletins.

'Bloodless' recalls a passage in an essay of a year earlier, 'The English People':

> The temporary decadence of the English language is due, like so much else, to our anachronistic class system. 'Educated' English has grown anaemic because for long past it has not been reinvigorated from below. The people likeliest to use simple concrete language, and to think of metaphors that really call up a visual image, are those who are in contact with physical reality. (*CEJL*, III, p. 43)

And in a memorable formulation at the end of the essay,

> Language ought to be the joint creation of poets and manual workers, and in modern England it is difficult for these two classes to meet. (*CEJL*, III, p. 46)

There is surely a literary echo here, a recollection of Wordsworth's design in the *Preface to Lyrical Ballads* (1800) for a language of poetry based on the 'plainer and more emphatic language' of people in 'humble and rustic life' who 'hourly communicate with the best objects from which the best part of language is originally derived'.[4]

The stress on the clear, the concrete and the visual looks forward to the remarks in 'Why I Write' of three years later, quoted at the beginning of this chapter.

Demotic speech, then, is clear, visual, concrete, colloquial, popular. We can add a further attribute, vigour, if we interpret the sexual and genetic stereotypes with which Orwell slurs the upper-class accent: 'bloodless', 'anaemic', 'reinvigorate' and 'effeminate' (*CEJL*, III, p. 46) connote lack of virility. Demotic speech is vigorous, masculine.

SPOKEN AND WRITTEN LANGUAGE, AND STANDARD ENGLISH

We can now see how J.B. Priestley could in Orwell's view be effective as a broadcaster: 'his Yorkshire accent, which he probably broadened a little for the occasion' (*CEJL*, III, p. 167) connoted demotic speech, and engaged his audience in a radio context that was dominated by the '"educated", upper-class accent', which was, for the likes of the 'gang of navvies eating their bread and cheese in a pub' (ibid, p. 163), literally a turn-off.

The problem which Orwell now confronted was how to incorporate the qualities of demotic speech into the public language of the ruling class. 'Propaganda and Demotic Speech' is much concerned with the problem of making scripted broadcast language accessible and popular – understandably, since Orwell had recently spent a little over two years at the BBC – and in this essay Orwell discusses a number of technical possibilities for democratising speech on radio. But the issue which became more and more a preoccupation with him in the late 1940s was the reform of prose style towards the clarity and vigour of what he called demotic speech. Orwell recognised the radical scale of the problem. As early as 1938 he had registered the sharp distinction that exists between writing and speech: they are two separate modes – even, as he phrased it, two languages. The distinction is first articulated almost as an aside in a letter to his friend Jack Common:

As to the great proletarian novel, I really don't see how it's to come into existence. The stuff in *Seven Shifts* is written from a prole point of view, but of course as literature it's bourgeois literature. The thing is that all of us talk & write two different languages,

& when a man from, say Scotland or even Yorkshire writes in standard English he's writing something quite as different from his own tongue as Spanish is from Italian. I think the first real prole novel that comes along will be spoken over the radio. (20 April 1938: *CEJL*, I, pp. 348–9)

The distinction between written and spoken is made the foundation of his argument in two key later essays, 'The English People' (1943; *CEJL*, III, 42) and 'Propaganda and Demotic Speech' (1944; *CEJL*, III, 164–5).

Actually Orwell merges two separate distinctions. The first is technical, the second ideological. Technically, speech and writing are two different *modes*. Linguists have, regrettably, traditionally paid little attention to the difference: they have tended to say somewhat complacently that speech is the primary mode – since it precedes writing both in the history of mankind and in the linguistic development of the individual – and that writing is therefore a derived reflection or representation of speech. Orwell would have appreciated the subsequent irony that, having taken this line, linguists usually work with bookish, grammatically correct, invented examples, excusing themselves by asserting that speech is full of grammatical mistakes (and is therefore somehow subordinate to writing)!

Anyone who has tried to put a transcription of spontaneous speech down on paper, or has read transcriptions prepared by linguists, will be immediately impressed with how different the structure of speech and that of writing really are.[5] Speech is not just simpler, nor is it 'slip-shod' [*sic*] as Orwell puts it; it differs systematically from written language in many ways. The overall organisation of sentences is different, spoken utterances often having long and complex syntactic structures organised in a serial, narrative way. But intonation (the rises and falls in the pitch of the voice) chops up speech into a series of relatively short units of information. Nouns and verbs are used differently, written language being more nominal, especially employing lots of 'nominalisations', nouns formed from verbs. Vocabulary is different in other ways; writing has a higher proportion of multi-syllabled words. Lexical density is higher in writing than in speech, that is to say, the proportion of 'content words' (words with full meaning, such as 'cat' and 'imagine', as opposed to 'function words' such as 'and' and 'to') to the total of words as a whole, is higher. Pronouns and other words which apply to people and things are handled much more explictly in writing. Speech is more repetitive. And so on. These and other differences have in fact been studied only recently. A pioneer in this work has been the linguist M.A.K. Halliday, who has made a start on identifying the areas of description needed for a proper grammar of spoken English.[6]

The grammatical differences between the spoken and written modes are readily related to the physical differences between the two media – the speed of speech, the possibility of mis-hearing, the rapid fading and general impermanence of the signal; the cognitive differences between producing writing and speech, e.g. difficulty of pre-planning or editing speech; similarly the quite different relationships between addressor/addressee, and between these participants and their contexts, in the two modes.

Speech and writing are then 'two different languages', as Orwell puts it, in the fundamental sense that the same kinds of linguistic structures cannot be used in the two modes. There is in effect a basic problem for a writer, whether of documentary or fiction, who wishes to communicate the texture of human social life: the structures of speech will not go into printed form. In effect they look unnatural or comic. As we have seen, 'dialect speech' in novels, including Orwell's, is constructed by a set of literary conventions so that an experienced, familiar, fiction-reader will receive them 'as if' speech. 'Realistic' dialogue of this kind has a limited role in Orwell, as we would expect. More generally, the disparity between spoken and written linguistic structures is the cause of Orwell's despair about 'the great proletarian novel': the experience of the working class can be communicated only in speech, but the written format transforms it to 'bourgeois literature'. And here we come to the second opposition between written and spoken in Orwell's thinking, what I called the 'ideological' distinction.

The 1938 letter to Jack Common (pp. 25–6 above) equates written or printed English with Standard English. Thus the regional-dialect speaker has a double problem in writing: not only must s/he lose the linguistic markers of speech, for the technical reasons just discussed, s/he is also forced to write in a dialect which is the property of a different (higher) class. For Orwell, Standard English existed in a variety of forms which he found distasteful. There is official English or what he calls 'Stripe-trouser': 'this dreary dialect, the language of leading articles, White Papers, political speeches, and BBC news bulletins' ('The English People', 1943, *CEJL*, III, 43, cf. 133). His later essays make it clear that he also associates Standard English with the writings of intellectuals, including scientists, and particularly socialist intellectuals: as his rejection of Soviet totalitarianism and its admirers became more decisive, he developed a strong hatred for 'Marxist English, or Pamphletese' (*CEJL*, III, p. 133). Standard English, like the upper-class accent, symbolised for Orwell privilege, power, disregard for the people, intolerance. Above all it meant the avoidance and suppression of thought.

His analysis is hostile, but essentially well-founded: the concept of Standard English has since the eighteenth century been the construct of the élite in government, education, and publishing, and it is still a controversial issue today. The official thinking about English language education in the National Curriculum introduced in England in 1988 clearly has it that, if they are to 'do well' in life, children had better acquire 'Standard English', leaving their local varieties to the playground and the home. Since it is virtually impossible for teachers to change their charges' accents, this prescription can only really apply to writing, which, by the application of the red pen, can be subjected to norms of correctness. So we have in effect another opposition between speech and writing, writing being associated with the norms appropriate to opportunity and privilege, speech with local or class values that must be purged from writing.[7]

Orwell's objections to Standard English are basically political, and ultimately moral: it is an instrument of power, and an enemy of humane values because of its rejection of the qualities of 'demotic speech'. Worse still, Standard English threatens criticism and freedom by inhibiting concrete, independent thought.

'A CATALOGUE OF SWINDLES AND PERVERSIONS': THE ILLS OF 'STANDARD ENGLISH'

From 1943 Orwell wrote a series of diatribes against the official, commercial, political and intellectual varieties of English, which he lumped together as 'Standard English' and condemned as 'the deadliest enemy of good English' (*CEJL*, III, 43). As he enumerates the faults, he seems, superficially, to be voicing conservative sentiments, writing as a representative of what Milroy and Milroy (see note 1) call the 'guardians' of good English, defenders of the language against the incursions of the new.[8] What is unconventional in Orwell is the deter-

mined anti-authoritarianism which fires his statements on bad wri.
ing. Unlike the guardians of English generally, his motives for wanting
to stem the decline of English are far from conservative.[9]

We may briefly list the faults he finds with written English:[10]

- **Dead metaphors** are condemned, particularly ones which have
  become part of political jargon: 'jackboot', 'toe the line', 'stab in
  the back'. They are used with no consciousness of the original
  meaning, and convey no vivid image.
- **Borrowings** from American English ('cop', 'escalator'); from
  European languages 'to give an air of culture and elegance' (*joie
  de vivre, esprit de corps, Weltanschauung*); Greek and Latin words
  and derivatives used pretentiously in scientific writing; clumsily
  translated German and Russian phrases in Marxist writings.
- **Archaisms**, especially those used in writing about war. Orwell's
  central insight about archaism in this context is that it is a technique of *euphemism*, a way of avoiding speaking of the horrors
  of modern warfare while still 'glorifying war': '"We will not sheathe
  the sword" sounds a lot more gentlemanly than "We will keep on
  dropping blockbusters", though in effect it means the same.'
- **Jargon**, specialised terms marking a particular expertise, used
  unnecessarily and excessively in ordinary communication. 'Doctors, scientists, businessmen, officials, sportsmen, economists, and
  political theorists all have their characteristic perversion of the
  language.' The clichés of Marxist political rhetoric were a particular abomination to Orwell.
- **Meaningless words**, a broad enough category, but Orwell instances
  specifically the vacuities of art criticism and literary criticism:
  'romantic', 'plastic', etc., words so devoid of meaning that opposites
  can be asserted of the same object without contradiction: 'When
  one critic writes, "The outstanding features of Mr X's work is
  [*sic*] its living quality", while another writes, "The immediately
  striking thing about Mr X's work is its peculiar deadness", the
  reader accepts this as a simple difference of opinion'.

Two general points may be made about these faults (in Orwell's
view) of usage. First, a writer who commits them is not thinking
properly, not concentrating on the precise ideas s/he wishes to convey. Second, the majority of these faults boil down to the use of
verbal materials lifted from other people's language, allowing the

writer to avoid taking any real responsibility: it is an easy way out. Orwell's anger against linguistic abuse is especially high when he condemns a further prose laziness, the use of *ready-made phrases*. The practice is vividly evoked in two memorable passages in 'Politics and the English Language':

> [P]rose consists less and less of *words* chosen for the sake of their meaning, and more of *phrases* tacked together like the sections of a prefabricated hen-house.

> [M]odern writing at its worst does not consist in picking out words for the sake of their meaning and inventing images in order to make the meaning clearer. It consists in gumming together long strips of words which have already been set in order by someone else, and making the results presentable by sheer humbug. (*CEJL*, IV, pp. 159, 163)

He instances 'in due course', 'take the earliest opportunity, 'the answer is in the affirmative', 'render inoperative', 'exhibit a tendency to', etc.; his examples of worn-out metaphors like 'take up the cudgels for', 'ride roughshod over', are essentially the same practice. These defunct metaphors 'may once have been fresh and vivid, but have now become mere thought-saving devices, having the same relation to living English as a crutch has to a leg'.

In 'The English People' Orwell generalises: 'Whoever writes English is struggling ... against vagueness, against obscurity, against the lure of the decorative adjective, against the encroachment of Latin and Greek, and, above all, against the worn-out phrases and dead metaphors with which the language is cluttered up' (*CEJL*, III, p. 42). A writer who succumbs to these tendencies of modern English loses the qualities of prose 'like a window pane': concrete detail is lost to abstraction or sheer meaninglessness, vividness gives way to vagueness, simplicity gives way to pretentious elaboration. And these are not simply stylistic flaws, but cognitive failings: the writer is not thinking.

LANGUAGE AND THOUGHT

The question of how language and thought interrelate is\
dously difficult in the philosophy and psychology of language
to set up the question with a simple dualism of 'language' on the
one hand and 'thought' on the other is liable to pre-structure the
discussion, although in presenting Orwell's views this happens not
to be particularly harmful since he tends to discuss the matter in a
simple dualistic way.

Still oversimplifying, one may be either a 'realist' or a 'nominalist'. A nominalist believes that things, or our ideas of them, do not
have a naturally discrete existence or structure of their own, but are
shaped by the vocabulary that we have available for talking about
them. Orwell was not a nominalist, and it is crucial to realise that it
is an essentially nominalist theory of how language might influence
thought that he attacks with a biting satire as 'Newspeak' in *Nineteen Eighty-Four*.

The metaphor of the window pane with which we started, and
the frequent mentions of clarity, vividness, precision, concreteness
as desirable properties of prose, indicate that Orwell held a fundamentally *realist* view. Things exist, and English has perfectly good
names for them: one of his repeated complaints is that we borrow
unnecessarily from French, or Greek, to name objects that are already
named. Orwell does not complain that renaming *changes* the nature
of a thing, but that it can obscure our knowledge of that thing.

His essay 'New Words' of 1940 (*CEJL*, II, pp. 17–27) gives a
clear understanding of his position; it is a calm piece of work, not
yet troubled by his preoccupation with the link between corrupt
language and totalitarianism which dominated his essays of the late
1940s. 'New Words' is a call for the invention, perhaps by several
thousand volunteers, of 'a vocabulary which would accurately reflect the life of the mind' (ibid, p. 21). We readily invent new
words for 'material objects', Orwell says, but not for abstractions
or mental processes. He prefaces this call with a theory of mind
involving two processes: 'reasonable' thoughts which move logi-
cally as on a chess-board, and a 'disordered, un-verbal world', on
which he asks us to reflect:

> Examine your thought at any casual moment. The main move-
> ment in it will be a stream of nameless things – so nameless that

one hardly knows whether to call them thoughts, images or feelings. In the first place there are the objects you see and the sounds you hear, which are in themselves describable in words, but which as soon as they enter your mind become something quite different, and totally indescribable. (*CEJL*, II, p. 18)

Orwell's 'realistic' philosophy is manifest here. There exist 'objects' – recall the 'solid objects' and 'surface of the earth' of 'Why I Write' – about which we have feelings and thoughts. Thought is 'a stream of nameless things'; these 'thoughts-about-things' (so to speak) are 'indescribable'. The next stage of Orwell's argument concerns the inadequacy of language. He maintains that 'feelings . . . are generally admitted to be subtler than words' (ibid, p. 19); words are not 'a direct channel of thought' (ibid, p. 21). The topic of the essay is a sparse area of English vocabulary, which he thinks can be remedied, but he is soon into the struggle of writing, his perennial theme:

> For anyone who is not a considerable artist (possibly for them too) the lumpishness of words results in constant falsification . . . A writer falsifies himself both intentionally and unintentionally. Intentionally, because the accidental qualities of words constantly tempt and frighten him away from his true meaning. He gets an idea, begins trying to express it, and then, in the frightful mess of words that generally results, a pattern begins to form itself more or less accidentally. It is not by any means the pattern he wants, but it is at any rate not vulgar or disagreeable; it is 'good art'. (ibid, p. 20)

The argument turns to truth and lying. Existing language lets the writer down by offering pre-formed patterns, and 'lies will fall into artistic shape when truth will not'. Language by its lack of resources and by its temptations to laziness (offering ready-made patterns) fails the writer and his reader. The writer is not really thinking, and the reader 'constantly sees meanings which are not there' (ibid, p. 21).

It is important to recognise the limits to Orwell's position, its basic straightforwardness. Orwell's realism extended to a commitment to historical facts, for which he required a precise and truthful expression. The faults of language as he analysed them inhibited the expression of truth, and the reception of truth by readers and hearers. This problem he regarded as an intense danger given the authoritarian tendencies of modern states: the nature of language, in his view, made it possible for those in control of the state to render truth inaccessible. Even in his most strident essay on this topic, 'Politics and the English Language', he carefully noted that he was concerned with 'merely language as an instrument for expressing and not for concealing or preventing thought' (*CEJL*, p. IV, p. 169). He did *not* suggest that language might mould reality in some specific way (the nominalist position), as some commentators – misconstruing the import of Newspeak in *Nineteen Eighty-Four* – have suggested. His simple realism – words fail the truth of facts, and thus corrupt thought – makes his presentation of Newspeak less ambiguous but no less dramatic: Newspeak is an absurdly projected nominalism, a false belief that language can be manipulated to channel thought absolutely. We will return to this topic in the final chapter.

'AN INSTRUMENT WHICH WE SHAPE FOR OUR OWN PURPOSES'

Orwell believed (contrary to mainstream linguistics since Saussure, though he was not to know that[11]) that language could be controlled by its users if they wanted to. It is, he says, false to regard language as 'a natural growth'; we should see it as 'an instrument which we shape for our own purposes' ('Politics and the English Language', *CEJL*, IV, p. 156). He maintains that thinking that language usage cannot be changed is a complacency which amounts to a reprehensible political quietism at a time when writers should speak fearlessly.

If we agree with Orwell that language is an instrument, it can be misused deliberately; hence the provisional plausibility of Newspeak: a regime so confident of itself could, insanely, believe that it could manipulate language, and its users, by such a grand design. Orwell offers occasional indication that he suspected conscious, conspiratorial, misuse of language. His phrasing 'swindles and perversions' implies a conscious intention to swindle and pervert. On the same page of 'Politics and the English Language' he claims that 'words of this kind [*democracy, socialism, freedom*, etc.] are often used in a consciously dishonest way' (*CEJL*, IV, 162). The sense of conspiracy and deliberate malpractice is strong in this essay, but the dominant focus is laziness and complicity: politicians write and speak in this dishonest, stale, way because it is easier: it saves thought.

'The point is that the process is reversible' (*CEJL*, IV, 157). We have seen that Orwell sketches practical schemes for regenerating language and making it a better medium for thought: the project for coining words for mental states, carefully thought out (if naive) even to the point of advising that words should sound appropriate to their meanings; the schemes for bringing broadcast and public-speaking English more into line with demotic speech; and above all, the constant advice to writers on how to use English to allow them to think for themselves:

   i. Never use a metaphor, simile or other figure of speech which you are used to seeing in print.

   ii. Never use a long word where a short one will do.

   iii. If it is possible to cut a word out, always cut it out.

   iv. Never use the passive where you can use the active.

   v. Never use a foreign phrase, a scientific word or a jargon word if you can think of an everyday English equivalent.

   vi. Break any of these rules sooner than say anything outright barbarous. (*CEJL*, IV, 169)

This apparently mundane advice, which is basically similar to what is routinely drilled into apprentice writers and journalists, takes on an urgency of a higher level in the context of Orwell's ethical arguments.

4 A Personal Voice

In Chapter 1 I referred to one of the major and most attractive features of Orwell's writing, the individual, colloquial, forthright style, clearest in those essays in which he expounds his views on some subject that moves him. In this chapter I will try to show how this voice is achieved linguistically. My starting-point and main source of evidence in this chapter are the essays. But we must bear in mind that, if the idea of an 'Orwellian' personal style has any validity, it applies also to the third-person narratives, and to first-person writing in which the persona is not Orwell himself, such as the novel *Coming Up for Air*. The 'window pane' and 'demotic speech' requirements, if they mean anything, apply to any genre of his prose, and not just to the first-person essay, the closest form to speech. In later chapters, we will be looking at the Orwellian voice as it appears in the full-length books, interacting with other styles of writing and particularly in the context of the language of narration.

Bernard Crick in his biography of our subject offers one view of Orwell's stylistic development. He quotes from the first published essay, 'A Farthing Newspaper' (1928; see p. 8 above) and comments on 'the pithy use of ordinary phrases', 'irony', 'pseudo-precision', 'all devices found frequently in his famous essays':

> His first journalism was thus closer to his mature style than were his early novels. It seems as if he then regarded his journalistic style as merely workmanlike and still strove to achieve a 'literary style'. It took him some years to discover that he already possessed something much finer than what he thought he was still seeking.[1]

Crick proposes that the vigorous journalistic style is the basis for Orwell's singular achievement, and that it was there from the beginning; that the style of the great essays of the 1940s is essentially the same; that the 'modernist' trials of the 1930s novels were the misguided effort of an apprentice writer who as yet had not recognised his personal strength. There is much that is plausible in this account: Crick has identified the essence of Orwell's personal voice, observed that it was there from the beginning, and interestingly suggested that it was possible in or even was shaped by the permissive journalistic context in which he first published.

Crick's presentation needs however to be somewhat qualified. It suggests that the early novels were an aberration, a deviation from Orwell's true path, mere apprentice work, embarrassingly florid and derivative. Such a view may be partly supported by Orwell's negative feeling toward some of them in 'Why I Write' – but that is the much later hindsight of 1946. Orwell's novels of the 1930s are not juvenilia, they are part of a responsible practice of writing, the exploration of a number of techniques of narrative in which Orwell was both conscientious and in touch with major literary work of his time. (Crick's acknowledgement of the importance to Orwell of Joyce's *Ulysses* as a technical model in fact testifies to this.)[2] A second problem with this account is the implication that Orwell's 'true' style was 'natural', and not a product of the craft of writing: but Orwell's later essays on the English language, discussed in the previous chapter, clearly indicate that all writing for him was a conscious, crafted, practice. Third, Crick's account is restricted to the first-person essay and commentary in Orwell; it does not explain how the Orwellian style translates into the third-person narrative novels where – at least in the last two novels – his personal vision and style achieve a fusion of political writing and art.

A distinction made by Orwell in 'Why I Write' and occasional references elsewhere, and taken up by Crick (see note 1), is between 'purple' and 'plain' styles:

> I wanted to write enormous naturalistic novels with unhappy endings, full of detailed descriptions and arresting similes, and also full of purple passages in which words were used partly for the sake of their sound. And in fact my first complete novel, *Burmese Days*, which I wrote when I was thirty but projected much earlier, is rather that kind of book.
> [O]f later years I have tried to write less picturesquely and more exactly. *(CEJL*, I, 25, 29)

The quest for simplicity of expression is part of the triumph of the Orwellian voice (and that is why *Animal Farm* is so central to his craftsmanship). Another major force working on his style is his idea of demotic speech. But in order to understand the nature of the personal voice more clearly, and its relationship with other voices in Orwell's texts, it will be helpful to arm ourselves with some more technical linguistic concepts. It is convenient to introduce some ideas from sociolinguistics in a group at this point, though some of them will be more applicable in later chapters.

LINGUISTIC VARIETIES

In this section I will briefly introduce the following linguistic ideas: *mode, register, sociolect, idiolect*. These terms are drawn from general linguistic theory. They are independent of Orwell, neither based on his language theories nor limited to his language practice. I give them a distinct prominence here in the belief that they will not only help us to understand the Orwellian style, but also prove useful to the readers of this book in their other critical work on the language of literature.

'Mode', 'register', 'sociolect' and 'idiolect' come from 'variety theory' in sociolinguistics: they refer to four different ways in which a language varies within itself as it is used in different situations. Other important variety terms include 'dialect' (on which the terms 'sociolect' and 'idiolect' are based), and 'style'. The latter, 'style', means roughly a distinctive or characteristic manner of writing or speaking. The term has an inherent imprecision because of its traditionally varied usage in literary criticism;[3] it will be found in this book (e.g. 'Orwellian style' in the previous paragraph) where exactness is not crucial and a more technical linguistic term might be intrusive: 'Orwellian style' signifies in technical terms 'Orwellian idiolect'.

We have already encountered 'mode' in the discussion of speech and writing in the previous chapter. Different modes correspond to the two different channels of communication, speech and writing: language is structured differently according to the physical characteristics of the channels, and according to the way language users relate to the channels. For example, conditions of planning and memory differ for the two media, and therefore different arrangements of language are required: a reader can backtrack in a way that a listener can not, and so a writer can (for example) begin a clause, interrupt it with another one, and resume the first idea later; a different syntax is implied. The dichotomy of speech versus writing is fundamental,

as Orwell knew. Some linguists have suggested that there are inter-
mediate modes, such as script (written language designed to be read
as if spoken), transcript (spoken language written down), etc., but
these are not really separate modes, only compromises between the
two basic modes: adaptations of one to make it sound or look like
some variety of the other one. Written language can be adapted to
simulate an oral mode, and Orwell's 'demotic speech' is such an
adaptation: in his written prose he incorporates cues or signs which
recall an ideal pattern of speech, a no-nonsense mode of plain speaking,
dissociated from the class markers of effeteness, evasion and authoritarianism, and from the pretentious bookishness of academic and
political writing.

The second term, 'register', was popularised by the linguist
M. A. K. Halliday, who employs it to refer to a variety of language
distinguished 'according to use' as opposed to language 'according
to user' – the latter is a *dialect* (regional variety) or, by analogy, a
sociolect (class variety).[4] Registers differ according to what you are
doing with language, what your subject matter is, what your relationship with your addressee is. The theory of register suffers from
a degree of vagueness, in that there are many undecidable and bor-
derline situations where it is not easy to say that a certain text is in
one register or another. However, 'register' is intuitively very suggestive, and it does in a general way make sense to talk about registers
associated with very distinctive situations such as, for example,
advertising, religion, academic writing, teaching, economics, chemistry,
etc. To avoid the problem of indeterminate cases, we will restrict
'register' to specialised and recognisable functional varieties such
as these. Such registers are constantly cited or parodied in Orwell –
for example, the instances of academic and political writing quoted
in 'Politics and the English Language' (*CEJL*, IV, pp. 156–70), or
the many parodies of registers of official language in *Nineteen Eighty-
Four* (see Chapter 10).

Register intersects with mode in a way which is very pertinent to
Orwell, in that there are some registers which are associated with
one mode rather than the other, and some registers which are in
general unwelcome in one mode or the other. For example, the legal
register of contracts, insurance policies and the like is unspeakable,
and conversation is generally unprintable. Certainly, trying to speak
or write something from the other mode produces some very peculiar effects, as readers may discover by simple experiment. Thus,

Orwell's attempt to situate oral registers in written mode posed considerable technical problems. On the other hand, there are advantages when, within a novel, he is parodying and mocking some non-narrative register such as political speaking: in the context, the alien register sticks out like a sore thumb, and seems to take on an intrinsic peculiarity.

As we have seen, *sociolects* and *idiolects*, like *dialects*, are properties of the users of language rather than the uses to which language is put. A sociolect is a variety of language which relates to membership of a social group: the distinctive language of the aristocracy, or of Cockneys, of doctors, of the unemployed young, and so on. Orwell's objection to the 'plummy voice' is a dislike of a sociolect, the language of those who hold positions of economic prestige or administrative power. His campaign for 'demotic speech' is the championing of another sociolect, and some of the linguistic strategies which make his prose style distinctive involve building fragments of this sociolect into the written mode (which officially resists it).

An *idiolect* is the linguistic idiom of an individual, his/her linguistic 'fingerprints'. We can recognise the voices of friends and acquaintances over the telephone by registering an individual cluster of features of accent, voice quality, typical words and habitual constructions of syntax. An idiolect is a product of dialect and sociolect and other more idiosyncratic features. When I speak of Orwell's 'personal voice' I am proposing that his writing projects an impression of a consistent idiolect. This idiolect draws on the reader's knowledge of mode in evoking an oral model; on register in preferring the vocabulary of informal conversation; on sociolect in using words which he thought characteristic of working-class speech.

Interestingly, Orwell himself was very aware of people's idiolects, and his writings are full of comments on and attempts to render idiosyncratic aspects of speech style: idiolectal differentiation is a prominent feature in *Down and Out*, for example. On idiolectal characterisation in Orwell, and also the rendering of sociolects, see also Chapters 6–8.

Modes, registers, dialects, sociolects and idiolects are different but overlapping kinds of linguistic varieties. There is a simple and crucial general point which can be made about all these concepts. From the perspective of the listener or reader, it takes only a little detail to suggest that a piece of language is in one variety or another. The impersonal pronoun 'one', for instance, can be used, as it is by the popular Press, to suggest the sociolect of the British Royal family. A technical term implies an appropriate technical register: 'prognosis', 'pathology', 'surgical procedure' connote the register of medicine. A single sound can stand for a whole accent: an actor who wants to sound 'Northern' may use the short open vowel /æ/ in words like 'class' and 'dance', while pronouncing a distinct /r/ in words such as 'card', 'girl' suggests rusticity, and 't^{h}ing' for 'thing' is a shorthand for Irishness. Features such as these may be called *cues*. In a very economical way, a cue will summon up a listener's or reader's pre-existing knowledge of the variety concerned: it will cause the alert reader to access a *model* of a variety and of the situations in which it is typically used.[5]

The economy of cue and model is very useful for a writer. Orwell could assume that his readers would already possess knowledge of pertinent varieties, and would be able to access a model of a variety when presented with some minimal cue. Only small signs are necessary to encourage accessing of a model; the text does not have to be saturated with variety markers, an over-marking which would impede reading. This principle is easiest to grasp in relation to social-group stereotypes which figure in his novels: Paddy the Irishman in *Down and Out*, or the various classes of Burmese and English in *Burmese Days* (see also, Chapters 6 and 7). But the principle of cue and model is also relevant to the 'personal voice'. In real life, a person's idiolect can be recognised by the slightest sign, the smallest fragment. Orwell's writing creates an impression of a consistent personal voice by markers which can be used very sparingly. A single word will evoke his voice for a reader who is familiar with this writer. Note how the vernacular word 'kip' is suddenly inserted into a matter-of-fact narrative context in this extract from *Homage to Catalonia*:

One day in February we saw a Fascist aeroplane approaching. As usual, a machine-gun was dragged into the open and its barrel cocked up, and everyone lay on his back to get a good aim. Our isolated positions were not worth bombing, and as a rule the few Fascist aeroplanes that passed our way circled round to avoid machine-gun fire. This time the aeroplane came straight over, too high up to be worth shooting at, and out of it came tumbling not bombs but white glittering things that turned over and over in the air. A few fluttered down into the position. They were copies of

a Fascist newspaper, the *Heraldo de Aragón*, announcing the fall
of Malaga.

That night the Fascists made a sort of abortive attack. I was
just getting down into kip, half dead with sleep, when there was
a heavy stream of bullets overhead and someone shouted into the
dug-out: 'They're attacking!' (*Catalonia*, pp. 43–4)

The demotic model is suddenly triggered by this slangy, non-literary word, and the colloquial phrase 'half dead with sleep' which
follows it, bringing the personal voice more directly to our attention and enhancing the immediacy of the bombing attack which is
about to be narrated.

EXAMPLES OF THE PERSONAL STYLE

At this point I want to offer an informal discussion of the stylistic
features of some extracts from the *Collected Essays, Journalism and
Letters*, drawing from the analysis a preliminary list of features of
the personal style which can then be applied to other texts. There is
the problem of choosing a representative sample. Even within the
essays and other non-fiction, Orwell practised a number of genres,
for different types of publication with a variety of readerships, and
involving the projection of different images of himself. There are
semi-autobiographical narratives such as 'A Hanging' and 'Shooting an Elephant'; angrily polemical works like 'The Prevention of
Literature' and 'Politics and the English Language' written with certain
types of politician and intellectual clearly in mind; quiet personal
reflections such as 'Some Thoughts on the Common Toad' or 'The
Moon under Water' (his ideal and imaginary pub); book reviews;
didactic writings more concerned to *explain* something to a specific
audience, such as 'The English People', or the 'London Letters' to
the American magazine *Partisan Review*, and some of the war broadcasts; his weekly column 'As I Please' in *Tribune* from December,
1943 to January, 1945, arguably one of his most individual and
attractive achievements and perhaps the most 'essayistic' in form.
The *Collected Essays, Journalism and Letters* contains a range of
other forms: letters with many different purposes and styles; notes;
diary entries. Finally we ought to remind ourselves that the non-
fictional prose output also contains radio scripts, some to be read

by Orwell and some by other people.[6] These have their own distinctive features.

The various genres within the above wide range have different rhetorical requirements and produce variations of stylistic form. Thus it would be unrealistic to look for one 'typical passage' illustrating the essence of Orwell's style. To do so would in any case miss an important point about the Orwellian voice, implicit in the theory of model and cue. The personal voice is at its purest and most observable in the essays, but it is not a uniform quality always totally characterising the writing: it is an impression, a model which readers will recognise under a variety of forms of expression. Cues are placed in writings within different registers so that the reader can sense the overt, or the underlying, presence of the distinctive Orwellian voice with its consistent values.

I have selected three short extracts from the better-known essays, somewhat different in overall stylistic impression, but each containing some of the cues or markers of the ubiquitous Orwellian voice.

I It was perfectly clear to me what I ought to do. I ought to walk up to within, say, twenty-five yards of the elephant and test his behaviour. If he charged I could shoot, if he took no notice of me it would be safe to leave him until the mahout
5 came back. But also I knew that I was going to do no such thing. I was a poor shot with a rifle and the ground was soft mud into which one would sink at every step. If the elephant charged and I missed him, I should have about as much chance as a toad under a steam-roller. But even then I was not think-
10 ing particularly of my own skin, only the watchful yellow faces behind. For at that moment, with the crowd watching me, I was not afraid in the ordinary sense, as I would have been if I had been alone. A white man mustn't be frightened in front of 'natives'; and so, in general, he isn't frightened. The sole thought
15 in my mind was that if anything went wrong those two thousand Burmans would see me pursued, caught, trampled on and reduced to a grinning corpse like that Indian up the hill. And if that happened it was quite probable that some of them would laugh. That would never do. There was only one alternative. I
20 shoved the cartridges into the magazine and lay down on the road to get a better aim. ('Shooting an Elephant' [1936], *CEJL*, I, p. 270)

Extract I, from the justly famous 'Shooting an Elephant', is more literary than the other two extracts below: a first-person story, perhaps based on Orwell's personal experience but essentially written to conform to a fictional genre and to appear in a literary magazine, *New Writing*. The narration is carried by a sequence of simple action verbs, either infinitive or simple past tense: walk, test, charged, leave, sink, charged, missed . . . shoved, lay down. As oral narration conventionally is, and as speech actually is, the style is dominated by verbs rather than nouns (and there are only half a dozen adjectives in the whole extract: decorative description is avoided). Note however that until the last sentence these verbs refer to hypothetical conditions rather than performed actions: Orwell is reporting not what he did, but what he thought about doing, and what responses he anticipated. Thus the passage is strongly subjective, with the narrator very present in repeated use of the pronoun 'I'. There are also a considerable number of predicates conveying thought, mental states, and judgement: clear, knew, thinking, afraid, frightened, thought. The use of verbs relating to emotional experience and thought processes is a major part of the linguistic process of constructing the impression of the voice of an individual subjectivity.

The syntax of extract I has the simplicity that Orwell required of prose that aspired to the demotic voice. Sentences and clauses are short – a quick reading of extract III will give a sense of the contrast in this respect. Information is presented in the short units which are characteristic of speech:

> If he charged/ I could shoot,/ if he took no notice of me/ it would be safe to leave him/ until the mahout came back.

Moreover, the general syntactic construction is *paratactic*: clauses and phrases of the same status are added on as the sentence proceeds, without the complex dependency, and the reversal of main and subordinate clauses, which characterise the *hypotactic* organisation of much printed prose (but cf. III).

The vocabulary is concrete and simple, avoiding abstract or very general words, and avoiding polysyllables except in such very ordinary words as 'particularly', 'alternative'. Among this very mundane vocabulary, there are a few cues to the colloquial register which is typical of Orwell: 'poor shot', and 'shoved' discreetly connote a casualness which rejects the social propriety of a more pretentious prose. And there is just one of the concrete homely metaphors (he rations them) which are one of Orwell's trade-marks, the toad and the steam-roller in line 9.

There is a distinctive sentence in lines 13–14:

A white man mustn't be frightened in front of 'natives'; and so, in general, he isn't frightened.

The contracted negatives 'mustn't' and 'isn't' are markers of speech. A writer who uses such contractions – against the advice of generations of English teachers – is highlighting a personal tone for the purposes of argument. This as-if-speech sentence has the character of a *saying*, a piece of oral wisdom giving one of the rules of behaviour by which the colonial administrators conducted their relationship with 'natives'. The effect here is to draw attention to the way colonialism falsifies the self, creating an artificial gap between the 'white man' and the 'natives' based on the coloniser's need to behave with unnatural authority for fear of rebellion.

Extract II contains some of the above features, and others; it is overall different in tone but unmistakeably Orwell:

II Get hold of a dozen of these things, preferably McGill's – if you pick out from a pile the ones that seem to you funniest, you will probably find that most of them are McGill's – and spread them out on a table. What do you see?

5   Your first impression is of overwhelming vulgarity. This is quite apart from the ever-present obscenity, and apart from the hideousness of the colours. They have an utter lowness of mental atmosphere which comes out not only in the nature of the jokes but, even more, in the grotesque, staring, blatant quality of the

10   drawings. The designs, like those of a child, are full of heavy lines and empty spaces, and all the figures in them, every gesture and attitude, are deliberately ugly, the faces grinning and vacuous, the women monstrously parodied, with bottoms like Hottentots. Your second impression, however, is of indefinable

15   familiarity. What do these things remind you of? What are they so like? In the first place, of course, they remind you of the barely different postcards which you probably gazed at in your childhood. But more than this, what you are really looking at is something as traditional as Greek tragedy, a sort of sub-

20   world of smacked bottoms and scrawny mothers-in-law which
     is a part of western European consciousness. ('The Art of Donald
     McGill' [1942], *CEJL*, II, pp. 184–5)

Orwell is commenting upon the very British genre of comic or
'seaside' postcards. We are again very much in the presence of a
speaker, but this time he is constructed not by the foregrounding of
the 'I' and his feelings and reactions, but by what we might call a
dialogic attitude.[7] By this I mean that the voice implied by the writing
is directed toward an imaginary, but apparently specific, addressee;
everything which is said takes its tone from a dramatic stance towards
an assumed reader. By incessantly calling on a 'you' (lines 2, 3, 4,
and throughout this extract), Orwell defines a precise space for the
reader to occupy. Orders – 'get hold of' (line 1), 'spread them out',
(line 4) – and schoolmasterly questions ('What do you see?' line 4,
'What do these things remind you of? What are they so like?' lines
15–16) suggest an energetic interrogator who is putting great pressure on the reader to agree with Orwell's interpretation of this cultural phenomenon; note the sheer physicality of those two imperatives:
'get hold of', 'spread them out'. The Orwellian colloquialism in
vocabulary is there: 'a dozen', 'these things' (is this dismissive, or
simply informal?), 'pick out', 'a pile', 'bottoms', etc. But the casual
style swiftly erupts into a storm of apparently uncompromising condemnation (from line 5) which is entirely typical of Orwell (see pp.
55ff. below on Orwell 'over the top'). His picture of the style of
the postcards seems to be deliberately hyperbolic in its negativity:
'overwhelming vulgarity', 'ever-present obscenity', 'hideousness';
there is a string of Orwellian negative terms – 'lowness', 'grotesque',
'staring', 'blatant', 'heavy', 'empty', 'ugly', 'vacuous' and so on;
and almost every judgement has its intensifier – 'utter', 'monstrously',
etc. The overstatement suggests passionate opinion on the part of
this strident rhetorician, but it is inevitably ironised by the comic
triviality of the subject-matter.

The spoof rhetoric reaches a climax with the semi-rhyming phrase
'bottoms like Hottentots', followed by a shift of register, and thus
tone, of a kind Orwell often employs to keep his readers on their
toes. Just as Orwell will suddenly insert a vernacular term to cue
the demotic tone, so he will often make the reverse shift, dropping
in a learned or abstract word or phrase. The polysyllabic and vague
'indefinable familiarity' is in a quite different register, and sets up

the reader for a more intellectual reinterpretation of comic post-cards. Like Greek tragedy, they express deep cultural archetypes, 'a part of western European consciousness'. Of course Orwell knows he is exaggerating: later in the essay he rephrases the generalisation more modestly, in terms of British stereotypes of marriage, and of people's instinct to revolt against virtue. Here the tongue is kept in the cheek: it is a 'sub-world' with no psychological depth, harbour-ing nothing darker than the prosaic comic reality of 'smacked bot-toms and scrawny mothers-in-law' (line 20). This typical Orwellian colloquialism reverses the register once again, puncturing the pre-tentiousness without destroying the claim. The extract is a deliber-ately rhetorical passage from early on in the essay, and its purpose is to engage the reader in an argument which is at first glance ab-surd, and which must never be taken wholly seriously in the man-ner of the intellectuals. There is an important cultural significance to this apparently trivial, popular, art-form, Orwell goes on to ar-gue, but to be over-serious would risk destroying enjoyment of an essentially saturnalian genre.[8] They are after all an essentially hol-iday form, a cocky expression of carnival.

My three sample passages come from three distinct phases and sections of Orwell's career and preoccupations. The first presents in narrative form one detail of his sense of the predicament of the British official in colonial administration, and springs from his ex-perience in the Burmese police. The second reflects his affection for things ordinary and traditional in English life, and his absorbing desire to understand them rather than take them for granted. The mood is prominent in his prose writings of the early 1940s. The third extract comes from a period of focused political conscious-ness in the later 1940s, when his analysis of the evils of totali-tarianism was crystallising, and when he was specifically moved by the inhibiting effects of conformism on independent thought, and on writing.

The differences in the styles stem from these circumstances, and probably from the different characters of the three magazines for which he was writing. The Orwellian persona is still detectably present in Extract III, but it is less oral, more in the character of an argu-mentative printed mode. The passage comes about half-way through an essay some fifteen pages long; by this time, an ongoing rhetoric has been established:

III Consider, for example, the various attitudes, completely incompatible with one another, which an English Communist or 'fellow-traveller' has had to adopt towards the war between Britain and Germany. For years before September 1939 he was
5 expected to be in a continuous stew about 'the horrors of Nazism' and to twist everything he wrote into a denunciation of Hitler: after September 1939, for twenty months, he had to believe that Germany was more sinned against than sinning, and the word 'Nazi', at least so far as print went, had to drop right out
10 of his vocabulary. Immediately after hearing the 8 o'clock news bulletin on the morning of 22 June 1941, he had to start believing once again that Nazism was the most hideous evil the world had ever seen. Now, it is easy for a politician to make such changes: for a writer the case is somewhat different. If he
15 is to switch his allegiance at exactly the right moment, he must either tell lies about his subjective feelings, or suppress them altogether. In either case he has destroyed his dynamo. Not only will ideas refuse to come to him, but the very words he uses will seem to stiffen under his touch. Political writing in
20 our time consists almost entirely of pre-fabricated phrases bolted together like the pieces of a child's Meccano set. It is the unavoidable result of self-censorship. To write in plain, vigorous language one has to think fearlessly, and if one thinks fearlessly one cannot be politically orthodox. ('The Prevention of Literature' [1946], *CEJL*, IV, pp. 88–89)

Here we have essentially a written rather than oral model, but with the individuality, the implied authenticity, of the personal voice systematically cued. The extract starts dialogically, with a request to 'consider' seeming to assume that the essayist has a right to expect a cooperative reader. 'Consider . . .' is from a didactic, authoritarian register, the language of the lecture-room. Also authoritarian is the style of *generalisation*: from lines 4–5 Orwell asks us to accept as true a series of general statements about the English Left, all very tendentious but offered as fact for the purposes of this argument. In line 14 he shifts the application of the generalisations from politicians to political writers, then from the dilemma of the individual writer to the characteristics of political writing generally. Three generalisations of unmistakable moral force end our extract, but this is not in fact a rhetorical climax, since Orwell goes on for

another dozen lines: 'It might be otherwise in an "age of faith"...';
typically – Orwell finds it difficult to stop, characteristically he (in
Norfolk dialect) 'runs on'.

To turn now to syntax, I suggested on p. 43 that the reader might
get a sense of the contrast of styles by making an informal syntactic comparison between extracts I and III. The sentences in extract
III are much longer, and they contain many subordinate clauses,
which often precede main clauses and thus necessarily hold interpretation of the whole sentence in suspense: for example, the sentence 'If he is to switch...' beginning in line 14, and 'To write...',
line 22. Often, major constituents are interrupted by interpolated
phrases, for example in lines 1–2 'completely incompatible with
one another' separates 'attitudes' from the relative pronoun which
refers to it, and also stretches the distance between 'attitudes' and
the verb of which it is the object, 'adopt'. It will be obvious that
such syntactic complexity (characteristic of *hypotaxis*) lends itself
to processing by the eye rather than the ear, because short-term
memory is under strain and one may need to backtrack in order to
check the drift of a sentence. (I am particularly conscious of back-
tracking in the apparently climactic sentence 'To write...', line 22,
where because of main/subordinate clause inversions, and the paral-
lelism between the two halves of the sentence which encourages
comparison of their contents, the whole complex of cause–effect
relationships is not immediately transparent.)

If Orwell is not expecting his reader to access an oral model
here, but to take the essay fairly as a piece of political *writing*, the
demotic requirement has to be supplied by the vocabulary. There
is, I think, no jargon except what is attributed to his targets, and
ironised, like 'the horrors of Nazism' (lines 5–6) and 'the most hideous
evil' (line 12) or the cliché 'more sinned against than sinning' (line 8).
Abstract words like 'allegiance' (line 15) and 'self-censorship' (line 22)
are clear rather than vague or gestural. There is the exaggerated
Orwellian precision of 'Immediately after hearing the 8 o'clock news
bulletin on the morning of 22 June 1941' (lines 10–11). There are
colloquial words and phrases such as 'in a stew' (line 5) and 'tell
lies' (line 16), the latter particularly salient because of its juxtaposition with the higher-register phrase 'subjective feelings'. And there
are the familiar concrete metaphors, 'dynamo' (line 17) and 'Meccano
set' (line 21). (This is one variant from a system of mechanistic
metaphors applied to the 'ready-made phrases' which so angered
him: see p. 30 above.)

I have introduced the idea of 'authority' in discussing extract III; on reflection, it is also very relevant to Extract II. The sense of a person speaking behind the pages of prose is cued by many devices, but the structures that are used to establish a claim of authority are of major importance: for example the generalising structures that are the basis of the rhetoric of III. Also important is the kind of *modality* deployed. Modality is the linguistics of judgement: the set of devices in language through which speakers/hearers express attitudes towards their subject-matter and toward their addressees. Modality is treated in both logic and grammar, and traditionally four types of modal attitudes are recognised:

1. The speaker's knowledge of, or claim about, the *truth* of a statement or the *factuality* or the *likelihood* of an event.
2. His or her views on the *desirability* or otherwise of a state of affairs.
3. Attitudes towards the *obligations* and *duties* of participants in events being written/talked about.
4. The giving of *permission*.

Let us note immediately that the way writers handle modal elements of language is the foundation of our sense of them as authority-figures. Modality is always present in speech and writing, but may be a discreet background feature, or highlighted and stressed. A writer who affirms, or even strongly insists on, the factuality of what s/he is writing about (type 1); who pronounces judgements on it (type 2); who talks about what people must and must not do (type 3); and who allows that they *may* do certain things (type 4): such a writer clearly claims a role of authority, the possession of wisdom which must be made known to readers. Orwell is very much such a writer; foregrounded modality is very much a defining feature of his personal voice.

The authoritarian stance, built largely through modality, is a quality of his idiolect, but also comes from a pre-existing register. Orwell is in a tradition of English writers who make strong claims of historical, moral and psychological knowledge. One branch of this tradition is the personal, opinionated, essay on diverse subjects, famously established by Francis Bacon in the early seventeenth century; obviously Orwell's own output as an essayist and journalist makes him a central twentieth-century example of that genre. The second relevant branch of this authoritarian tradition of discourse is the 'omniscient author' most familiar in the nineteenth-century novel, in the works of Dickens, George Eliot, and Hardy, for example. The omniscient 'author' is in fact the linguistically constructed voice of a *narrator* who appears to know everything about the story and the characters, including their thoughts and motives, and to possess a broad and profound knowledge of the world and the culture, and of norms of behaviour, thus being qualified to make ethical comments on the characters and to utter philosophical-style pronouncements (see further, Chapter 8, p. 137, and Chapter 10, p. 187).

Generalisation is one expression of authoritarian modality because the writer claims the universal truth (wherever applicable) of the statement s/he makes. The distillation of this is the proverb. But modality is more specifically associated with two other areas of English structure: *modal auxiliary verbs*, and certain types of *adjectives* and *adverbs* which have modal and evaluative meanings. Modal auxiliaries are the little words like 'can', 'will', 'should' which often precede main verbs in English. Modal adjectives include 'certain' and 'probable', and corresponding to them are their adverbial forms 'certainly', 'probably'. It is essential however to grasp that the presence of modal meaning does not depend on the presence of a modal auxiliary: modality is *always* present, whether or not overtly expressed. In the absence of a modal auxiliary, a statement is read as being modalised 'it is a fact that': so in extract III/4, the sentence beginning 'For years before . . .' is read as 'It is a fact that for years before . . .'. Unmarked modality like this is the way a writer or speaker communicates commitment to the assumed, matter-of-fact truth of what s/he says, with no expression of uncertainty ('might', 'probably') admitting doubt, nor any indication of over-confidence ('must', 'certainly'). Unmarked modality is a pervasive characteristic of Orwell's writing, and indicates confidence in his judgements; it is most obvious on the many occasions when he modalises as plain facts statements which are obviously highly subjective, partial, impressions. Extract II is an excellent example, particularly the second paragraph: outrageous, hyped-up judgements are worded as unquestionable statements of fact generally applicable to the postcards. We will return to this feature of Orwell's authoritarian rhetoric in the section on Orwell 'over the top'.

Where modality is marked by a modal auxiliary verb, some specific modal meaning is expressed or stressed. We can illustrate this from the extracts. For convenience I repeat extract I here, with the modal elements picked out in **bold**:

I It was perfectly clear to me what I **ought to** do. I **ought to** walk up to within, say, twenty-five yards of the elephant and test his behaviour. If he charged I **could** shoot, if he took no notice of me it **would** be safe to leave him until the mahout came back. But also I knew that I was going to do no such thing. I was a poor shot with a rifle and the ground was soft mud into which one **would** sink at every step. If the elephant charged and I missed him, I **should** have about as much chance as a toad under a steam-roller. But even then I was not thinking particularly of my own skin, only the watchful yellow faces behind. For at that moment, with the crowd watching me, I was not afraid in the ordinary sense, as I **would** have been if I had been alone. A white man **mustn't** be frightened in front of 'natives'; and so, in general, he isn't frightened. The sole thought in my mind was that if anything went wrong those two thousand Burmans **would** see me pursued, caught, trampled on and reduced to a grinning corpse like that Indian up the hill. And if that happened it was quite probable that some of them **would** laugh. That **would** never do. There was only one alternative. I shoved the cartridges into the magazine and lay down on the road to get a better aim.

For Orwell, this passage is quite strongly marked modally. Two areas of modal meaning are expressed. The very prominent 'would', with variants 'should' and 'could', indicates, with no great confidence, possibilities and likely consequences if certain actions were performed: the modality can be sensed as apprehensiveness and uncertainty on the part of the narrator, and it is an important determiner of the tone of the passage. The other modal meaning is about obligation or duty. The repetition of 'ought to' at the beginning alerts us to this dimension. It appears initially to refer to what would be the best, or most successful, thing for the narrator to do in this dangerous situation, but then 'mustn't' in the sentence on which I commented earlier adds the dimension of social responsibility: the narrator is conscious not only of the practicalities of the situation, but of his duty as a 'white man', being scrutinised by 'natives', to act decisively. So the sense of indecision and anxiety comes largely from the marked modality, producing a subjective tone quite different from the confidence of the modally unmarked extract II.

Extract III is again marked modally, but with quite different options chosen from the systems of modal meanings. Again I repeat the passage, with the modals highlighted:

III   Consider, for example, the various attitudes, completely incompatible with one another, which an English Communist or
'fellow-traveller' **has had to** adopt towards the war between Britain
and Germany. For years before September 1939 he was expected
to be in a continuous stew about 'the horrors of Nazism' and to
twist everything he wrote into a denunciation of Hitler: after September 1939, for twenty months, he **had to** believe that Germany
was more sinned against than sinning, and the word 'Nazi', at
least so far as print went, **had to** drop right out of his vocabulary. Immediately after hearing the 8 o'clock news bulletin on
the morning of 22 June 1941, he **had to** start believing once again
that Nazism was the most hideous evil the world had ever seen.
Now, it is easy for a politician to make such changes: for a writer
the case is somewhat different. If he **is to** switch his allegiance at
exactly the right moment, he **must** either tell lies about his subjective feelings, or suppress them altogether. In either case he
has destroyed his dynamo. Not only **will** ideas refuse to come to
him, but the very words he uses **will** seem to stiffen under his
touch. Political writing in our time consists almost entirely of
pre-fabricated phrases bolted together like the pieces of a child's
Meccano set. It is the unavoidable result of self-censorship. To
write in plain, vigorous language one **has to** think fearlessly, and
if one thinks fearlessly one **cannot** be politically orthodox.

I have already commented on the authoritarian force of generalisations in this passage. Every assertion Orwell makes is offered as
true in all cases to which it is applicable, without exception: every
'Communist or "fellow-traveller"' behaves in these ways, political
writing in our time has universally these characteristics. The assert-
iveness of the generalisations is heightened by the modal auxiliaries I have emboldened, signifying *obligation* and *necessity*. Orwell
presents his communists, fellow-travellers, politicians and political
writers – and those who might wish to behave more morally – as in
the thrall of unavoidable forces. The communist or fellow-traveller
is compelled, presumably by his peers and by political orthodoxy,
to adopt certain attitudes but to reverse them at the drop of a hat;
the political writer's language necessarily goes dead if he is orthodox, and 'plain, vigorous language' depends on personal fearless-
ness. In Orwell all this is *necessarily* so: his modality bombards us
with inevitability.

We can experience in extracts II and III two further aspects of Orwell's personal style: *negativity*, and over-statement or *hyperbole*. Both features are well-illustrated in extract II. The many words with negative meanings, or at least negative connotations, are shown in *italics*, the intensifiers which produce hyperbole **bold**. The word 'monstrously' seems to realise both dimensions simultaneously:

Your first impression is of **overwhelming** *vulgarity*. This is quite apart from the **ever-present** *obscenity,* and apart from the *hideousness* of the colours. They have an **utter** *lowness* of mental atmosphere which comes out not only in the nature of the jokes but, even more, in the *grotesque, staring, blatant* quality of the drawings. The designs, like those of a child, are **full** of *heavy* lines and *empty* spaces, and **all** the figures in them, **every** gesture and attitude, are deliberately *ugly,* the faces *grinning and vacuous,* the women **monstrously** *parodied, with bottoms like Hottentots.*

Negativism and hyperbole are major characteristics of Orwell's 'naturalistic' styles: see the following chapter on 'sordid realism' and on 'hyperrealism'. They are also features of Orwell's 'over-the-top' journalism, to be discussed in the next-but-one section of this chapter. First let us summarise informally some of the main aspects of the personal voice.

LINGUISTIC MARKERS OF ORWELL'S IDIOLECT

The personal voice is cued in a variety of stylistic contexts. It is at its most overt in the essays, but even there, as we have seen, it expresses itself in different stylistic envelopes, from quiet, reflective narration to strident cultural critique and to syntactically elaborate political commentary. The idiolect is not a single, consistent style, but a sense of an individual presence constructed in the mind by an experienced reader of our author. This sense is triggered by the presence of a selection of features or cues: only some need to be present – and perhaps interspersed with quite different stylistic markers – to evoke the persona.

So far we have noticed markers of the following kinds:

- *Oral markers*   suggestions of the presence of a speaking voice. These include contractions ('mustn't') and colloquialisms ('kip'); paratactic (additive) syntax, though hypotaxis (subordination and embedding) is not excluded; short phrases, clauses and sentences, suggesting the intonation and the information structure of speech. As we will see in the following section, Orwell is also fond of an extreme of parataxis, long lists of words or phrases, called by Ringbom 'series'.[9]

- *Lexical register*   a predilection, no doubt motivated by his ideal of 'demotic speech', for vernacular diction: short, concrete, colloquial words and homely similes, blunt adjectives and comments. A single vernacular word will work strikingly to evoke the voice when dropped into a more formal, writerly, context. Orwell sometimes reverses the strategy, inserting the odd high-register word in a low-key or neutral context.

- *Subjectivity*   markers of the presence of a person with thoughts and feelings and strong points of view. The tentativeness and introspection conveyed by mental-process verbs and adjectives in 'Shooting an Elephant' is one manifestation of subjectivity, relatively infrequent but certainly a style found elsewhere, for example in parts of the first-person narrative *Homage to Catalonia*. Orwell is more usually confident to the point of authoritarianism: we have seen how this tone is communicated by modality, particularly generic sentences and other generalisations, and strong words of judgement (see below). One important set of cues which were prominent in the 'The Art of Donald McGill' fall in the area of *dialogism*. Orwell will call up the presence of an imaginary reader by addressing him as 'you', by firing questions and imperatives: an aggressive, didactic tone recalling the teacher or the demagogue.

- *Hyperbole and negativity*   Orwell's language tends toward overstatement, stridency and negativity. When he condemns, he does not do so by halves. The extract from 'The Art of Donald McGill' on which I commented above is entirely characteristic in its dominant negative judgement screwed up to a high pitch by intensifiers. We will take a closer look at Orwell's negativism and exaggeration in the next section.

ORWELL OVER THE TOP

Because of his political views, and his outspoken expression of them, Orwell has always been a controversial writer. He has attracted committed partisanship, from George Woodcock for example, who appropriated Orwell's own metaphor of 'the crystal spirit' to represent his qualities;[10] and he has been just as strongly condemned – as a traitor to the Left, for example, a point of view which in relatively recent years still dominated some critical accounts of his work, for example, the book by the Marxist critic the late Raymond Williams.[11]

In view of the controversial nature of the content of his writings, it is imperative to try to take a balanced view of Orwell's style, particularly in thinking about the 'personal voice' and the ideal of prose like a 'window pane'. Orwell's style in fact bears little resemblance to a window pane, certainly not a clean one. As we will see in the next chapter, when he is writing in documentary mode he sometimes achieves a sharp presentation of detail, so that in a sense one can 'see through' his prose to the material reality of what he is writing about. That is one sense of 'clarity', but it is not the predominant style. When he is writing down his own views, in his own voice, he is forthright and blunt: honesty and courage are signalled.[12] This is perhaps another sense of 'clarity': that he does not dissimulate, but says what he thinks. However, the style is not calm and dispassionate, it is a highly coloured polemic. The tendentious and emotional potential in Orwell should have been emerging in this chapter: it is there in the generalisations, the modality, the vocabulary, the overwhelming negativity and exaggeration. Often this potential leads Orwell 'over the top', to excessive claims and stridently abusive judgements. We can illustrate and analyse this tendency quite briefly, introducing some fresh examples and one or two more points of linguistic description.

Part One of *The Road to Wigan Pier* (1937) reports Orwell's observations on poverty and on working and housing conditions in the North of England. Part Two is a long essay which begins autobiographically with an account of his youthful feelings about 'the poor', and of his Burmese experiences which changed his perceptions. It proceeds to a lengthy and highly charged condemnation of the political intelligentsia, with particular vitriol reserved for those who, in his opinion, were betraying the ideals of Socialism. Here is a flavour:

The only thing *for* which we can combine is the underlying ideal of Socialism; justice and liberty. But it is hardly strong enough to call this ideal 'underlying'. It is almost completely forgotten. It has been buried beneath layer after layer of doctrinaire priggishness, party squabbles, and half-baked 'progressivism' until it is like a diamond hidden under a mountain of dung. The job of the Socialist is to get it out again. Justice and liberty! *Those* are the words that have got to ring like a bugle across the world. For a long time past, certainly for the last ten years, the devil has had all the best tunes. We have reached a stage when the very word 'Socialism' calls up, on the one hand, a picture of aeroplanes, tractors, and huge glittering factories of glass and concrete; on the other, a picture of vegetarians with wilting beards, of Bolshevik commissars (half gangster, half gramophone), of earnest ladies in sandals, shock-headed Marxists chewing polysyllables, escaped Quakers, birth-control fanatics, and Labour Party backstairs-crawlers. Socialism, at least in this island, does not smell any longer of revolution and the overthrow of tyrants; it smells of crankishness, machine-worship, and the stupid cult of Russia. Unless you can remove that smell, and very rapidly, Fascism may win. (*Wigan Pier*, pp. 189–90)

This is not as scathing as some other passages in Part Two, but it is strident, polemical and abusive. Typographically, the italics, the quotation marks and the exclamation mark signal an intensity in pitch and stress of the voice above the level of flat prose. Syntactically, there are some three-part structures, which are a hallmark of rhetoric: 'doctrinaire priggishness, party squabbles and half-baked "progressivism"'; 'crankishness, machine-worship, and the stupid cult of Russia'. At one point the series of three phrases erupts into a list or series, highly typical of Orwell at his most passionate or damning: 'vegetarians with wilting beards, . . . Bolshevik commissars . . ., shock-headed Marxists . . ., escaped Quakers, birth-control fanatics, and Labour Party backstairs-crawlers'. This list contains some of Orwell's pet hates: the modern sensitivity winces at his jibes against birth control and vegetarianism. It is characteristic of Orwell that he treats these targets *stereotypically*,[13] using plurals to suggest that all Marxists (vegetarians, etc.) are the same, and evoking a simplified, generalising visual image very much as a cartoon caricaturist such as Biff or Posy Simmonds does: 'wilting beards', 'shock-headed', 'sandals'. A final point on listing is that this syntax suggests that the objects named in the list are all pretty much the same for present purposes: a list is a *levelling* structure. (More examples of lists will be examined below.)

Finally, the vocabulary merits brief comment. There is an abundance of negative terms, usually plain blunt words in the demotic vein, but some from a schoolboy register: 'half-baked', 'stupid'; such words abound in Orwell's most intemperate writing. Typical also, and here more contrived, is the imagery of excrement and odour: 'dung ... smell ... smell'. Earlier in Part Two of *Wigan Pier* he had dwelt on his boyhood disgust for dirt and stink, a disgust which he and his fictional heroes convey throughout his writing career:

> You watched a great sweaty navvy walking down the road with his pick over his shoulder; you looked at his discoloured shirt and his corduroy trousers stiff with the dirt of a decade; you thought of all those nests and layers of greasy rags below, and, under all, the unwashed body, brown all over (that was how I used to imagine it), with its strong, bacon-like reek. (*Wigan Pier*, p. 112)

This distaste (and his *guilt* about his distaste) generates a good deal of Orwell's negative vocabulary and imagery.

There is in the over-the-top sections of *Wigan Pier* also an *animal* vocabulary and imagery which betrays another of Orwell's negative preoccupations, and a stylistic source for parts of his later major writing. In demotic English, animals are frequently the vehicles for abuse. A Chinese official regards everyone else as 'worms' (p. 113); Professor Saintsbury is like a 'little worm', a 'skunk' (p. 118); Orwell in his boyhood hated the 'hoggishly rich' (p. 120); in the literary world, people get on by 'kissing the bums of verminous little lions' (p. 144); middle-class Socialists are 'mingy little beasts' (p. 153); Communists flock to 'progress' 'like bluebottles to a dead cat'; the Fascist objective is 'a world of rabbits ruled by stoats'; Fascism and Communism are like 'rats and rat-poison' (p. 195); schemes of class-cooperation are reminded that 'the cat does not cooperate with the mouse' (p. 200). Elements of *Animal Farm* and *Nineteen Eighty-Four* are in this imagery.

Here, drawn from *Wigan Pier*, is a typical catalogue of Orwellian abuse applied to people and projects:

thick-skinned, odious little snob, ass, cock-virgin, soggy, half-baked, thoroughly flabby, boneless, mealy-mouthed, spurious, bunkum, cranks, gutless, even feebler, dull, empty windbags, fat-bellied, swindle, vulgar, ignorant and half-baked, little fat men, frightful debauchery of taste, filthy, bare-ass savage, dullness, flabbiness, pimpled followers, Romantic fools, mealy-mouthed, humbug, prig, priggishness . . .

And some series:

For several years . . . England was full of half-baked antinomian opinions. Pacificism, internationalism, humanitarianism of all kinds, feminism, free love, divorce-reform, atheism, birth-control – things like these were getting a better hearing than they would get in normal times. (*Wigan Pier*, p. 121)

hygiene, fruit-juice, birth-control, poetry, etc. (ibid, p. 142)

every fruit-juice drinker, nudist, sandal-wearer, sex-maniac, Quaker, 'Nature Cure' quack, pacifist, and feminist in England. (ibid, p. 152)

machines to save work, machines to save thought, machines to save pain, hygiene, efficiency, organization, more hygiene, more efficiency, more organization, more machines . . . (ibid, p. 169)

is it work to dig, to carpenter, to plant trees, to fell trees, to ride, to fish, to hunt, to feed chickens, to play the piano, to take photographs, to build a house, to cook, to sew, to trim hats, to mend motor bicycles? (ibid, p. 172)

when a human being is not eating, drinking, sleeping, making love, talking, playing games, or merely lounging about . . . (ibid, p. 173)

In a healthy world there would be no demand for tinned foods, aspirins, gramophones, gaspipe chairs, machine guns, daily newspapers, telephones, motor-cars, etc., etc. . . . (ibid, pp. 179–80)

Most of the objects, classes of person, processes and ideas listed in these series represent Orwell's hates. It is not difficult to read from *The Road to Wigan Pier* (and from Orwell's other writings) a coherent intellectual and moral position which makes his aversions comprehensible. He dislikes middle-class socialists, for example, because of their pretensions and affectations, which have alienated them from working people – a callously accepted alienation, in his view, given the dire conditions in the North which have so shocked him. He dislikes machines for a number of reasons: they displace craft; they offend against his nostalgia for what he believed was a more natural, human and creative world; they are naively accepted by the intellectual Left as a key symbol of socialist progress. And so on. In each case, we can see what he is getting at by attacking these things, in terms of his own strongly articulated views. The use of list structures, however, is an extreme and absurd technique of criticism. Lists lack logic and discrimination. They reduce everything to the same level, and therefore are offensive to some of things listed, which quite obviously have merit outside of this context: Quakers and tinned food, for instance. If Orwell is not making clear discriminations in this list, it is because he is proceeding in a tone of raucous mockery; it is, however, close to intemperance and intolerance.

5 Versions of Realism

In Chapters 5 to 8 I will discuss some stylistic features of the seven books which were published between 1933 and 1939. Orwell's productivity in this period was astonishing: one book a year, each taking a few months to write, despite other commitments, recurrent serious illness, poverty, several changes of home base, a research trip to the North of England, fighting in the Spanish Civil War . . . Each book seems to have been written straight out, with no overlapping: if the pace seems frantic, there was the gain of concentrated focus, a condition which will be appreciated by any writer who has to grapple with a number of simultaneous projects.

Orwell frequently revalued his books with hindsight reflections, with a tendency to *de*value them.[1] Critics also practise a kind of retrospection. Their vantage-point is the high territory of *Animal Farm* (1945) and *Nineteen Eighty-Four* (1949) which have of course enjoyed a phenomenally greater acclaim than the 'early' books. From this perspective, the seven books written and published in the 1930s might be seen as hastily-written, ragged, pot-boilers, inferior to the 'masterpieces' and interesting primarily as anticipating, in theme and/or in style, the two most popular books. Now it seems to me valid to find in the 1930s works numerous foreshadowings, both in ideas and in techniques, of the two major books; to regard some aspects of them as stages in the working-out of what we know were Orwell's preoccupations in his last years. However, this should not lead to the dismissal of the early fiction and documentary writings as try-outs by an apprentice. As a matter of fact, each of the early books was a distinct piece of writing, usually relating to some specific section of experience in Orwell's own life, or phase in the development of his political and artistic thinking. Each has its own models, and strategies of composition, and these are quite various: they deserve an attempt at understanding in their own terms. To grant the first seven books this minimal respect is not to deny that they have faults: they have been criticised, variously, for flat characterisation, uncertainty of point of view, unmotivated stylistic shifts and narrative transitions, and intrusive commentary. However, it is by no means the case that all these uncertainties of technique afflict all the early books. Every one of them has been acclaimed by different critics and reviewers at some time during its history, and all have remained in print since popular editions were published after Orwell's death. There is a strong tradition of appreciative literary criticism which, quite justifiably, finds reasons to admire Orwell's early fictional and documentary output as a whole.[2]

Four aspects of the language of the 1930s books will be examined. In this chapter I will demonstrate, largely with reference to *Down and Out in Paris and London*, *The Road to Wigan Pier*, *Burmese Days* and *Coming up for Air*, three interlinked styles of 'realistic' writing, which I will call **descriptive realism**, **naturalism** (or 'sordid realism'), and **surrealism** (or 'hyperrealism'). In Chapter 6 the subject will be 'voices of the other', Orwell's representation of modes of speech which differ from standard English, and the importance of stylistic and social heteroglossia in his work. In Chapter 7 I will look at another set of topics: literary strategies relating to description and figurative language, and will develop the discussion of 'voices of the other' (heteroglossia). Chapter 8 will examine the linguistic construction of narrative point of view, a subject which becomes of fundamental importance in *Animal Farm* (Chapter 9) and *Nineteen Eighty-Four* (Chapter 10).

Let us remind ourselves of the dates and sequence of the books concerned:

- *Down and Out in Paris and London*, 1933
- *Burmese Days*, 1934
- *A Clergyman's Daughter*, 1935
- *Keep the Aspidistra Flying*, 1936
- *The Road to Wigan Pier*, 1937
- *Homage to Catalonia*, 1938
- *Coming Up for Air*, 1939

Then, after a gap occupied by collections of essays, by journalism and by BBC work, there followed *Animal Farm* (1945); finally, in his Jura and hospital days, he wrote *Nineteen Eighty-Four* (1949).

Though each has an individual occasion and technique, the books of the 1930s may be divided for the purposes of stylistic discussion into two groups. Four of them, *Burmese Days*, *Clergyman's Daughter*, *Aspidistra* and *Coming Up for Air*, are novels more or less strictly speaking: they are fictionalised narratives told in the third person, or in one case, *Coming Up for Air*, a first-person narration in which the speaker is a character and not an Orwell-toned narrator.

The other three (*Down and Out*, *Wigan Pier* and *Catalonia*) are mixed genres, part-autobiography, part-documentary or reportage, part-commentary or general essay. In all of them Orwell figures directly, but in various guises and speaking in different voices. All three versions of 'Orwell', however, can be best seen as involving variants of the 'personal voice' of the previous chapter, that personal voice by which the man Blair constructed himself as the writer George Orwell, an observer of, and commentator on, his life and times.

Each of these three books makes very specific demands of its reader, who must adjust his or her expectations to each text: no pre-existing generic model will fit. There is no familiar form to bring to these works, unlike the case of, for example, *Burmese Days*, where the reader will not be let down if s/he brings a foreknowledge of the 'colonial novel' of the Kipling (or even Burgess) tradition, or more specifically Forster's *A Passage to India* (1924). Each of the three books must be read – to use a phrase which seems necessary but surely abhorrent to Orwell as a piece of pretentious academic jargon – *sui generis*, one of a kind. No single generic label and assumptions will fit any of them properly: *Down and Out* is an anonymised fragment of personal autobiography, has a slight narrative continuity but digresses to documentary and commentary. When Orwell has some general points to make, he boldly breaks off from the narrative and starts up again in a first-person essayistic style: ch. 22 opens 'For what they are worth I want to give my opinions about the life of a Paris *plongeur*' (p. 117); ch. 32, 'I want to put in some notes, as short as possible, on London slang and swearing' (p. 170); ch. 36, 'I want to set down some general remarks about tramps' (p. 203). *Wigan Pier*, which was commissioned as a report rather than a story, is also of mixed genre. It has a fictionalised personal opening, a mass of documentation (including photographs, though these were not taken in the areas he visited)[3], and passages in a plain realistic style; but as we have seen, Part Two of *Wigan Pier* shifts abruptly and stridently to a polemical and abusive style. *Homage to Catalonia* is a narrative account of Orwell's experiences in the Spanish Civil War, but also contains set descriptive passages and elements of travelogue, and is interrupted by political analyses and documentary quotations (especially chs. 5 and 11). He declares:

If you are not interested in the horrors of party politics, please skip; I am trying to keep the political parts of this narrative in separate chapters for precisely that purpose. (*Catalonia*, p. 46)

'Artistic' integration is not prominently on the agenda. None of these three books is strongly driven or unified by story, none is consistently essay, or description, or analysis; each mixes all these, and other ingredients, in various proportions.

The seven books published in the 1930s encompass a variety of genres, and three of them, *Down and Out*, *Wigan Pier* and *Catalonia*, settle to no recognisable prior form. Relatedly, they manifest a remarkable variety of *stylistic* techniques between them, and individually, each includes a range of styles. The juxtaposition of distinct styles within one work may be called **heteroglossia**: it is a feature of Orwell's writing in all his books except *Animal Farm*, and its artistic and political significance will be discussed in Chapter 10 in relation to *Nineteen Eighty-Four*. In the present and the following two chapters we will identify some of the elements of the heteroglossic mix.

THE THREE 'REALISMS': BRIEF CHARACTERISATION

The first thing to acknowledge is that the three versions of realism are not watertight distinct styles but overlapping stylistic models: it is not possible to find absolutely clear instances, to say that one style starts here in the text and ends there, to be replaced by some other clear style, say 'demotic' or 'lyrical'. The three styles of realism (as generally with 'styles') are 'models' in the sense introduced in Chapter 4 (p. above). Key features or cues – which may be just single words or phrases, or individual phonetic or metaphoric usages, symbols, etc. – encourage the reader to experience a part of the text as a particular kind of representation of the world. The reader's previous literary and other linguistic experience, including in this case familiarity with the writer's usual practices, brings the models to a reading of the text, and they are activated by the liaison of the pre-existing model and the textual cues.

Descriptive realism is a realism of physical particularity, a focus on what he called 'solid objects and scraps of useless information' (p. 19 above). This 'descriptive realism' is less obviously literary than the more sensationalist 'sordid realism', but no less crafted. It is an illusion of clarity and precision created by certain linguistic techniques including focus on detail or 'microscopism'; the enu-meration of facts; and a preoccupation with textures, spatial dimensions and other material considerations. Orwell's work has been much admired for the concreteness and memorability of his descriptions of settings and places. His ideal of prose as clear as a window pane comes to mind, but as we will see at the end of this chapter, description is not readily separable from the narrator's views and values, so the clarity is often not perfect.

Naturalism has later nineteenth-century literary origins[4] and consists of a focus on suffering and on physical squalor in people and places. Extremes of sensation are evoked: dirt, smell, noise, light and dark, heat and cold, violent movement, crowding, confinement, physical contact (sensations to which Orwell seems to have had powerful personal aversions). The style is hyperbolic, and relies to a considerable extent on metaphor, evocative adjectives and intensifying phrases; the tone is generally negative or condemnatory, a tendency which meshes well with Orwell's dominant discontent and anger.

Surrealism in Orwell's writing is, as I have tried to suggest by the alternative term 'hyperrealism', a stage beyond naturalism. In hyperrealism the assault on the senses is intensified and diversified, and there are odd juxtapositions of images suggesting a more discordant world, one more difficult to figure out, than the real world. Metaphors and similes, often unusual and opaque, are common. Sensory experience is presented in terms of a fictional or alien world: in the passages to be examined below, there are evocations of hell, or a lunar landscape. Symbolism is constantly hinted, though usually in an imprecise way. Surrealism is usually achieved through descriptions of sights and scenes, but once, in a Joycean chapter of *A Clergyman's Daughter*, Orwell tries for the only time a surrealistic effect based on a disorienting medley of voices (see Chapter 6, fourth section).

In Chapter 7 we will examine a fourth style of descriptive writing which could not be called 'realistic', the **picturesque**, the highly visual and colourful evocation of unusual, striking, scenes and landscape, often exotic. The picturesque is prominent in *Burmese Days* and found in passages of *Homage to Catalonia*; it is a style which Orwell, with hindsight, confessed to rather than admired. There is a less spectacular, more rural, variant which I have called **pastoral**,

well-illustrated in *Coming Up for Air* but occurring at romantic
moments elsewhere.

Both the 'descriptive' and the 'sordid' models of realism persist
throughout Orwell's writings up to and including his final novel,
Nineteen Eighty-Four. In the early works there are prominent 'set
pieces' of description in one or the other mode, but sometimes they
are tendencies rather than utterly distinct, and are often interwoven,
or just cued by some significant detail. 'Surrealism' or 'hyperrealism'
is not simply an indulgence of Orwell's early, experimental, work,
but has a specific function in *Nineteen Eighty-Four* as communicating Winston Smith's dreaming and hallucinatory states (Chapter
10, pp. 192–3).

DESCRIPTIVE REALISM AND THE SENSE OF 'PLACE'

Orwell's writing has frequently been praised for the precision and
memorability of his descriptions of settings and locations, particularly those that convey the minutiae of English life; for example,
J. R. Hammond: 'his undoubted talent lay in the power to evoke a
setting with such clarity that the picture remains in the mind long
after the book has been laid aside'.[5] Hammond may here be recalling a comment of Orwell on Dickens that he quotes elsewhere:

> Much that he wrote is extremely factual, and in the power of
> evoking visual images he has probably never been equalled. When
> Dickens has once described something you see it for the rest of
> your life. (*CEJL*, I, 485)

Details such as the following, from the opening pages of *Coming
up for Air*, abound in Orwell:

> ○ Down below, out of the little square of bathroom window, I could
> see the ten yards by five of grass, with a privet hedge round it
> and a bare patch in the middle, that we call the back garden.
> There's the same back garden, same privets, and same grass, be-
> hind every house in Ellesmere Road. Only difference – where
> there are no kids there's no bare patch in the middle ...
> Our dining-room, like the other dining-rooms in Ellesmere Road,
> is a poky little place, fourteen feet by twelve, or maybe it's twelve

by ten, and the Japanese oak sideboard, with the two empty decanters and the silver egg-stand that Hilda's mother gave us for a
wedding present, doesn't leave much room. (*Coming up for Air*,
pp. 7, 10)

These two fragments, inserted in George Bowling's account of a
morning at his house, contribute, with other jigsaw pieces, to an
overall description of the spiritless modern housing estate where he
and his family live. Because the description is given in bits, the
details remain prominent: a few nouns list the salient points, and
because they are few in number and in very brief passages, they are
highlighted: 'grass', 'privet', 'bare patch', 'Japanese oak sideboard',
'the two empty decanters and the silver egg-stand'. There is in fact
space for extra detail to be mentioned and not lost: the bathroom
window is not simply a viewing point on the garden, it is a 'little
square'; the sideboard is 'Japanese oak'. The dimensions, both of
the garden and of the dining-room, are specified, as is very common in Orwell.

Orwell's finest descriptions are of settings that typify the life of
a traditional, even vanished, England; they are often *remembered*
by the narrator, not just observed, and for this reason are charged
with a kind of evocative power. *Coming up for Air* contains a chain
of nostalgic passages in which the hero and narrator George Bowling recalls his childhood impressions of his family's home and shop
(his father was an animal feed merchant):

The very first thing I remember is the smell of sainfoin chaff.
You went up the stone passage that led from the kitchen to the
shop, and the smell of sainfoin got stronger all the way. Mother
had fixed a wooden gate in the doorway to prevent Joe and
myself...from getting into the shop. I can still remember standing
there clutching the bars, and the smell of sainfoin mixed up with
the damp plastery smell that belonged to the passage. It wasn't
till years later that I somehow managed to crash the gate and get
into the shop when nobody was there. A mouse that had been
having a go at one of the meal-bins suddenly plopped out and
ran between my feet. It was quite white with meal. (*Coming up
for Air*, (pp. 35–6)

Note the use of smells to prompt memory; the simple details that nevertheless give an image and a texture: 'the stone passage', 'a wooden gate'; the clear focus on a single mouse 'quite white with meal'. The child George progresses to the shop:

> And the shop itself, with the huge scales and the wooden measures and the tin shovel, and the white lettering on the window, and the bullfinch in its cage – which you couldn't see very well even from the pavement, because the window was always dusty – all these things dropped into place one by one, like bits of a jigsaw puzzle. (ibid, p. 36)

The jigsaw metaphor (which I borrowed above) is instructive. Knowledge, here the boy's mental map of his home surroundings, is a whole picture which is constituted from 'bits' of sensory experience which become integrated as they snap into place: they cease to be isolated fragments, but acquire meaning when they are understood as functioning in relation to one another. This is as good a theory of the way readers integrate and interpret textual description as it is of the way children make sense of the bits of the world.[6] We recover the individual 'bits' from the text; in Orwell, these are characteristically given in very simple and concrete noun phrases (hence the feeling of visual precision):

> the shop, the huge scales, the wooden measures, the tin shovel, the white lettering on the window, the bullfinch in its cage, the pavement, the windows... always dusty.

The scales, measures and shovel are the implements for scooping, weighing and serving for an old-fashioned 'corn and seed merchant' like George's father; the white applied lettering is characteristic of pre-war shop fronts; the window is dusty, not through any slovenliness but because the goods in which the shop deals are dusty, dry animal feeds stocked in bulk. Orwell highlights the separate components – which are therefore distinct as they are read and remembered – and the reader makes the connections as s/he reconstructs the fictional world which the boy is remembering.[7] From a few spare references to a coherent set of physical objects, each mentioned with precision, we build a picture of an old-fashioned shop, and an atmosphere. The fact that we know that the scene is remembered by the narrator with affectionate nostalgia helps us to imagine this atmosphere, without Orwell having to mention explicitly the feeling by any adjectives or adverbs of attitude and evaluation. The plain, concrete yet suggestive style dominates this section of *Coming up for Air*, and is carried very effectively in some quite sensitive sections, for example, the description of the kitchen and his mother's work within it (pp. 48–9).

An additional small point which might be noticed is that each of the descriptions quoted so far contains one reference to something slightly odd or puzzling: the 'silver egg-stand' and 'the bullfinch in its cage'. These slight incongruities complicate the tone somewhat: the grotesque egg-stand hints at George's hostility to his mother-in-law, while the pet bullfinch domesticises a commercial setting (it is presumably an advertisement for the bird-seed that George's father sells). Both references, slightly off-beat, may act as short-cuts to retrieve the setting from our memory store.

Interiors, settings and scenes are described in this lucid and economical but suggestive way throughout Orwell's writings. I would like to quote two more examples here, two interiors from Orwell's first true novel, *Burmese Days* (1934), famed for the landscape descriptions discussed in Chapter 7 below. There is a shading here into other kinds of writing, judgemental in the first, and symbolic in the second. First, the basic account of the 'white man's Club' in colonised Kyauktada, Burma:

> Inside, the Club was a teak-walled place smelling of earth-oil, and consisting of only four rooms, one of which contained a forlorn 'library' of five hundred mildewed novels, and another an old and mangy billiards table – this, however, seldom used, for during most of the year hordes of flying beetles came buzzing round the lamps and littered themselves over the cloth. There was also a card-room and a 'lounge' which looked towards the river, over a wide veranda; but at this time of day all the verandas were curtained with green bamboo chicks. The lounge was an unhomelike room, with coco-nut matting on the floor, and wicker chairs and tables which were littered with shiny illustrated papers. For ornament there were a number of 'Bonzo' pictures, and the dusty skulls of sambhur. A punkah, lazily flapping, shook dust into the tepid air. (*Burmese Days*, p. 19)

The second passage describes the bedroom in the quarters of John Flory, the central protagonist in *Burmese Days*:

> The bedroom was a large square room with white plaster walls, open doorways and no ceiling, but only rafters in which sparrows nested. There was no furniture except the big four-poster bed, with its furled mosquito net like a canopy, and a wicker table and chair and a small mirror; also some rough book-shelves containing several hundred books, all mildewed by many rainy seasons and riddled by silver fish. A *tuktoo* clung to the wall, flat and motionless like a heraldic dragon. Beyond the veranda eaves the light rained down like glistening white oil. Some doves in a bamboo thicket kept up a dull droning noise, curiously appropriate to the heat – a sleepy sound, but with the sleepiness of chloroform rather than a lullaby. (ibid, pp. 47–8)

As the intricate and well-devised narrative of the novel unfolds, quite a lot of action occurs in these two locations, particularly at the Club; and the basic function of these two passages is to map out in an introductory way the structure and contents of the settings. As is common in Orwell's descriptions of places, the style is basically nominal: a framework of nouns listing the main features of the rooms and what was contained in them – four rooms, billiard-table, lamps, card-room, lounge, veranda, bamboo chicks, coconut matting, wicker chairs and tables, papers, pictures, skulls, punkah; white plaster walls, open doorways, etc. The verbs introducing these nouns might not be noticed: they are largely 'was' and 'were', plus 'contain' in both passages; significant is the avoidance of any more informative verbs, or decorative ones: even simple locative verbs like 'stood', or 'placed', are absent, and there is a marked scarcity of prepositions indicating spatial relationships between the objects listed, only 'towards' and 'beyond'. Just enough information is given to allow readers to understand the use of these spaces in future scenes: the four rooms of the Club are carefully distinguished, so that we can construct how, later, the English with their sexual and political tensions occupy parts of this building in their various role-playings and crises.

But the sparse description means also sparseness of the rooms and objects described: Flory's bedroom, it is hinted, is under-furnished by British standards; the Club is tatty and institutional; there is nothing personal, nothing luxurious. Some simple negative words carry a large weight of meaning: '*only* four rooms', '*open* doorways', '*no* ceiling', '*only* rafters', '*no* furniture'. In the description of the Club, a string of adjectives indicate seediness and neglect: 'forlorn', 'mildewed', 'old and mangy', 'littered', 'unhomelike', 'dusty', 'tepid'. Both places are infested, with sparrows, flying beetles, silver fish, a 'tuktoo'. These locations are both described and judged, and they are judged negatively: they symbolise the dehumanisation of the English in Burma, and are fitting settings for the inadequacies of social and sexual relationship which their situation brings about, and particularly for the racism which is enacted in the book. In describing the Club, Orwell lays the ground for a critique of it and its members; this typical mixture of description and evaluation will be discussed in the final section of the present chapter.

The second passage, the description of Flory's bedroom, moves from a matter-of-fact account of the room to an evocation of a mood symbolised by the light and the sound of the Burmese natural world. Orwell's correlation of the characters' feelings and the sensations of landscape and climate in *Burmese Days* will be discussed in Chapter 7.

NATURALISM AND SURREALISM IN *DOWN AND OUT IN PARIS AND LONDON*

Down and Out has its sources in Orwell's personal travels of 1927–9: his voluntary tramping in the East End of London, followed by eighteen months trying to live as a writer in Paris, where he became genuinely destitute and worked as a *plongeur* or dishwasher.[8] Orwell vouched for the authenticity of the book: 'nearly all the incidents described there actually happened, though they have been rearranged' (*Wigan Pier*, p. 133). The English and French experiences have been transposed. The book starts in a poor quarter of Paris with depictions of a hotel and bar and its neighbourhood, and of various eccentrics (his term) who live at or frequent the hotel and bistro. By Chapter 3 the narrator has lost his money; he teams up with Boris, a Russian waiter, to search for work, and the next several chapters follow their adventures and financial decline until they secure work at a hotel. Boris is a caricature, a Dickensian grotesque; their hunt for a job, a picaresque farce. The structure so far is rambling and anecdotal, a series of comic or pathetic incidents, and curious tales narrated by the 'eccentrics'.

Chapter 10 has the narrator and Boris employed at the 'Hôtel X', and here begins a section of some sixty pages depicting the hotel and restaurant world seen from below. This sequence can be regarded as the imaginative centre of the book. Orwell devotes great descriptive and poetic energy to presenting the squalid conditions of the kitchens; the power hierarchy in the work force, with the lowest grade, the *plongeurs* (at which level Orwell was employed) being essentially slaves; the cheating of, and contempt for, customers. In his review, C. Day Lewis commented 'if you wish to eat a meal in a big hotel without acute nausea, you had better skip pp. 107–109'.[9] Here is art as political writing. There are a number of often-quoted set pieces, including recurrent treatments of a motif that clearly preoccupied Orwell: his vision (from a position of privilege) of labour and working life as a descent into hell; there is a version of inferno at his first entrance into the Hôtel X:

> He led me down a winding staircase into a narrow passage, deep underground, and so low that I had to stoop in places. It was stiflingly hot and very dark, with only dim, yellow bulbs several yards apart. There seemed to be miles of dark labyrinthine passages – actually, I suppose, a few hundred yards in all – that reminded one queerly of the lower decks of a liner; there were the same heat and cramped space and warm reek of food, and a humming, whirring noise (it came from the kitchen furnaces) just like the whir of engines. We passed doorways which let out sometimes a shouting of oaths, sometimes the red glare of a fire, once a shuddering draught from an ice chamber. (*Down and Out*, p. 54)

The narrator moves from the Hôtel X to a pretentious but filthy and disorganised restaurant; the squalor and chaos are again portrayed in detail. He escapes by borrowing the money to return to England, but before he relates his return he offers a chapter of 'opinions about the life of a Paris *plongeur*' (Ch. 22).

The book continues with a rambling account of life among tramps and beggars in London (which in Orwell's real life was a voluntary descent undertaken before his trip to Paris). The procedure and structure are similar to the first part: Orwell puts his narrator in association with two low-life characters, Bozo the 'screever' or pavement artist, and Paddy the tramp, and takes the reader from location to location, describing lodging houses and 'spikes' ('casual wards' for the homeless) with a documentary detail that foreshadows *Wigan Pier*.

He ends with an essay on the social and economic conditions of tramps. This is a direct treatment of one aspect of the theme of the book (destitution), voiced in the form of a commentary. Critics have expressed their dissatisfaction with this essay, treating it as a deviation from a predominantly fictional mode. But the narrative fiction – the low-life stories peopled with Dickensian oddities – is itself only an instrument, as Orwell clearly announced in the first chapter:

> I am trying to describe the people in our quarter, not for the mere curiosity, but because they are all part of the story. Poverty is what I am writing about, and I had my first contact with poverty in this slum. The slum, with its dirt and its queer lives, was first an object-lesson in poverty, and then the background of my own experiences. It is for that reason that I try to give some idea of what life was like there. (*Down and Out*, p. 5)

The dominant mode of representation in the first part of *Down and Out* is naturalistic: 'sordid realism'. Significantly, Orwell invokes Zola, whom we know (note 4) he much admired: 'I wish I could be Zola for a little while, just to describe that dinner hour' (ibid, p. 64; peak demand at the hotel, frenzied activity in the kitchen). The point is not whether Orwell emulated Zola's style in detail, but that his descriptive model is in general terms naturalistic in the Zola mode, and therefore literary in character.

The opening description of the street and the hotel where the narrator lived is a characteristic evocation of 'noise and dirt', the keynotes of Orwell's representation in the Paris section:

> The Rue du Coq d'Or, Paris, seven in the morning. A succession of furious, choking yells from the street. Madame Monce, who kept the little hotel opposite mine, had come out on to the pavement to address a lodger on the third floor. Her bare feet were stuck into sabots and her grey hair was streaming down.
>
> *Madame Monce:* 'Salope! Salope! How many times have I told you not to squash bugs on the wallpaper? Do you think you've bought the hotel, eh? Why can't you throw them out of the window like everyone else? *Putain! Salope!'* ... Quarrels, and the desolate cries of street hawkers, and the shouts of children chasing orange-peel over the cobbles, and at night loud singing and the sour reek of the refuse-carts, made up the atmosphere of the street.

It was a very narrow street – a ravine of tall, leprous houses, lurching towards one another in queer attitudes, as though they had all been frozen in the act of collapse . . . My hotel was called the Hôtel des Trois Moineaux. It was a dark, rickety warren of five storeys, cut up by wooden partitions into forty rooms. The rooms were small and inveterately dirty, for there was no maid, and Madame F., the *patronne*, had no time to do any sweeping. The walls were as thin as matchwood, and to hide the cracks they had been covered with layer after layer of pink paper, which had come loose and housed innumerable bugs. Near the ceiling long lines of bugs marched all day like columns of soldiers, and at night came down ravenously hungry, so that one had to get up every few hours and kill them in hecatombs. Sometimes when the bugs got too bad one used to burn sulphur and drive them into the next room; whereupon the lodger next door would retort by having *his* room sulphured, and drive the bugs back. It was a dirty place, but homelike, for Madame F. and her husband were good sorts. The rent of the rooms varied between thirty and fifty francs a week. (ibid, pp. 1–2)

The 'realism' here is of a very literary kind. The verbless opening sentence 'The Rue du Coq d'Or . . .' is like the title of a picture, or a scene-setting opening stage-direction: Orwell signals that he is to embark on a word-painting of 'the atmosphere of the street'. A second verbless sentence follows, conveying an impression rather than a narrative report of an event; further on, the sentence beginning 'Quarrels . . .', though finite (culminating in a verb that completes it), is dominated by a string of noun phrases which offer a series of discrete sensory impressions. We saw in the previous chapter that the list or series is a favourite stylistic device of Orwell's. It is here used to suggest a crowding of sensory stimuli; we will encounter some more spectacular lists later.

Three other simple linguistic strategies dominate this impressionistic technique of 'sordid realism'. The first is a set of nouns and verbs, in a colloquial register, designating unpleasant, intrusive or low-life objects, sensations and actions:[10]

yells, bare feet, squash bugs, throw [bugs] out of the window, quarrels, cries, shouts, orange-peel, singing, reek, refuse-carts, cracks, bugs (x 4), kill, burn sulphur.

The second strategy is effected through the adjectives, and is highly typical of Orwell: the passage is suffused by adjectives offering consistently negative judgements; none severe in itself, but together producing an overwhelmingly gloomy effect:

> furious, choking, bare, grey, desolate, loud, sour, narrow, leprous, queer, dark, rickety, small, dirty, thin, loose, too bad, dirty.

Once again this is, apart from 'desolate' and 'leprous', a vernacular register, part of Orwell's way of maintaining contact with 'demotic speech'. And the oppressive negativity foreshadows the gloom of such later books as *Aspidistra* and *Nineteen Eighty-Four*. Only at the end are positive evaluations offered: 'homelike', 'good sorts'.

A third feature of this version of naturalism is a general heightening of sensation carried by some of the adjectives which suggest some extreme state of affairs, or at least a high level of energy output or sensation (for example 'furious', 'choking', 'loud', 'tall'), and by intensifiers:

> very narrow, inveterately, as thin as, layer after layer, innumerable, long, all day, ravenously, every few hours, too bad.

We can begin to see in this passage how Orwell's style tends toward hyperbole, even exaggeration and stridency. Later, in the set descriptive passages on hotel kitchen life, his use of these linguistic resources results in sensationalism or surrealism rather than naturalism, as we will see.

This realism is done in one of Orwell's mixed styles. Part of the vocabulary is 'low'; the tone is urgent as if the speaking voice wishes to break through. There may be seeds of the descriptive realism of *Wigan Pier*: the bugs on the pink paper are observed microscopically, the rents of the lodgings are stated in a matter-of-fact way, but without the foregrounded precision of the room dimensions and family budgets of *Wigan Pier*. But the painterly opening sentence, the traces of a high-register vocabulary ('sabots', 'leprous', 'hecatombs'), and the high-profile metaphors, encase the realism in a literary frame. There are two set-piece metaphors, the first extensive and complex, but ostentatious and laboured:

a very narrow street – a ravine of tall, leprous houses, lurching towards one another in queer attitudes, as though they had all been frozen in the act of collapse.

The first part of the complex metaphor, 'ravine', invokes landscape to picture the geometry of the street; that visual field is then replaced by an image drawn from human disease to convey the texture of rotten, broken plaster; 'lurching' makes the houses lean and jerk like drunks; 'frozen' arrests the lurching motion, but in this sensorily confusing context the normal suggestions of ice, coldness, hardness are irrelevant or not activated – the final part of the metaphor remains dead because the context does not motivate it. The second set metaphor is more unified:

long lines of bugs marched all day like columns of soldiers

The image is visually precise, not dissipated like the previous one; and the military metaphoric vehicle evokes purpose and threat. But it is presented comically: the bugs are mocked by the disproportionately elevated classicism 'hecatombs' and by the farce of smoking them backwards and forwards from room to room. The unexpected learned word 'hecatomb', which stands out in the vernacular context, is a typical Orwell strategy: from time to time he drops in a strikingly erudite word which many readers will have to look up (I did: a hecatomb was a Greek or Roman ceremonial sacrifice of 100 oxen). Orwell's extreme stylistic self-consciousness and his respect for the colloquial would rule out mere display of cleverness: the aim seems to be comic here, while elsewhere a learned polysyllable seems to serve to unsettle the style, to keep the reader alert.

The 'naturalistic' style of the opening, then, is far from 'documentary'. It is decorative, hyperbolic, and whimsical in tone. This is also a literary set piece, a passage of atmospheric writing which prefigures the Zolaesque kitchen descriptions at the centre of the book; it differs from them in its interweaving of distaste and humour. One of these set pieces has been excerpted earlier; I will extend the quotation here:

He led me down a winding staircase into a narrow passage, deep underground, and so low that I had to stoop in places. It was stiflingly hot and very dark, with only dim, yellow bulbs several yards apart. There seemed to be miles of dark labyrinthine passages – actually, I suppose, a few hundred yards in all – that reminded one queerly of the lower decks of a liner; there were the same heat and cramped space and warm reek of food, and a humming, whirring noise (it came from the kitchen furnaces) just like the whir of engines. We passed doorways which let out sometimes a shouting of oaths, sometimes the red glare of a fire, once a shuddering draught from an ice chamber. As we went along, something struck me violently in the back. It was a hundred-pound block of ice, carried by a blue-aproned porter. After him came a boy with a great slab of veal on his shoulder, his cheek pressed into the damp, spongy flesh. They shoved me aside with a cry of *'Sauve-toi, idiot!'* and rushed on. On the wall, under one of the lights, someone had written in a very neat hand: "Sooner will you find a cloudless sky in winter, than a woman at the Hôtel X. who has her maidenhead." It seemed a queer sort of place. (*Down and Out*, pp. 54–5)

Some elements of the style of the first passage are intensified here: naturalism is raised to hyperrealism. There is, for example, the crowding and diversity of violent and unpleasant sensations, hurled at the reader in rapid lists of noun phrases: 'heat and cramped space and warm reek of food, and a humming, whirring noise', 'sometimes a shouting of oaths, sometimes the red glare of a fire, once a shuddering draught from an ice chamber'. There is the heightening of impression through constant intensifiers: 'narrow', 'deep', 'so low', 'stiflingly hot', 'very dark'. The extremes of heat, cold, noise, confinement and darkness hold the passage together as one of Orwell's literary visions of hell,[11] quite explicit on the next page as he moves to describe the kitchen:

The kitchen was like nothing I had ever seen or imagined – a stifling, low-ceilinged inferno of a cellar, red-lit from the fires, and deafening with oaths and the clanging of pots and pans.

Remarkably, this highly picturesque and impressionistic writing, with a strong literary heritage in images of hell, is achieved with a very ordinary vocabulary. The vocabulary is neutral (e.g. 'low', 'stoop', 'cramped', 'staircase', 'passage', 'doorways') or vernacular ('shoved', 'queer'). Much of it is native in origin rather than Latin or French.

There is little figurative language, certainly none of the ostentatious metaphors or similes found elsewhere in Orwell. Much of the vocabulary is of one or two syllables only; often a whole clause or sentence is constructed in this mainly monosyllabic mode:

> there were the same heat and cramped space and warm reek of food ... After him came a boy with a great slab of veal on his shoulder, his cheek pressed into the damp, spongy flesh.

There is one foregrounded classical polysyllabic word, 'labyrinthine', but its meaning and its connotations of the Minotaur are entirely appropriate in the context.[12]

The relationship between language and context, and what the context does to our perception of style, is important here.[13] A piece of language – a sentence, a paragraph, a text – has certain objective and describable structural characteristics: its words may be short or long, native or foreign, concrete or abstract, vernacular or technical, and so on; they are arranged in a certain syntax, an ordering of words and phrases. But a description of the objective features of a text's language does not predict what significance they may have for the writer and for readers within different contexts of discourse. Similar linguistic characteristics may have – will have – different social and rhetorical meanings depending on the nature of the text as a whole, its cultural context and the expectations of its readers. To take the sentence about the boy with the slab of veal, its language is objectively 'simple' in a number of ways which could be exactly stated. In the context of a literary inferno, however, the sentence carries complicated and rather sinister connotations: the anonymous boy is a diabolical helper like the 'twelve cooks [who] skipped to and fro' at the 'furnaces' on the next page; the unconcerned intimacy of his living face and the dead flesh is not only gruesome but also surreal. Suppose, however, that the context were different: Orwell might perhaps have described work at an abattoir. In that context, the sentence about the boy carrying the veal might be experienced very differently, as a plain, matter-of-fact account of a routine act of work, unpleasant in itself but without the connotations suggested by the context of the diabolical kitchen.

This example suggests that the *language* of literary naturalism and its hyperreal extension may not be markedly different from that of the descriptive realism for which Orwell is praised, and that is

the case at least for *Down and Out*. The plain and vernacular basis
for the descriptive style is also present in the more elevated styles.
I will simply illustrate this fact with a passage from *Down and Out*,
reserving a more detailed treatment of descriptive realism for the
discussion of *Wigan Pier*, below. This is Orwell's first description
of conditions in a common lodging house:

[T]he boy led me up a rickety unlighted staircase to a bedroom.
It had a sweetish reek of paregoric and foul linen; the windows
seemed to be tight shut, and the air was almost suffocating at
first. There was a candle burning, and I saw that the room measured
fifteen feet square by eight high, and had eight beds in it. Already
six lodgers were in bed, queer lumpy shapes with all their own
clothes, even their boots, piled on top of them. Someone was
coughing in a loathsome manner in one corner.

When I got into the bed I found that it was as hard as a board,
and as for the pillow, it was a mere hard cylinder like a block of
wood. It was rather worse than sleeping on a table, because the
bed was not six feet long, and very narrow, and the mattress was
convex, so that one had to hold on to avoid falling out. The sheets
stank so horribly of sweat that I could not bear them near my
nose. Also, the bedclothes only consisted of the sheets and a cot-
ton counterpane, so that though stuffy it was none too warm. Several
noises recurred throughout the night. About once in an hour the
man on my left – a sailor, I think – woke up, swore vilely, and
lighted a cigarette . . . [other noises] . . . Once when [the man in
the corner] struck a match I saw that he was a very old man,
with a grey, sunken face like that of a corpse, and he was wearing his trousers wrapped round his head as a nightcap, a thing
which for some reason disgusted me very much. (*Down and Out*,
pp. 131–2)

Like the other passages discussed, this one conveys a range of
sensory impressions, with a strong emphasis on their effect on the
narrator – here, a consistent and powerful sense of physical disgust,
unrelieved by any comedy or symbolism such as is found in the
other extracts. We will see below that 'realistic' representation in
Orwell is very much something experienced in the senses and feelings rather than coldly observed and recorded. There is always a
very emotive tone: involvement and opinion are never far away when

Orwell writes of the life of the poor. The impression of realism coexisting with the thread of judgement and feeling comes from an insistence on particularity of reference: here, the measurements of the room, the count of eight beds and six lodgers in them, the bed 'not six feet long', the texture and geometry of objects – 'lumpy shapes', 'hard as a board', 'cylinder', 'narrow', 'convex', 'sunken face', and so on. Orwell is also fond of material arrangements that the reader has to work at to visualise: 'his trousers wrapped round his head as a nightcap', a precise, grotesque and defamiliarising image.[14]

NATURALISM IN *HOMAGE TO CATALONIA*

In the next section of this chapter I will discuss some heightened versions of 'realistic' writing, and the way they carry social and political judgement. But before moving on from the subject of naturalism or 'sordid realism', it is appropriate to refer to its place in the third of the 'mixed genre' books that Orwell wrote in the 1930s, *Homage to Catalonia* (1938). In December, 1936, Orwell 'had come to Spain with some notion of writing newspaper articles, but I had joined the militia almost immediately, because at that time and in that atmosphere it seemed the only conceivable thing to do' (*Catalonia*, p. 8). *Catalonia* is his record of the time and the atmosphere (a word which recurs in the book), of his very physical experiences of warfare in the trenches and of violent turmoil in Barcelona; and his discussion of the politics of the various parties involved in the Spanish Civil War, and of British responses to the War.

Orwell was conscious that Spain, like Wigan, Paris, Burma and the London of the destitute, was unknown territory to his middle-class English reader. In this book, Spain in civil war has to be communicated physically to those who have not had his privilege of direct experience, and discussed politically for those who may be misled by foreign commentators who have not observed directly. We are concerned with the former aspect of the work, the communication of material conditions and atmosphere. He writes:

> I wish I could convey to you the atmosphere of that time. I hope I have done so, a little, in the earlier chapters of this book. It is all bound up in my mind with the winter cold, the ragged uniforms

of militiamen, the oval Spanish faces, the morse-like tapping of machine-guns, the smells of urine and rotting bread, the tinny taste of bean-stews wolfed hurriedly out of unclean pannikins. (*Catalonia*, p. 103)

These phrases are shorthands or mnemonics for scenes and topics that are detailed earlier in the book. Orwell conveys the squalid physical experience of the trenches, the filth and cold and deprivation, in considerable detail; also the devastation of the areas around the front, and of the villages and buildings touched by the War. Here is one such piece of naturalistic description:

[Alcubierre had] . . . the peculiar squalid misery of the Aragonese villages. They are built like fortresses, a mass of mean little houses of mud and stone huddling round the church, and even in spring you see hardly a flower anywhere; the houses have no gardens, only back-yards where ragged fowls skate over the beds of mule-dung. It was vile weather, with alternate mist and rain. The narrow earth roads had been churned into a sea of mud, in places two feet deep, through which the lorries struggled with racing wheels and the peasants led their clumsy carts which were pulled by strings of mules, sometimes as many as six in a string, always pulling tandem. The constant come-and-go of troops had reduced the village to a state of unspeakable filth. It did not possess and never had possessed such a thing as a lavatory or a drain of any kind, and there was not a square yard anywhere where you could tread without watching your step. The church had long been used as a latrine; so had all the fields for a quarter of a mile around. I never think of my first two months at war without thinking of wintry stubble fields whose edges are crusted with dung. (Ibid., p. 19)

The hallmarks of naturalism are here as they are in many passages of the book: references to mundane or unpleasant things, 'mud', 'mule-dung', 'lavatory', 'drain', 'latrine', 'dung'; negative adjectives, 'squalid', 'mean little', 'ragged', 'vile', 'clumsy', etc.; an almost exaggerated judgement as in 'peculiar', 'a mass of', 'even', 'unspeakable'. This kind of naturalism is a prominent style in the early parts of *Homage to Catalonia*: the accounts of life in the trenches offer a strong and repulsive physical evocation, with great particularity, and are a strength of a book that has been much admired.

REALISM, JUDGEMENT AND SYMBOLISM IN *THE ROAD TO WIGAN PIER*

Although the passages from *Down and Out* and *Catalonia* just quoted are naturalistic in technique, heightened in tone, and convey, as so often in Orwell, repulsion, they are at least 'concrete' and 'objective' in their detailing of shape, texture, measurement and the narrator's sensory perceptions. In relation to this concreteness, we may recall Orwell's later reflection that 'So long as I remain alive and well I shall continue to ... love the surface of the earth, and to take pleasure in solid objects' (cf. Chapter 3, p. 19 above). In *Wigan Pier* there are more passages of naturalistic description of this kind: based in objective observation but emphasising squalor and his response to it:

> There were generally four of us in the bedroom, and a beastly place it was, with that defiled impermanent look of rooms that were not serving their rightful purpose ... We were therefore sleeping in what was still recognisably a drawing-room. Hanging from the ceiling there was a heavy glass chandelier on which the dust was so thick that it was like fur. And covering most of one wall there was a huge hideous piece of junk, something between a sideboard and a hall-stand, with lots of carving and little drawers and strips of looking-glass, and there was a once-gaudy carpet ringed by the slop-pails of years, and two gilt chairs with burst seats, and one of those old-fashioned horsehair armchairs which you slide off when you try to sit on them. The room had been turned into a bedroom by thrusting four squalid beds in among this other wreckage. (*Wigan Pier*, p. 5)

The precision of reference that is the foundation of any realistic style is so obvious as to need little comment: the little drawers and strips of mirror, etc., help the reader to visualise the nameless piece of Victorian furniture; the simile of dust 'like fur' is precisely evocative for anyone who has entered a long-neglected attic or cellar; the rings on the carpet suggest a careful observer who makes his survey at eye-level and ceiling, and then *looks downward* to complete his survey. But, like the previous passage, this is by no means straightforward description. It retains the sordid component of naturalism (dust, slop-pail, etc.), and it is framed in a suffusion of value-judgement in words from the negative end of Orwell's demotic vocabulary: 'beastly', 'defiled', 'hideous', 'junk', 'squalid', 'wreckage'.

The origin of *Wigan Pier* was a commission from the publisher Victor Gollancz to report on the conditions of poverty and unemployment in the North. Orwell spent two months visiting Wigan, Barnsley and Sheffield, two months of intensive observation of industrial, mining, and domestic conditions and of local political activity. He gathered a mass of observations, some of which are recorded in documentary fashion in *Wigan Pier*: on unemployment figures, for example:

> Take the figures for Wigan, which is typical enough of the industrial and mining districts. The number of insured workers is round about 36 000 (26 000 men and 10 000 women). Of these, the number unemployed at the beginning of 1936 was about 10 000. But this was in winter when the mines were working full-time; in summer it would probably be 12 000. Multiply by three, as above, and you get 30 000 or 36 000. The total population of Wigan is a little under 87 000; so that at any moment more than one person in three out of the whole population – not merely the registered workers – is either drawing or living on the dole. (*Wigan Pier*, p. 68)

Elsewhere in the book he reproduces his notes on individual houses, with dimensions and inventories of furniture (ibid, pp. 44–8, 59–60), gives examples of household budgets (p. 83), tabulates the rates of unemployment benefit (pp. 68–9) and so on. He explains in more or less factual terms the procedures of mining using a mechanical coal-cutter (pp. 27–8), describes a caravan-dwellers' colony with some precision (pp. 54–5), gives a general characterisation of workers' housing (p. 45).

Although the passages quoted to show that Orwell *could* write in a plain, referential, style, the realism of the book is hardly documentary overall. His political conscience was too demanding for the plain style, requiring a rhetoric of outrage which could not be kept under restraint until the polemical Part Two. Even passages of straightforward reportage are generally framed with authorial judgement, and the judgemental frame is more typically Orwell in style than the document or description within the frame. Often Orwell *precedes* a description with a pointed negative evaluation, so that it is bound to be read in terms of those values; for example, his chapter on housing begins:

> As you walk through the industrial towns you lose yourself in labyrinths of little brick houses blackened by smoke, festering in planless chaos round miry alleys and little cindered yards where there are stinking dust-bins and lines of grimy washing and half-ruinous WCs. (*Wigan Pier*, p. 45)

This is the style of sordid realism, driven by Orwellian guilt about the condition of the poor; he then particularises, but the detail is of course smeared by the preceding judgement:

> The interiors of these houses are always very much the same, though the number of rooms varies between two or [*sic*] five. All have an almost exactly similar living-room, ten or fifteen feet square, with an open kitchen range; in the larger ones there is a scullery as well, in the smaller ones the sink and copper are in the living-room. At the back there is the yard . . . (*Wigan Pier*, p. 45)

We read a text in terms of what we have already experienced; and we read a part of a text in terms of what has gone before. This is true of the book as a whole, not merely individual passages such as the one just quoted. The sensationally squalid opening chapter, a devastating naturalistic account of Orwell's lodging above a tripe shop, gives immediate notice that the book is not going to convey a material reality calmly while leaving readers to make up their own minds, but that it will voice its author's outrage and shame at Northern working-class life in no uncertain terms (hence the polemical Part Two, which I briefly characterised in the preceding chapter, is well expected from the beginning). A celebrated passage from the first chapter is in principle 'realistic' in its microscopic detail, but communicates primarily an oratorical expression of disgust:

> in the middle of the room was the big kitchen table at which the family and all the lodgers ate. I never saw this table completely uncovered, but I saw its various wrappings at different times. At the bottom was a layer of old newspaper stained by Worcester Sauce; above that a sheet of sticky white oil-cloth; above that a

green serge cloth; above that a coarse linen cloth, never changed and seldom taken off. Generally the crumbs from breakfast were still on the table at supper. I used to get to know individual crumbs by sight and watch their progress up and down the table from day to day. (*Wigan Pier*, p. 7)

The opening chapter of *Wigan Pier* (so resented by generations of Wigan readers!) has plenty of objective reference, plenty of linguistic precision, but the overall effect is one of sordid realism, and this sets the keynote of the book: it is hardly the spotless window pane of documentary; the pane is etched by authorial feeling, and we cannot see the scene except through his emotions.

The chapter also contains another noted image: it has a high visual precision of a quality Orwell often achieves, but it is not descriptive realism because the passage is shot through with expression of pathos, guilt and distaste:

The train bore me away, through the monstrous scenery of slag-heaps, chimneys, piled scrap-iron, foul canals, paths of cindery mud criss-crossed by the prints of clogs. This was March, but the weather had been horribly cold and everywhere there were mounds of blackened snow. As we moved slowly through the outskirts of the town we passed row after row of little grey slum houses running at right angles to the embankment. At the back of one of the houses a young woman was kneeling on the stones, poking a stick up the leaden waste-pipe which ran from the sink inside and which I suppose was blocked. I had time to see everything about her – her sacking apron, her clumsy clogs, her arms reddened by the cold. She looked up as the train passed, and I was almost near enough to catch her eye. She had a round pale face, the usual exhausted face of the slum girl who is twenty-five and looks forty, thanks to miscarriages and drudgery; and it wore, for the second in which I saw it, the most desolate, hopeless expression I have ever seen . . . She knew well enough what was happening to her – understood as well as I did how dreadful a destiny it was to be kneeling there in the bitter cold, on the slimy stones of a slum backyard, poking a stick up a foul drain-pipe. (*Wigan Pier*, pp. 16–17)

What we have here, despite its clarity of detail, is not description but symbolism: the 'slum girl' (an interesting category in itself) and everything about her stand for the degradation and hopelessness Orwell perceives in this Northern town. As for Orwell himself, he is enclosed in the train, and escaping; there is something of the voyeur's eye about his vision. His confidence about her typicality is patronising.

The first part of *Wigan Pier* begins, as we have seen, with a naturalistic description of the tripe-shop lodging; it ends with surreal landscapes of Wigan and Sheffield. The slag-heaps of Wigan are presented as a 'lunar landscape' (his phrase):

> The canal path was a mixture of cinders and frozen mud, criss-crossed by the imprints of innumerable clogs, and all around, as far as the slag-heaps in the distance, stretched the 'flashes' – pools of stagnant water that had seeped into the hollows caused by the subsidence of ancient pits. It was horribly cold. The 'flashes' were covered with ice the colour of raw umber, the bargemen were muffled to the eyes in sacks, the lock gates wore beards of ice. It seemed a world from which vegetation had been banished; nothing existed except smoke, shale, ice, mud, ashes and foul water. (*Wigan Pier*, p. 95)

And then Sheffield:

> At night, when you cannot see the hideous shapes of the houses and the blackness of everything, a town like Sheffield assumes a kind of sinister magnificence. Sometimes the drifts of smoke are rosy with sulphur, and serrated flames, like circular saws, squeeze themselves out from beneath the cowls of the foundry chimneys. Through the open doors of foundries you see fiery serpents of iron being hauled to and fro by redlit boys, and you hear the whizz and thump of steam hammers and the scream of iron under the blow. (*Wigan Pier*, p. 96)

Orwell professes to be showing the 'ugliness' (his word) of these industrial scenes, but the descriptions (which are much more extended than my quotations, totalling nearly three pages), dense with metaphors and allusions, achieve a conventional literary beauty. In fact the sources are literary, notably Dickens's surrealist evocation of 'Coketown' in *Hard Times*:

It was a town of red brick, or of brick that would have been red if the smoke and ashes had allowed it; but, as matters stood it was a town of unnatural red and black like the painted face of a savage. It was a town of machinery and tall chimneys, out of which interminable serpents of smoke trailed themselves for ever and ever, and never got uncoiled. It had a black canal in it, and a river that ran purple with ill-smelling dye, and vast piles of building full of windows where there was a rattling and a trembling all day long, and where the piston of the steam-engine worked monotonously up and down, like the head of an elephant in a state of melancholy madness.[15]

The 'serpents' metaphor seems to indicate Orwell's specific indebtedness to this passage; indeed the stylistic influence of Dickens was considerable and various, and we will see another aspect of it in the next chapter. But the point of the present comparison is simply that, in his descriptive writing, even treating a concrete material subject such as an industrial town, Orwell is definitely a literary rather than a documentary writer.

6 Voices of the Other

In the last two chapters we have seen Orwell, from the earliest days of his writing career, developing an individual style of writing modelled on his idea of 'demotic speech'. In the essays and in the argumentative and non-narrative sections of his full-length books, the Orwellian voice is the medium of expression for a consistently negative set of attitudes towards modern life: condemnation of commercialism, of bureaucracy, of technology, of fashionable socialism, of totalitarianism, of urban and suburban life, etc. It is not the object of the present book to treat the thematic concerns of Orwell's books or to criticise his politics or his prejudices, though it must be noted that his view of socialism is stereotyped and naive, and his slights on several categories of people, particularly Jews and homosexuals, are distasteful. The point is that Orwell discovered and deployed an effective and instantly recognisable style for saying what he had to say. He is one of those writers who creates a *persona*, an impression of a consistent and coherent individual subjectivity speaking in its own linguistic manner and voicing a definite world-view. Other writers who have created memorable personae include Chaucer, Wordsworth, Thackeray, Yeats, Larkin. As we have seen with Orwell, the idiolect of the persona is capable of a range of tones, from quiet reflection to strident ranting. And it can be adapted to be the basis of further styles.

The personal style is extended in his narrative writings in two directions. We saw in the previous chapter that it is the basis of heightened, metaphorically elaborated, realism or naturalism (which is of course still the utterance of an Orwellian narrator). The second direction in which he projects his morose, angry, individual voice is toward the presentation of fictional characters, principally the heroes of *Coming Up for Air, Keep the Aspidistra Flying* and *Nineteen Eighty-Four*. In all three books the central character is an imaginative creation based on Orwell's own beliefs, dislikes and anxieties, and the characterisation is achieved partly by calling up Orwell's mental landscape by cues to his personal style.

HETEROGLOSSIA

We now turn to the argument of this chapter, in which the demotic style is studied not in the foreground, but is seen as a background and a framing presence. The Orwellian voice acts as a foil to other, very different, linguistic manners, which contrast significantly with it: against the linguistic constancy of the Orwellian point of view Orwell displays a cacophony of what I call here 'voices of the other'.

Speech is prominent in Orwell's fictional books right from the beginning. *Down and Out*, for example, is a very 'oral' novel: voices – French, Russian, Cockney and Irish – abound. It begins with a slanging match in the street; there is shouting and quarrelling in many other scenes in the Paris section, and a carnivalistic street scene in London with soap-box speakers and heckling. Throughout the book, the narrative (such as it is) is constantly interrupted for characters whose speech is said to hold special idiosyncrasies to deliver lengthy anecdotes or reflections on their experiences. Often the sole function of a character is to act as a vehicle for these oral narratives: this would be the case of Charlie, for instance, who plays no part in the plot but has two stories to tell (chapters 2 and 18), or the waiters Valenti and Jules (chapters 15 and 19). The narrator's companions Boris, Paddy and Bozo also have a lot of speech, but they do have genuine roles in the plot or in the education of the narrator. *Burmese Days* tries to distinguish the speech of Burmese, Indian, and Eurasian people, not to mention white colonisers of different mentalities who are to some extent individualised; *A Clergyman's Daughter* produces distinct social dialects in the speech of the various middle- and upper-class characters (Dorothy's father, the Reverend Hare, and her cousin, Sir Thomas Hare, speak quite differently), and there are also Suffolk countrymen and Cockney and Irish hop-pickers, not to mention a variety of minor oddities such as Mrs Creevy the school-keeper and the various oafish parents who set upon Dorothy. These early books are full of characters with eccentric speech habits, and characters who speak with the tones of a class or a region, and the practice persists in Orwell's more accomplished work, if less prominently: the cameo caricature Mr Cheeseman in *Aspidistra* is typical – his first utterance to Gordon is 'Ot c'n I do f'yer!'; the practice is structurally and ideologically important in *Nineteen Eighty-Four*, as we will see.

In name, character and language Mrs Creevy and Mr Cheeseman

recall Dickens, who was almost certainly Orwell's model for this gallery of linguistic eccentrics. It would be laborious to track down precise sources for Orwell's caricatures and grotesques, however, and it is more important to understand the general principle of design that led Orwell to present this plurality of individual and class voices. We can then see how some of these 'voices of the other' function in individual novels.

Orwell's multi-voiced novels, like those of Dickens, are *heteroglossic*. The idea of heteroglossia in fiction originates with the Russian linguist Mikhail Bakhtin; it emerged, with some related concepts, in the late 1920s, but Bakhtin's ideas only became known in the West in the 1970s. Bakhtin saw the classic European novel of the nineteenth century as 'monologic', its viewpoint dominated by the attitudes of an omniscient author speaking in a single tone of voice. He credited Dostoevsky with pioneering a new form of fiction in which the author's or narrator's language displays an awareness of the language and the points of view of others. Heteroglossia, which expresses itself superficially as the inclusion of other varieties, is the 'other-directedness' of the author's speech in such fiction, its orientation towards the language and views of characters whose values are alien to those of the central narrating point of view.[1]

We may return to Orwell. We saw in Chapter 3 that he was acutely conscious of speech differences, and of the essential distinction between speech and print. He shared with Bakhtin the insight that different manners of language – different dialects, sociolects and idiolects – signify different social and personal world-views: his reaction to upper-middle-class speech overheard in hospital (p. 23 above) gives this a striking formulation. At the other end of the social scale, he was fascinated with the Cockney dialect, and included representations of it in his books where appropriate, from *Down and Out* right through to *Nineteen Eighty-Four*. Yet he felt that it was despised, even by its own speakers, for what it signified. Early works, principally *Down and Out* and *Clergyman's Daughter*, include a lot of dialect, mainly Cockney, painstakingly rendered. I have suggested that this dialect speech is included not to typify any specific social values such as solidarity, simplicity, craftiness, etc., but largely to dramatise difference as such: to make evident to his readers that a world beyond their ken existed in the slums of London and Paris. The letter to Jack Common quoted above (pp. 25–6) seems to despair of the possibility of rendering 'proletarian' (Orwell's word) experience in the novel, in the words of the people concerned. Though there are in the English novel conventions for indicating non-Standard dialects,[2] the result always looks odd and unnatural, because speech will not go into writing, and writing is anyway dominated, in English, by the Standard. Heteroglossia in Orwell is a reminder to the narrator, or the central character, and to the reader, that alien worlds exist: the foreignness of their speech and thought qualifies the narrative point of view, unsettles it, removes its absoluteness. What the Cockneys, Irish and 'eccentrics' in *Down and Out* actually *think* is largely unanalysed, nor are the ideas of those who speak fine shades of 'native' English in *Burmese Days* clearly distinguished. Orwell wants his readers to be aware of foreign and uncomprehended social worlds. Sometimes, as we will see, he comments on these alien world-views expressed in speech, but usually the speakers are fixed, externally observed, caricatures.[3] At least this is the case with the 'Dickensian' characters, Cockneys, Irish, etc., in the early works.

But some of the alien voices in Orwell's work are analysed and condemned, by comment and by parody: upper-class and affected varieties, and above all varieties of political speech and writing. We will discuss the negative treatment of alien voices in *Burmese Days* in Chapter 7, with more treatment of this topic in the chapters on *Animal Farm* and, particularly, *Nineteen Eighty-Four*.

LITERARY REPRESENTATION OF SPEECH

In Chapter 3, I pointed out that speech and writing are substantially different modes of language, and that Orwell had the insight (more so than academic linguists) to see this. He regarded them as so distinct as to merit the description of distinct 'languages'. His particular complaint was that Standard English dominated writing, so that non-standard varieties, and thus their (to him) desirable moral and political qualities, could not find expression in the written mode. This is an acute point, well worth consideration in studies of ideology in fiction. But for the novelist there is a more basic technical problem stemming from the modal difference: it is, as Norman Page puts it:

> the central dilemma of the writer of dialogue: he seeks to create by the use of one medium the effect of language used in another,

and if there is a means by which this can be accomplished, however incompletely, it is certainly not by the slavish reproduction of the features of actual speech.[4]

Spontaneous speech accurately transcribed into print gives an impression which seems 'wrong' in the context of a book. Even the language of a 'good speaker', talking quite carefully, will contain mistakes, loose ends, changes of course, opaque references, and so on, which cause no problem in face-to-face communication through speech in context, but when rendered in print suggest disorganisation, tentativeness and vagueness. Yet speech – monologue and dialogue – seems to be an indispensable attraction of the modern novel, a source of realism and vitality. To create the illusion of speech, a novelist does not construct a text which aims to simulate a transcription. As Leech and Short observe after characterising the 'normal non-fluency' of ordinary speech:

> it may be concluded that real conversation is unlikely to be promising material for literary employment, and that it must strike an observer who has an eye on the aesthetic capabilities of language as sloppy, banal, and ill-organised.[5]

The novelist employs a set of linguistic conventions which has evolved with the development of the novel from the eighteenth century: readers as well as novelists have a knowledge of these conventions, and reading according to these conventions allows us to accept printed monologue and dialogue 'as if' speech. The conventions cover a wide variety of styles of speech, including the representation of different types of dialect. Speech in printed fiction is a linguistic artifice.

There is a useful distinction in linguistics between 'unmarked' and 'marked' forms. An unmarked form is the usual or default state of affairs, the marked form is exceptional, even deviant: a plural noun is marked by comparison with the singular, and this shows in the ending: *horse, horses*; references to females are often marked, a fact which is objectionable to feminists: *actor, actress*. As for speech in novels, the unmarked form is a kind of neutral, unnoticeable Standard English based on sentence constructions and vocabulary which are both simple: the complex syntax of prose, based on subordination of clauses (hypotaxis), and indeed the long sentences, are avoided;

so are learned and technical terms. The narrative frame of the fiction may be marked by hypotaxis and high-register vocabulary, but the speech of the characters must not include these signals, unless the author wants them to sound bookish. The normal non-fluencies of speech, which appear even in educated speech, are edited out, because, in printed dialogue, they conventionally send out negative signals about class, education and intelligence. 'Unmarked' conversation in the novel is not like real speech, and it does not risk its head above the parapet of the prose architecture which frames it. Leech and Short (pp. 163–5) demonstrate very succinctly and effectively how the illusion of plain conversation is constructed in a passage of dialogue from D. H. Lawrence, but they note also that, though subdued and unostentatious, it is rich in literary and psychological meanings.

We are more concerned here, and especially in relation to heteroglossic Orwell, with *marked* forms of speech representation. Marked speech in fiction contains deviations from the patterns of written language which are *intended* to stand out from the prose frame of the narrative, to be noticeable, drawing attention to a different cultural world from that encoded in 'Standard English' and from that encoded in Orwell's 'demotic' prose style. By the time Orwell was writing, there was established in the English novel a range of conventions for different kinds of speech marking: a range of traditional meanings for marked speech, and a range of cues that could be inserted in the language to suggest these meanings. There were already readers experienced in the marked speech styles developed by the likes of Henry Fielding, Sir Walter Scott, Emily Brontë, Mrs Gaskell, Charles Dickens, Thomas Hardy. The conventions of marked speech representation were (and are) used for a variety of functions. A prominent function of marking is the suggestion of the language of a region, a dialect, from Scots to Lancashire to Cockney. In British English – in reality and in fiction – regional accents, and particularly those of the large urban areas, are inextricably bound up with questions of class: dialect speakers tend to be the poor and the working classes, and that is a message which is strongly conveyed in English fiction, where the framework of narrative language is Standard, middle-class English for a middle-class readership. Thus the cues for dialect tend to get mingled with signals of uneducated English: not the routine unfluencies which according to Leech and Short characterise speech generally, but specific ungrammaticalities which conventionally suggest 'illiteracy' – 'we was', 'I don't want no . . .', 'I aren't' and so on. This English symbolises an uneducated subculture mingled with a regional culture. The speech of other social groups ('sociolects') also has its conventional forms in fictional dialogue, conventions usually shared with dramatic literature which, in English, has since the sixteenth century been very powerful in the development of sociolectal speech stereotypes. Fops, pedants, politicians, the British nobility, the military and other élites had strongly coded speech habits in literature well before Orwell, and he draws on the repertoire of conventions: Sir Thomas Gale in *A Clergyman's Daughter*, Westfield in *Burmese Days*, the homosexual bookshop customer in *Keep the Aspidistra Flying*, the 'well-known anti-Fascist' lecturer in *Coming Up for Air*, and numbers of other political speakers, are among Orwell's characterisations based on 'higher' sociolects.

Norman Page's book *Speech in the English Novel* is a clear and well-illustrated introduction to conventions for the handling of dialects, sociolects and idiolects in fiction, which cannot be dealt with in any more detail here.

ENGLISH DIALECTS AND ACCENTS IN THE EARLY FICTION

In this section we will examine Orwell's treatment of speech in some of his early books, particularly his representations of Cockney, of Irish English, and his indications of idiolects – personal styles – and some sociolects – social group styles or mannerisms. Our sources will be *Down and Out* and *A Clergyman's Daughter*, in both of which non-standard speech is presented in a particularly raw, foregrounded way.

Down and Out is one of the most self-conscious books in its treatment of speech that I know. Orwell constantly comments on the speech mannerisms of his characters:

'R., an Englishman' is alluded to: he 'talked in a refined, woman-ish voice' (p. 5);

a waiter, Jules, 'had a spluttering, oratorical way of talking' (p. 102);

his Irish companion, Paddy, 'would keep up a monologue . . . in a whimpering, self-pitying Irish voice' (p. 152);

'Bozo had a strange way of talking, Cockneyfied and yet very lucid and expressive' (p. 163).

These descriptions are not necessarily followed up with any attempt to mimic the individual speech patterns, although everyone's speech is heightened, liberally peppered with exclamations, French phrases, sentimentalities, oaths and obscenities. Here is Boris, Orwell's Russian companion:

'Ah, but I have known what it is to live like a gentleman, *mon ami*. I do not say it to boast, but the other day I was trying to compute how many mistresses I have had in my life, and I made it out to be over two hundred. Yes, at least two hundred . . . Ah, well, *ça reviendra*. Victory is to him who fights the longest. Courage!' etc. etc. (p. 21, Orwell's 'etc. etc.')

Or, in similar vein, Valenti, a waiter:

'You know, *mon p'tit*, this hotel life is all very well, but it's the devil when you're out of work. I expect you know what it is to go without eating, eh? *Forcément*, otherwise you wouldn't be scrubbing dishes. Well, I'm not a poor devil of a *plongeur*; I'm a waiter, and *I* went five days without eating, once. Five days without even a crust of bread – Jesus Christ!' (p. 82)

The speech styles of the Paris characters, energetic, exclamatory, colourful, are not in fact much differentiated, but Orwell constantly says that they are queer, eccentric, and this relentless attention to speech and mannerism (including gesture and dress) encourages the reader to experience the text as highly oral, dramatic, and potentially idiolectal. The illusion of dramatic and individualistic speech is formed not so much by an idiosyncratic transcription of language as by a combination of two elements: the speech forms themselves, and the way they, and the characters who utter them, are glossed in the narrator's own commentary and in speech-introducing formulae. Apart from mentioning supposed individualities, he almost always identifies a person as Irish, or Cockney, or Russian, French, or whatever: thus the reader's imagination is drawn to apply the appropriate stereotype of dialect speech or of foreignness, compensating for the fact that the speech passages are relatively sparsely marked with cues of dialect. This economy, this reliance on the reader's knowledge of stereotypes, is a common technique, by no means restricted to Orwell. One part of the rationale is that it is more effective, more engaging, to let the reader do much of the work; another, that an over-heavy use of dialect notation in the text is liable to make it impenetrable, a problem of which novelists were conscious from the early days of rendering dialect.[6]

The second part of *Down and Out*, narrating Orwell's experiences roughing it in London, displays a similar enhanced consciousness of speech, this time of the regional/social dialect Cockney. Cockney also figures prominently in Orwell's novel of two years later, *A Clergyman's Daughter*; both books include also representations of the speech of destitute Irish in England. Both dialects are there because they symbolise poverty and ignorance, material and intellectual states beyond the experience of the narrator and the reader (and, in *A Clergyman's Daughter*, of the heroine). These early novels tend to put the dialect speech on display, almost like specimens; and in this spirit of distant curiosity, Orwell even includes in *Down and Out* a chapter of 'notes . . . on London slang and swearing' (ch. 32).

Cockney has a peculiar importance historically and in modern English – and the reasons for its importance explain Orwell's fascination with this variety. Cockney is 'the traditional working-class dialect of London . . . associated particularly with the innermost suburbs of east London . . . the broadest form of London local accent'.[7] It is one of three British English accents with its own name (the others are 'Scouse' [Liverpool] and 'Geordie' [urban North-East]), and its unique prominence in folk-linguistic consciousness, its unique symbolic value, stems from its geographical, social and ideological relationships with Standard English. In the London region the variety known as Standard English developed from the late fourteenth century: a London standardisation of East Midlands dialect was assured by the political and economic dominance of the capital, and the cultural importance of the region.[8] Standard written English, and its recent associated accent, 'Received Pronunciation', have developed as the property and the badge of the middle and upper classes of the South-East. Cockney has developed alongside the 'high' version of London English as its working-class antithesis and challenge.

Cockneys (the speakers and the speech share this name) are regarded as articulating values which are foreign to the Standard: quickness, wit, the secretiveness of a closed community, bluntness, and impatience with privilege, with officialdom, and with cultivated attitudes. (See further, below, pp. 104–5, on Cockney as 'antilanguage'.)

Given these attitudes towards Cockney – attitudes of, as well as towards, its speakers – it is not surprising that an immense amount of attention has been paid to this dialect/sociolect from as early as the sixteenth century. There is a long tradition of comment, and of literary representation.[9] Crucial to the technique and the reception of a modern writer like Orwell was the latter, literary representation. As Norman Page shows,[10] regional and social dialects were very extensively explored and represented in novels in the nineteenth century: Northern, Scottish, West Country, East Anglian, but above all, Cockney. The importance of the novelist Charles Dickens, a giant in popularity, cannot be overestimated. Low-life Cockney characters have a memorable prominence in many of his novels: Sam Weller in *The Pickwick Papers* (1836–7), Jo in *Bleak House* (1853), Bill Sykes and Fagin's gang in *Oliver Twist* (1837–8). Page comments usefully on Dickens's achievement in developing a language which suggests Cockney speech:

> Dickens's primary concern was not, of course, the delineation of living speech. To create a Cockney idiom that would be readily identifiable, adaptable for a variety of characters, entertaining in itself, yet presenting no problems of comprehension in novels intended for a mass readership – this was the problem he set himself to solve . . . Dickens isolates and emphasizes certain features of pronunciation, indicates them orthographically often enough to signal the presence of the dialect, but makes no attempt at a complete or consistent reading. The reader who cares to read the text aloud, or to 'hear' it in his mind as he reads silently, will find enough phonological information thus provided to produce a distinctive effect, if not a completely convincing Cockney; but the signals never cluster so densely as to create . . . obstacles to rapid reading. (Page, *Speech*, p. 61)

This compromise is of course the sensible solution to the problem of representing dialect in writing so that it is distinctive, appears accurate, and does not become incomprehensible. Dickens's achievement was that he mastered the technique for Cockney, and thus provided readers with stereotypes and cues, and later novelists with a technical model which would work for readers whose eyes and ears had been trained by familiarity with the conventions which Dickens had established. Passages such as the following, from Jo the crossing-sweeper in *Bleak House*, are usually cited as examples of the technique. Note that the spelling is in fact more fussy and deviant, more informative about pronunciation, than Orwell's; Dickens's notation is more elaborate than has become usual in twentieth-century representations of dialect (though much less so than Shaw's, which is very difficult to read):[11]

'They're wot's left, Mr Snagsby', says Jo, 'out of a sov'ring as was give me by a lady in a wale as sed she was a servant and as come to my crossin one night and asked to be showd this 'ere ouse and the ouse wot him as you giv the writin to died at, and the berrin-ground wot he's berrid in. She ses to me, she ses, "are you the boy at the Inkwhich?" she ses. I ses, "yes", I ses. She ses to me, she ses, "can you show me all them places?" And she ses to me "do it", and I dun it, and she give me a sov'ring and hooked it.' (cited Wright, *Cockney Dialect*, p. 15)

It is necessary to distinguish features of a text which serve to suggest a specific dialect from features which are conventional to the literary representation of speech generally. In the latter class are spellings which are merely deviant, including Dickens's 'wot', 'sed', 'berrid' and 'dun': these do not indicate any difference of pronunciation from Standard, but simply suggest, in an impressionistic way, that the speaker is uneducated. Having filtered out phonetically irrelevant features, we may look for three, possibly four, kinds of indicator of a specific dialect or accent:

1. Dialect-specific spellings give cues to the phonology of the dialect itself: so ''ouse' and ''ere' cue the 'dropped "h" of Cockney'; 'wale' for 'veil' cues the interchange of the phonemes /v/ and /w/, which may have been a feature of early nineteenth-century London speech, but is certainly a much-used literary cue to Cockney in Dickens. There are no examples of Cockney vowels in this passage; but the vowel phonology of the Cockney accent contains some highly recognisable items which have risen to the

status of stereotypes, and we will find instances in Orwell.[12]

2. Syntactic, and particularly morphological, differences from Standard English, e.g. differences in verb forms, verb endings, or pronouns, multiple negation, etc. In the Dickens extract we find 'give' for 'given', 'as' for 'who', 'come' for 'came', etc. These are said to be markers of Cockney, and are certainly features of the stereotype of Cockney, and are deployed by Orwell. However, it must be realised that these syntactic and morphological deviancies are not *peculiar* to Cockney: they are features of non-standard 'General English', not tied to a region but widespread, and particularly characteristic of lower-class urban speech.[13] If a text is cued as Cockney by other markers (e.g. by phonetic spellings) or by narrator's comment, non-standard features will be perceived as markers of Cockney.

3. Lexical differences from Standard English, i.e. different words. Vocabulary differences are very important in traditional dialectology for distinguishing rural dialects, but are said to be less striking as features of urban dialects. However, Cockney is said to be characterised by an extensive vocabulary in the areas of slang and swearing,[14] and Orwell's chapter on London slang and swearing in *Down and Out* indicates that this was his view. In Jo's speech from *Bleak House* we find 'hooked it'; and there is an extensive underworld argot elsewhere in Dickens, especially in *Oliver Twist*. Slang might be considered a feature of style of speech rather than of the linguistic system itself.

4. Certain habits which are manifestly aspects of speech delivery rather than of the linguistic system are claimed to be characteristic of Cockney, manners of narrative or of argument.[15] For example, Wright (*Cockney Dialect*, p. 120), as if reporting his London field-work, states that 'In relating anecdotes the verb *to say* is repeated again and again, especially by Cockney women'. We find this precisely in the speech of Jo: 'ses ... ses ... ses ...'. Such stylistic features are not reliable predictors of a specific dialect: a Northern stand-up comedian could well play on 'says ... says ... says' in telling a story. Nevertheless, Orwell does play on this phrasing in extract 2. below, so the pattern may be conventional in cueing Cockney among other oral narrators.

If we turn now to some passages from Orwell, we find less marking for Cockney speech than we do in Dickens, but nonetheless his

Cockney speeches and dialogues do stand out from the narrative frame – there is sufficient marking to cue the dialect for anyone who is experienced in the previous models of literary representation of Cockney (especially Dickens). Here are some examples which include display or specimen passages, to illustrate his technique of 'transcription'; to start with, two passages from *Down and Out*:

1. The narrator looks for a bed while roughing it in London; these are the first scraps of Cockney in the narrative:

> I said I was stony broke and wanted the cheapest bed I could get.
>   'Oh,' said he, 'you go to that 'ouse across the street there, with the sign "Good Beds for Single Men." That's a good kip [sleeping place], that is. I bin there myself on and off. You'll find it cheap *and* clean.' . . . I entered a stone passage-way, and a little etiolated boy with sleepy eyes appeared from a door leading to a cellar. Murmurous sounds came from the cellar, and a wave of hot air and cheese. The boy yawned and held out his hand.
>   'Want a kip? That'll be a 'og, guv'nor.'
>   I paid the shilling . . . (*Down and Out*, pp. 130–1)

2. A self-contained passage reporting a monologue by a tramp, presumably a Londoner; this is 'display speech', one of a set of anecdotes with no narrative function:

> 'I ain't goin' far in —— Kent. Kent's a tight county, Kent is. There's too many bin' moochin' about 'ere. The —— bakers get so they'll throw their bread away sooner'n give it you. Now Oxford, that's the place for moochin', Oxford is. When I was in Oxford I mooched bread, and I mooched bacon, and I mooched beef, and every night I mooched tanners for my kip off of the students. The last night I was twopence short of my kip, so I goes to a parson and mooches 'im for threepence. He give me threepence, and the next moment he turns round and gives me in charge for beggin'. "You bin beggin'"', the copper says. "No I ain't", I says, "I was askin' the gentlemen the time", I says. The copper starts feelin' inside my coat, and he pulls out a pound of meat and two loaves of bread. "Well, what's all this, then?" he says. "You better come 'long to the station", he says. The beak

give me seven days. I don't mooch from no more ———— parsons.
But Christ! what do I care for a lay-up of seven days?" etc. etc.
(*Down and Out*, p. 190)

Cockney in extract 1 is cued by just one phonological feature,
the absent /h/ in ''ouse' and ''og'; by a non-standard verb, 'bin';
by slang ('kip', ''og'); and by a style feature, the tagged-on repetition of subject and auxiliary in one sentence, ',that is'. The last is
claimed by Wright (*Cockney Dialect*, p. 120) to be typical of Cockney, but is also found in other dialects. Notice how Orwell sharpens the contrast between the speech and the narrative frame, thus
highlighting the 'otherness' of the speech. First he reports the narrator's own speech in demotic style ('stony broke', 'cheapest'); but
he distances the narrator from the Londoner's speech by glossing
the slang ('kip' [sleeping place]', ''og . . . shilling'. He interpolates
a very literary fragment of narrative between the utterances of the
two Londoners, including one word, 'etiolated', from a very elevated
register of vocabulary – a startling shift of register which, as I have
already noted (Chapter 4, pp. 40–1), Orwell sporadically indulges in.

Extract 2. has only a little more in the way of phonetic spellings:
absent 'h' again, but only twice, and it is preserved in several places
where it might have been deleted; and the verb ending '-ing' consistently rendered as 'in'': both are stereotypes of Cockney, though
they occur in other dialects. There are plenty of non-standard markers:

> ain't, bin, off of, goes, mooches, give, bin, ain't, give, and the
> double negative don't . . . no more'

Swearing, represented by the '————', and slang, are very salient,
as they often are in Orwell's display passages of Cockney: 'kip',
'mooch' multiply repeated, 'beak', 'lay-up'. (Many of the Cockney
slang words Orwell attributes to his speakers are glossed in his chapter
on slang and swearing.) Finally, in extract 2 there are two features
which may be interpreted as markers of Cockney oral narrative, the
tagged-on ',Kent is', ',Oxford is', and the repetition of 'says' which
I have already mentioned.

What is noteworthy about these passages, then – and they are
typical of Orwell's treatment of the London vernacular – is that he

can suggest Cockney, and make it stand out from the framework of the narrative voice, with a quite sparing use of the conventional features of the literary version. He does not use purely symbolic spelling changes ('ses', etc.), and he makes little reference to the real, and potentially stereotypical, features of Cockney phonology such as 'mahth' for 'mouth', 'fing' for 'thing', 'fice' for 'face'. Non-standard verb and pronoun forms, and double negation, are made to work quite hard; as we have seen, they are not restricted to Cockney. But Cockney slang is emphasised, particularly in what I have called 'display speeches' such as extract 2, above, and the long speech by Nobby in 3, below. Since we are aware of the region and the cultural context in which the Cockney parts take place, and since we have the Dickens model in our heads, we access the dialect. And the dialect is foregrounded by the distance between it and the frame.

We will now look at a longer extract, this time from *A Clergyman's Daughter*; here, it seems, the use of dialect is more deliberately integrated with the scene and with the main character's state of mind.

3. In *A Clergyman's Daughter*, the central character, Dorothy Hare, is mysteriously transported from her father's rectory in Suffolk to London, where she regains consciousness in the street, suffering from amnesia. She has barely recovered her senses when she is accosted by two young men and a young woman, who first of all assume that she is 'ill' or 'batty', and that she, like them, is on the road; when they discover that she has a little money, they invite her to join them. The more articulate lad, Nobby, puts the suggestion:

'What I mean to say – how about you chumming in with Flo and Charlie and me? Partners, see? Comrades all, shoulder to shoulder. United we stand, divided we fall. We put up the brains, you put up the money. How about it, kid? Are you on, or are you off? Us three are going hopping, see – '

'Hopping?'

''Opping!' put in the dark youth impatiently, as though disgusted by Dorothy's ignorance. His voice and manner were rather sullen, and his accent much baser than Nobby's. 'Pickin' 'ops – dahn in Kent. C'n understand that, can't yer?'

'Oh, *hops*! For beer?'

'That's the mulligatawny! Coming on fine, she is. Well, kid, 'z I was saying, here's us three going down hopping, and got a job promised us and all – Blessington's farm, Lower Molesworth. Only we're just a bit in the mulligatawny, see? Because we ain't got a brown between us, and we got to do it on the toby – thirty-five miles it is – and got to tap for our tommy and skipper at night as well. And that's a bit of a mulligatawny, with ladies in the party. But now s'pose f'rinstance you was to come along with us, see? We c'd take the twopenny tram far as Bromley, and that's fifteen miles done, and we won't need skipper more'n one night on the way. And you chum in at our bin – four to a bin's the best picking – and if Blessington's paying twopence a bushel you'll turn your ten bob a week easy. What do you say to it, kid? Your two and a tanner won't do you much good here in Smoke. But you go into partnership with us, and you'll get your kip for a month and something over – and *we'll* get a lift to Bromley and a bit of scran as well.'

About a quarter of his speech was unintelligible to Dorothy. She asked rather at random:

'What is *scran*?'

'Scran? Tommy – food. I can see *you* ain't been long on the beach, kid.' . . .

'Come on, less get movin'! It's 'ar-parse two already. We don't want to miss that there —— tram. Where d'they start from, Nobby?'

'The Elephant,' said Nobby: 'and we got to catch it before four o'clock, because they don't give no free rides after four.'

'Come on, then, don't waste no more time. Nice job we'll 'ave of it if we got to 'ike it down to Bromley *and* look for a place to skipper in the —— dark. C'm on, Flo.' (*A Clergyman's Daughter*, pp. 85–7)

I have shortened a much longer scene to provide this extract. The speech of these East Enders is rendered generally by the techniques of literary Cockney that I illustrated from *Down and Out*, but with a distinction between the two male speakers. The chief marker of the idiolect of the main speaker, Nobby, is a dense use of slang: 'mulligatawny', 'kid', 'brown', 'on the toby', etc. There is a sprinkling of non-standard forms in his speech: 'us three', 'got', 'ain't', 'you was', 'easy', 'don't give no'. There are some indications of the contractions of syllables common to any kind of rapid colloquial speech: 's'pose f'rinstance'. There are in Nobby's speech no deviant spellings suggesting the classic phonological markers of stereotypical Cockney, not even a dropped 'h'. The treatment of Bozo's speech in *Down and Out*, said to be 'Cockneyfied and yet very lucid and expressive', is likewise phonologically unmarked. Nobby is clearly presented as, like Bozo, a 'better' class of Cockney speaker, certainly by contrast with Charlie ('the dark youth'). Despite Dorothy's incomprehension of a quarter of what Nobby says, she recognises him as a better speaker than Charlie, or at least Charlie's accent is 'much baser', and this sociolinguistic perception seems to reinforce her confidence in Nobby and her aversion to Charlie. In even the little that Charlie says, there are more radical indicators of the Cockney accent: dropped 'h': ''Opping,' ''ops,' ''ave,' ''ike'; '-ing' pronounced '-in': 'Pickin',' 'movin''; 'ah' where Standard Southern has 'ow': 'dahn'; the spelling ''ar-parse' probably indicating a pronunciation of the long 'a' with the tongue further back in the mouth than in Standard, a variant recognised by Wells (*Cockney Dialect*, p. 305). A little before our extract starts, Charlie's word 'just' is spelt 'jest'. A Cockney variant of this vowel (as in 'strut') is more like an open front 'a' sound (Wells, *Cockney Dialect*, p. 305), so a more appropriate spelling might be 'jast'. For a different purpose, Wells (ibid, p. 333) quotes a speech of Mrs Gamp in which 'such' is spelt 'sech', so there is a consistency. ('Just' is also spelt 'jest' in *Nineteen Eighty-Four*: pp. 75, 81, 83.) Whatever we are to make of this in strict phonetic terms, at least Orwell attributes to Charlie yet another non-Standard vowel form. By these devices Charlie is assigned a broader accent than Nobby; his speech also contains non-standard verb and pronoun forms, double negation, some slang, and swear words recorded as '———'.

The more deviant nature of Charlie's speech fits in with the way the two lads are distinguished from one another in dress and manner, foreshadowing differences in the parts they will play in the unfolding of the coming section of the story. This is how they first appear to Dorothy (first Charlie, then Nobby):

One of the youths was about twenty, narrow-chested, black-haired, ruddy-cheeked, good-looking in a nosy Cockney way, and dressed in the wreck of a raffishly smart blue suit and a check cap. The

other was about twenty-six, squat, nimble, and powerful, with a
snub nose, a clear pink skin and huge lips as coarse as sausages,
exposing strong yellow teeth. He was frankly ragged, and he had
a mat of orange-coloured hair cropped short and growing low on
his head, which gave him a startling resemblance to an orang-
outang. (*A Clergyman's Daughter*, p. 83)

Nobby, who has the most to say, seems to be the leader, and his
cheerful, confident manner encourages Dorothy to trust him. 'He
moved with a gambolling, ape-like gait, and his grin was so frank
and wide that it was impossible not to smile back at him.' The
dark-haired boy, Charlie, is sullen, sarcastic, impatient; he represents
the sinister and threatening element of this situation; his character
is in doubt from the outset, and indeed after three days on the road
to Kent, he and Flo decamp, stealing Nobby's 'bundle' and leaving
him and Dorothy without food.

In interpreting the speech differences in this way as signs of character differences, I am suggesting that we experience the representation of Cockney as functional rather than decorative or atmospheric
(as it seems to be in *Down and Out*). How is heteroglossia being
used to communicate Dorothy's experience? She has landed, Tardis-
fashion, in the New Kent Road, not knowing who she is; she is
confronted with a trio of young people whose speech – and appearance – are utterly foreign to what she knows from her village life
in Suffolk. Orwell makes it explicit that Nobby's language is partly
unintelligible to Dorothy, and particularly his use of Cockney slang,
in which the daily life and preoccupations of the hop-picking Londoner
are encrypted. This is the expression of a new world-view which
she is to learn in the processes of maturing and life-education which
are to be forced on her. The slang terms which mystify her signify
the major concerns of the vagrant causal worker, concerns of which
she is ignorant: comradeship ('chumming'); food ('tommy' – Tommy
Tucker sings for his supper – 'scran'); somewhere to sleep ('skipper', 'kip'); money ('brown', a copper coin, 'bob', 'tanner'); beg-
ging, borrowing and finding the means of life ('tap', 'on the beach'
i.e. beachcombing); walking ('toby', highway).[17] A high degree of
slang usage is mystifying to an outsider, and in order to appreciate
Dorothy's bemusement we have to make a historical jump from our
own knowledge to the life-experience of a person like Dorothy, a
young woman from a rural world (a clergyman's daughter), in the

1930s, before the age of universal mass media. Dorothy was living in a world which was seeing only the beginnings of radio and had no experience of television, computers, etc.; today we are familiarised to London speech by daily exposure on the media, whereas a person in Dorothy's situation would have to go to London to hear it. It could be argued that the mystification here is deliberate, that the slang is a code to conceal the thoughts and activities of an unofficial social group, with its fair proportion of beggars and thieves outside the law, and its market traders and other dealers on the margins of the law.[18] Thus the code transforms the standard language by substituting new lexical forms, the new forms express the concerns of the society while concealing them from the 'straight' world. The linguist M. A. K. Halliday calls such a code, set up in opposition to the norms of the official world, an **antilanguage**, its speakers belonging to an **antisociety**.[19]

According to Halliday, antilanguage is not only a device for secrecy, but is also a medium through which poetry and oratory can celebrate the values of the subculture. Literature from the underworld, in the unofficial slang vernacular of the society, has been recorded from the 'pelting speech' of Elizabethan vagabonds to the Rasta poets of today. Here is a taste of a poem in beggars' cant recorded by (probably) Thomas Dekker in 1612, followed by his 'translation' (I quote the first three verses of a poem in ten stanzas):

The Canting Song

Bing out bene morts, and tour, and tour,
    Bing our bene morts and tour;
For all your duds are binged a waste;
    The bene cove hath the lour.

I met a dell, I viewed her well;
    She was beneship to my watch:
So she and I did stall and cloy
    Whatever we could catch.

This doxy dell can cut bene whids,
    And wap well for a win,
And prig and cloy so beneshiply,
    All the dewse-a-vill within.

Thus for satisfaction of the readers, Englished.
Go forth brave girls, look out, look out,
   Look out, I say, brave conies,
For all your clothes are stolen, I doubt,
   Mad shavers share the monies.

I met a drab, I liked her well,
   My bowls did fit her alley,
We both did vow to rob pell-mell,
   And so abroad did sally.

This bouncing trull can rarely talk,
   A penny will make her ———:
Through any town which she doth walk,
   Nought can her filching 'scape.[20]

Orwell's fascination with the language of beggars and down-and-outs, and his realisation of its literary potential, has then a long ancestry. In the case of London speech, the antilinguistic strain of verbal art was transmitted in the nineteenth and earlier twentieth centuries in Cockney rhyming slang, street slang and other kinds of word-play, celebrated publicly in the music hall and in the turns of stand-up comics.[21] In this tradition, Nobby puts on a performance for Dorothy; he is showing off through speech, as he does through clothes and antics (and of course there is a sexual element in this display). He not only puts up a barrage of slang terms to puzzle and impress her, but also plays with words, notably the word 'mulligatawny':

That's the mulligatawny!
we're just a bit in the mulligatawny
that's a bit of a mulligatawny.

Mulligatawny is a kind of spicy soup, an exotic word, associated with an exotic culture. Nobby uses the word three different ways, first approvingly, then through rhyming slang, in the sense of 'in the soup', then in the sense of the slang word 'mull', muddle, problem. Dorothy clearly is as impressed by his verbal dexterity as by his grin, for she decides to 'chum' with these young people.
   Cockney is by far the most extensively used of dialects and

sociolects in Orwell's work, probably because of its antilinguistic character, its resistance to the official world, to privilege and power, resulting from its very specific historical relationship with Standard English. But we must not lose sight of the fact that in several of his books, including the two early ones discussed so far, *Burmese Days*, and *Nineteen Eighty-Four*, there is a plurality of voices of the other, even if some of the varieties are only briefly mentioned or lightly sketched. Heteroglossia, with its subversive and critical potential, is most obvious in multilingual or multidialectal societies (Kenya, Spain; capital cities, for example London, Paris); and Orwell creates multi-variety texts to replicate the heteroglossic situation.

He includes Irish characters among the tramps and the hop-pickers, diversifying the sources of poverty and ignorance: Paddy in *Down and Out*, Mrs McElligot in *A Clergyman's Daughter*. As usual, Orwell instructs the reader what stereotype to apply; Mrs McElligot gave advice 'in her base Dublin accent' (*Clergyman's Daughter*, p. 314); while Paddy is said to:

> keep up a monologue in this style, in a whimpering, self-pitying Irish voice:
> 'It's hell bein' on de road, eh? It breaks yer heart goin' into dem bloody spikes. But what's a man to do else, eh? I ain't had a good meat meal for about two months, an' me boots is getting bad, an' – Christ! How'd it be if we was to try for a cup of tay at one o' dem convents on de way to Edbury? Most times dey're good for a cup o' tay. Ah, what'd a man do widout religion, eh? I've took cups o'tay from de convents, an' de Baptists, an' de Church of England, an' all sorts. I'm a Catholic meself. Dat's to say, I ain't been to confession for about seventeen year, but I still got me religious feelin's y'understand. An' dem convents is always good for a cup o' tay...' (*Down and Out*, p. 151; cf. p. 208)

This passage – and other speeches by Paddy and by Mrs McElligot are absolutely consistent – is based on the same non-standard features of verbs, endings, pronouns, etc., that we found in Orwell's London speech. To this foundation are added two phonological features which are stereotypes of 'Irish brogue'. One is indicated in the spelling 'tay' for 'tea'. In this stereotype, the long vowel /i:/ of RP is replaced by the long vowel /e:/, not universally, but in certain typical words, of which 'tea' is one, 'Jesus' (spelt 'Jaysus') another. Wells (*Accents of English*, 2, p. 425) regards it as no longer current, but 'people sometimes put it on as a joke or as a conscious Hibernicism'. The other stereotype invoked by Orwell has a real basis in some varieties of Irish English (particularly lower-class, and particularly associated with Cork and with some parts of Dublin): the substitution of a dental or alveolar 'd' or 't' for voiced and voiceless 'th' respectively. This is of course represented in spellings such as 'de', 'dem', or, elsewhere in Paddy, 't'ree' for 'three', Mrs McElligot 't'inks' for 'thinks'. Having selected this marker (which is actually probably obligatory in written representation of uneducated Irish speech), Orwell is committed to spelling it with absolute consistency, and since these sounds are very frequent in English, the text comes out very strongly marked visually for the Irish accent. In fact, a very strange-looking written text is produced by notation of just one marker.

Other dialects are represented, in cameos, in the early books, but without any notation of appropriate markers, either realistic or stereotypical. Where are these speakers supposed to come from?

A. 'It's they *bells*, Miss,' he said . . .' They bells up in the church tower. They're a-splintering through that there belfry floor in a way as it makes you fair shudder to look at 'em. We'll have 'em down atop of us before we know where we are. I was up the belfry 'smorning, and I tell you I come down faster'n I went up, when I saw how that there floor's a-busting underneath 'em.'
B. 'Poor Pither! . . . him a-digging at his age, with his rheumatism *that* bad! Ain't it cruel hard, Miss? And he's had a kind of pain between his legs, Miss, as he can't seem to account for – terrible bad he's been with it, these last few mornings. Ain't it bitter hard, Miss, the lives us poor working folks has to lead? . . . Pither he says to me, when he comes home tired of a night and our rheumatism's bad, "Never you mind, my dear," he says, "we ain't far off Heaven now," he says. "Heaven was made for the likes of us," he says.' (*A Clergyman's Daughter*, pp. 32, 49–50)

Here we have a selection of non-standard features appropriate to the image of 'poor working folk': irregular pronouns and demonstratives ('us', 'they bells'), adverbs without the '-ly' ending ('terrible', etc.), irregular strong verb forms (past 'come', plural 'has').

Most of these non-standard markers occur in many different regional dialects, and some are found in the Cockney passages above. These markers do not specifically signify the regional dialect speech of the people in question, namely, the East Anglian dialect, for these are parishioners of Dorothy's father in Suffolk. Orwell – who should have known better, since he was living in Southwold while writing this novel – fails to use the common East Anglian form, which would be 'them bells'; Hughes and Trudgill observe that 'they' in this usage is unusual, but is found in Scottish dialects.[22] Mrs Pither's first person plural verb 'has to lead' is uncharacteristic of East Anglia, which in broad speech has no -s ending on verbs at all.[23] This feature also would have provided Orwell with an opportunity to insert a clear marker of Suffolk speech: the lack of -s in third-person-singular verbs is a strong marker of East Anglian speech, and a real Mrs Pither would say 'when he come home' and would report her husband's piety in the form 'he say . . . he say . . . he say . . . he say'. (By the way, the repeated 'say' form in oral narrative is, in my observation, as typical of East Anglian as it is of Cockney: see p. 98 above and reference.) A further missed opportunity concerns the -ing endings which are frequent in these extracts. Orwell tends to use the spelling 'in'' for Cockney, and this would be appropriate for East Anglian too, where it is pronounced /ən/ or even /n/.

The inaccuracy and underspecification of Orwell's rendering of Suffolk speech is a small criticism, since, as we have seen, it takes little in the way of explicit markers to persuade readers that a variety is 'on the page' when they are encouraged to expect it to be there. Orwell's 'Suffolk dialect' anyway remains distinct from his representation of London and of Irish speakers in this novel, and thus contributes individually to the heteroglossic pattern of the whole book.

EXPERIMENT IN POLYPHONY: THE TRAFALGAR SQUARE CHAPTER IN *A CLERGYMAN'S DAUGHTER*

So far, when illustrating dialect and sociolect representations in *A Clergyman's Daughter* and *Down and Out*, we have looked at the occurrence of Cockney, Irish and Suffolk as separate 'foreign voices' in specific narrative locations, and in relation to the narrator, the heroine, and the reader. Sometimes – usually the case in *Down and*

Out – a speech in some non-Standard variety of English may simply be put on display as illustration of a speaker from an unfamiliar social world; but the heteroglossic relationships become more functional as Orwell's narrative techniques become more sophisticated. Suffolk and Cockney are used in *A Clergyman's Daughter* to make specific points about the limitations of Dorothy's social and sexual experience. We will see that heteroglossia in *Burmese Days* is used to contrast the attitudes of the whites in Burma with those of the hero, John Flory, and to condemn their attitudes (Chapter 7, pp. 129–35). In Chapter 1 of *Keep the Aspidistra Flying*, a succession of customers of different social types pass through the bookshop minded by the snobbish poet Gordon Comstock; peculiar speech habits are sketched for each of them, and the function of this is to tell us something about the prejudices of the hero.

In addition to these specific dialogic relationships between the standard and the 'other', there is for each book a pattern or overall impression of heteroglossia, a modelling of a world in which a plurality of voices and views is manifest.

In one section of *A Clergyman's Daughter*, there is stylistic heteroglossia of a different and more intense kind. Chapter 3 (in which Dorothy has become penniless and homeless and, delirious with cold, spends the night with tramps in Trafalgar Square) uses a linguistic technique unprecedented in Orwell and never tried again by him: a sequence with no narrative commentary, simply the speech of a variety of characters printed like dialogue in a play script, and complete with stage directions; this device is maintained for a whole chapter of twenty-five pages. The technique is modelled directly on the 'Circe' or 'nighttown' episode of Joyce's *Ulysses*, a surrealist or hallucinatory sequence which has Bloom and Stephen among streetwalkers and other citizens of the night.[24] In 'Circe' a multitude of characters come and go in garishly lit, crowded, noisy streets, talking and singing, often to themselves; when they speak to one another, one utterance does not directly address the adjacent one, but the voices are woven so that several fragmentary conversations are interspersed and overlapping. (This is the structure which I wish to convey by 'polyphony'; see further, below.) No single, focusing viewpoint follows the conversations coherently. After an elaborate scene-setting teeming with discordant impressions, the whores call and are answered, children accost an idiot, oaths and shouts and singing merge. It is necessary to quote at length because the long stage directions contribute much to the surreal atmosphere (and that is a difference from Orwell's polyphonic text).

(*The Mabbat street entrance of nighttown, before which stretches an uncobbled tramsiding set with skeleton tracks, red and green will-o'-the-wisps and danger signals. Rows of flimsy houses with gaping doors. Rare lamps with faint rainbow fans. Round Rabaiotti's halted ice gondola stunted men and women squabble. They grab wafers between which are wedged lumps of coal and copper snow. Sucking, they scatter slowly. Children. The swan-comb of the gondola, highreared, forges on through the murk, white and blue under a lighthouse. Whistles call and answer.*)

[Dialogue and a longer surrealist stage direction.]

(*. . .Cissy Caffrey's voice, still young, sings shrill from a lane.*)

CISSY CAFFREY

I gave it to Molly
Because she was jolly,
The leg of the duck
The leg of the duck.

(*Private Carr and Private Compton, swaggersticks tight in their oxters, as they march unsteadily rightaboutface and burst together from their mouths a volleyed fart. Laughter of men from the lane. A hoarse virago retorts.*)

THE VIRAGO

Signs on you, hairy arse. More power the Cavan girl.

CISSY CAFFREY

More luck to me. Cavan, Cootehill and Belturbet. (*She sings.*)

I gave it to Nelly
To stick in her belly
The leg of the duck
The leg of the duck.

(*Private Carr and Private Compton turn and counterretort, their tunics bloodbright in a lampglow, black sockets of caps on their blond copper polls. Stephen Dedalus and Lynch pass through the crowd close to the redcoats.*)

PRIVATE COMPTON

(*Jerks his finger.*) Way for the parson.

PRIVATE CARR

(*Turns and calls.*) What ho, parson!
CISSY CAFFREY
(*Her voice soaring higher.*)

She has it, she got it,

Wherever she put it

The leg of the duck.

(*Stephen, flourishing the ashplant in his left hand, chants with joy the* introit *for paschal time. Lynch, his jockey cap low on his brow, attends him, a sneer of discontent wrinkling his face.*)
STEPHEN
Vidi aquam egredientem de templo a latere dextro. Alleluia.
(*The famished snaggletusks of an elderly bawd protrude from a doorway.*)
THE BAWD
(*Her voice whispering huskily.*) Sst! Come here till I tell you. Maidenhead inside. Sst.
STEPHEN
(*Altius aliquantulum.*) *Et omnes ad quos pervenit aqua ista.*[25] (Joyce, *Ulysses*, pp. 410–12)

The stylistic similarity of the Trafalgar Square chapter of *A Clergyman's Daughter* can readily be seen; here is the opening:

[SCENE: *Trafalgar Square. Dimly visible through the mist, a dozen people, Dorothy among them, are grouped about one of the benches near the north parapet.*][26]
CHARLIE [*singing*]: 'Ail Mary, 'ail Mary, 'a-il Ma-ary –
　　[*Big Ben strikes ten.*]
SNOUTER [*mimicking the noise*]: Ding dong, ding dong! Shut your
　　——— noise, can't you? Seven more hours of it on this ———
　　square before we got the chance of a setdown and a bit of
　　sleep! Cripes!
MR TALLBOYS [*to himself*]: *Non sum qualis eram boni sub regno
　　Edwardi!* In the days of my innocence, before the Devil car-
　　ried me up into a high place and dropped me into the Sunday
　　newspapers – that is to say when I was Rector of Little Fawley-
　　cum-Dewsbury . . .
DEAFIE [*singing*]: With my willy willy, *with* my willy willy . . .

MRS WAYNE: Ah, dearie, as soon as I set eyes on you I knew as you was a lady born and bred. You and me've known what it is to come down in the world, haven't we, dearie? It ain't the same for us as what it is for some of these others here.

CHARLIE [*singing*]: 'Ail Mary, 'ail Mary, 'a-il Ma-ary, full of grace!

MRS BENDIGO: Calls himself a bloody husband, does he? Four pound a week in Covent Garden and 'is wife doing a starry in the bloody Square! Husband!

MR TALLBOYS [*to himself*]: Happy days, happy days! My ivied church under the sheltering hillside – my red-tiled Rectory slumbering among Elizabethan yews! My library, my vinery, my cook, house-parlourmaid and groom-gardener! My cash in the bank, my name in Crockford! My black suit of irreproachable cut, my collar back to front, my watered silk cossack [*sic*] in the church precincts.

. . .

MRS WAYNE: Of course the one thing I *do* thank God for, dearies, is that my poor dear mother never lived to see this day. Because if she ever *had* of lived to see the day when her eldest daughter – as was brought up, mind you, with no expense spared and milk straight from the cow . . .

MRS BENDIGO: *Husband!*

GINGER: Come on, less 'ave a drum of tea while we got the chance. Last we'll get tonight –   coffee shop shuts at 'ar-parse ten.

THE KIKE: Oh Jesus! This bloody cold's gonna kill me! I ain't got nothing on under my trousers. Oh Je-e-e-*eeze*!

CHARLIE: [*singing*]: 'Ail Many, 'ail Mary . . .

SNOUTER: Fourpence! Fourpence for six —— hours on the bum! And that there nosing sod with the wooden leg queering our pitch at every boozer between Aldgate and the Mile End Road. With 'is —— wooden leg and 'is war medals as 'e bought in Lambeth Cut! Bastard!

DEAFIE [*singing*]: With my willy willy, *with* my willy willy –

MRS BENDIGO: Well, I told the bastard what I thought of 'im, any-way. 'Call yourself a man?' I says. 'I've seen things like you kep' in a bottle at the 'orspital,' I says . . .

MR TALLBOYS [*to himself*]: Happy days, happy days! Roast beef and bobbing villagers, and the peace of God that passeth all understanding! Sunday mornings in my oaken stall, cool flower scent and frou-frou of surplices in the sweet corpse-laden air! (etc.) (*A Clergyman's Daughter*, pp. 138–9)

Joyce opens his chapter with two long stage directions, one omitted here, which are part-descriptive, part-fantastic; Orwell does not use this technique to set the atmosphere of his surreal chapter. This is in a way surprising, since as we saw when discussing modes of realism in *Down and Out*, and in one passage in *Wigan Pier*, he had a taste and aptitude for a heightened naturalism of the senses verging on surrealism (Chapter 5). He does however use such stage directions later in the episode, when the tramps are moving around, and one passage, in which the defrocked clergyman Mr Tallboys celebrates a Black Mass (a clear parallel with 'Circe') is remarkably Joycean in its use of fantasy and heightened sensation:

> [*As he reaches the final word of the prayer he tears the conse-crated bread across. The blood runs out of it. There is a roll-ing sound, as of thunder, and the landscape changes. Dorothy's feet are very cold. Monstrous winged shapes of Demons and Archdemons are dimly visible, moving to and fro. Something, beak or claw, closes upon Dorothy's shoulder, reminding her that her feet and hands are aching with cold.*] (*A Clergyman's Daughter*, p. 157)

As far as the 'dialogue' is concerned, Orwell follows Joyce in both structure and texture. It is the structure of the relationships between speeches which I have called – adapting a term of Bakhtin's – 'polyphonic'. Polyphony in music is the interplay of distinct voices or musical lines occupying the same compositional segment – in performance, these voices sound simultaneously in one stretch of time. In speech many voices can coexist, but in a written text linguistic polyphony can only be *suggested*, of course, since written texts in-evitably proceed in a linear sequence. In Orwell, and to a large degree in Joyce, simultaneity of voices is implied by flouting the normal conventions which structure the linear organisation of con-versation. Everyday conversation stays fluent, coherent and coop-erative by adhering to a number of fairly strict conventions.[27] Speakers take turns in an orderly way; adjacent utterances relate to each other in connected 'moves', e.g. reply follows question, greeting follows greeting; one item is relevant in meaning and theme to its predeces-sor. These conventions are seriously disrupted in the Trafalgar Square sequence. At first sight, speeches appear to be arranged in no par-ticular order, either social or communicative. Each of the dozen or so participants is allocated a number of speaking spots, but the spots are not 'turns' since they do not relate to the adjacent spots of others. Sometimes the speakers are not addressing anyone else, just saying their bit, either to themselves (Mr Tallboys) or to no one in particular (Snouter, Mrs Bendigo). Mrs Wayne appears to be talking to Dorothy, but Dorothy does not respond. But even when they make no contact with others, individuals are consistent with themselves, either by repetition (Charlie, Deafie) or by continuity – Mr Tallboys harps on about his pleasures before he parted company with the Church, Mrs Wayne goes on about coming down in the world, Mrs Bendigo complains about her husband. Each has his or her theme, and it is as if the themes are being voiced simultaneously.

On closer inspection, there *are* conversations: these are intricately interleaved, with usually two going on at a time, and interrupted by stray remarks and snatches of song. Dialogue is more clearly detectable when the reader gets used to the habitual topics which preoccupy individuals. For example, a dialogue between Nosy Watson (who is obsessed with thieving and the police) and Charlie runs throughout a series of interruptions, a conversation about going to fetch tea, and a line of talk from Mrs Bendigo to which Mrs Wayne responds (pp. 142–3); the following 'exploded diagram' separates out the chains of dialogue, which are not immediately clear in the continuous text.

CHARLIE: 'Oo was it copped you, Nosy?
    THE KIKE: Oh Je-e-e-*eeze*!
    MRS BENDIGO: Shove up, shove up!
    Seems to me some folks think they've
    took a mortgage on this bloody seat.
    MR TALLBOYS: [*chanting*]: O all ye
    works of the Lord, curse ye the Lord,
    curse Him and vilify Him for ever!
    MRS MCELLIGOT: What I always say is,
    it's always us poor Catholics dat's down
    in the bloody dumps.
NOSY WATSON: Smithy. Flying Squad –
flying sod! Give us the plans of the
house and everything, and then had a van
full of coppers waiting and nipped the lot
of us. I wrote it up in the Black Maria:
    'Detective Smith knows how to gee;
    Tell him he's a —— from me.'

SNOUTER: 'Ere, what about our ——
tea? Go on, Kikie, you're a young 'un;
shut that —— noise and take the
drums. Don't you pay nothing. Worm it
out of the old tart. Snivel. Do the
doleful.

MR TALLBOYS [*chanting*]: O all ye
children of men, curse ye the Lord, curse
Him and vilify him for ever!

CHARLIE: What, is Smithy crooked too?

MRS BENDIGO: I tell you what, girls, I
tell you what gets *me* down, and that's
to think of my bloody husband snoring
under four blankets and me freezing in
this bloody Square. That's what *I* can't
stomach. The unnatural sod.

GINGER: [*singing*]: *There* they go – *in*
their joy – Don't take the drum with the
cold sausage in it, Kikie.

NOSY WATSON: Crooked? *Crooked?* Why,
a corkscrew 'ud look like a bloody
bradawl beside of him! There isn't one of
them double —— sons of whores in the
Flying Squad but 'ud sell his
grandmother for two pound ten and then
sit on her gravestone eating potato crisps.
The geeing, narking toe rag!

CHARLIE: Perishing tough. 'Ow many
convictions you got?

GINGER [*singing*]:
    There they go – *in* their joy –
    'Appy girl – *lu*cky boy –

NOSY WATSON: Fourteen. You don't stand
no chance with that lot against you.

MRS WAYNE: What, don't he keep you,
then?

MRS BENDIGO: No, I'm married to this
one, sod 'im!

CHARLIE: I got perishing nine myself.

The above display shows separate dialogues in the left and the right columns, overlapping, plus a number of disconnected exclamations, snatches of song and other bits of speech, on other topics including the tea-making, in the middle column, mixed in with the two dialogues at various points. I hope the diagram makes it clear that polyphony in this extract is not a random medley of voices, but a considerably crafted structure of utterances, dialogues and themes. The effect will be considered in a moment.

Also crafted is the *texture*, the detailed representation of individual voices. We have seen that very early in his career Orwell could render a range of sociolects and dialects. The majority of the characters in the Trafalgar Square scene are individually recognisable. The defrocked Mr Tallboys speaks a flowery, complex prose, full of allusions to the liturgy and the affairs of a churchman, including scraps of Latin (following Stephen in 'Circe'). Dorothy says very little, and her only longish contribution (p. 155) is polite and syntactically complex. Snouter's speech is so obscene that much of it has to be rendered by '——'. There are gradations of Cockney, from a 'high' version spoken by Mrs Wayne through the more marked version of Mrs Bendigo to the 'base' variety of some of the men speakers, including Charlie, Daddy and Ginger; Ginger's speech has the added dimension of slang, including a lot of rhyming slang – this is consistent and exclusive in his speech, testimony to the careful work of differentiation which Orwell put into the scene. Nosy Watson's language is full of the argot of crime, police procedure and prison. Mrs McElligot speaks broad Irish English, as she does in the hop-picking sequence earlier. Further differentiations among the characters come from catch-phrases, typical songs, and so on.

Chapter 3 of *A Clergyman's Daughter* is, then, composed entirely of (written-down) speech with stage-directions; each bit of speech is attributed to an identified individual character, and the words and topics of individuals are carefully chosen to form self-consistent idiolects; the diversity of the idiolects helps with the phonic separateness of the multiple voices in polyphony. When we read the text linearly, it seems to break the rules of conversational sequencing; but the voices overlap and interweave, and there *are* coherent conversations if the reader is alert enough. The overall effect that we can imagine is like the babble of a lot of people in one space, the so-called 'cocktail party effect' where everything is a blur except what you choose to concentrate on.

Critics usually say that one reason that speech is so important in the modern novel is that it gives an impression of realism (verisimilitude) and vitality. Is the dialogue of Chapter 3, then, 'realistic'? Of course it is not. It might be if it were a script for some quite different genre such as a radio play which has quite distinct audience expectations and competences, including (in radio modernism, post-Dylan Thomas, *Under Milk Wood*) the ability to perceive and to decode complex vocal polyphony. But this is a novel, in the British realist, humanist, tradition, and the genre has its own and distinctive conventions of verisimilitude. We do not expect polyphonic dialogue in the novel, nor do we expect dialogue to exist with such a marked absence of authorial frame. Paradoxically – as has been observed about 'Circe'[28] – the backgrounding of the discourse of narrator, and the defamiliarising switches between registers in the speech presentation, make the artificiality of the act of telling more obvious: this polyphonic discourse is estranging rather than mimetic. As has been observed repeatedly of the 'Circe' polyphony in *Ulysses*, the effect is surreal or hallucinatory. A central consciousness – Stephen/ Bloom in *Ulysses*, Dorothy here – is presented in a state of extreme, or extremely uncoordinated, sensory awareness in which the mundane world becomes fantastic. Dorothy is at her wits' end with tiredness and cold, disoriented by being thrust by her situation down into the hell of homelessness and pennilessness. The speech of her associates in the Square is, to her, a senseless cacophony. Speech is companionable and democratic for the other tramps, a medium of preservation, but it is for her a symbol of her alienation.

7 Further Aspects of Style

A theme of this discussion of the language of George Orwell has been the range of his linguistic achievement, the variety of styles in which he wrote, a variety which marks the differences between one book and another, and which is also manifested *within* each of the individual books (with the exception of one, *Animal Farm*). There is of course one consistent basis to the diversity. From his early writing days, and throughout his career, he established and maintained his *own* voice; though unmistakably individual, it encompasses a spectrum of tones from quiet appreciative reflection on traditional English life, as in his *Horizon* column 'As I Please', to the strident critique of fashionable socialism in the second part of *Wigan Pier* (Chapter 4). We have seen how the Orwellian style was adapted in various ways, used as the basis for a spectrum of 'realistic' styles from the plain to the surreal (Chapter 5). And under the heading of 'heteroglossia' we examined his representation of 'voices of the other', social dialects which seem to embody world-views alien to that of the framing narrating voice (Chapter 6). The present chapter will explore some further aspects of his stylistic virtuosity – and also develop some points already made – with reference to the early novel *Burmese Days*.

THE PICTURESQUE

Burmese Days (1934) is Orwell's first published novel and his second published book, *Down and Out* having appeared in 1933. But, apparently, neither of these was his first book-length writing. In his preface to the French translation of *Down and Out*, *La vache enragée* (1935), he maintains that he wrote two novels – which were not published, and do not survive in manuscript – while in Paris in 1928–9 (*CEJL*, I, pp. 137–8). Evidently he had learned a lot about the craft of writing in his Paris sojourn, for *Burmese Days* is a

119

most accomplished novel in most aspects of plot-construction, characterisation, and language.

It was the one of his early books that Orwell did not dismiss
entirely; writing to his American fellow-writer Henry Miller in 1936,
this is how he mentions it:

> That is the only one of my books that I am pleased with – not
> that it is any good *qua* novel, but the descriptions of scenery
> aren't bad, but of course that is what the average reader skips.
> (*CEJL*, I, 258)

In 'Why I write' he also refers to *Burmese Days* not entirely dep-
recatingly; when he was young:

> I wanted to write enormous naturalistic novels with unhappy end-
> ings, full of detailed descriptions and arresting similes, and also
> full of purple passages in which words were used partly for the
> sake of their sound. And in fact my first complete novel, *Bur-
> mese Days*, which I wrote when I was thirty but projected much
> earlier, is rather that kind of book. (*CEJL*, I, p. 25)

Burmese Days seems in fact to have been projected not long after
his return from Burma in 1927, for a 21-page manuscript concerning 'John Flory' in Burma exists, which according to Bernard Crick
can be dated either 1927–8 or 1928–9.[2] It is anyway understandable
to connect *Burmese Days* with Orwell's experiences as a young man
in Burma, which, according to the second part of *Wigan Pier* and
other comments, he found morally distasteful but politically illuminating; whatever his precise reasons for quitting the Imperial Indian
Police, it is clear that he was disgusted with and outraged by the
effects of imperialism on the ground, and guilty about his part in
the process.[3] One dimension to *Burmese Days* is its vigorous attack
on the behaviour and attitudes of the white community, an attack
conducted not by polemical commentary but by dramatising their
racism and bigotry in their actions and speech. The central character of the novel, John Flory, in a sense represents Orwell: he is
friends with an Indian doctor, enjoys the culture, and in general
does not share his white colleagues' values; he is full of anger,
frustration, and guilt about his own part in the practices of colonialism. Critics speak of Orwell's writing of the book as an 'act of

exorcism' of his Burmese past, or as an indictment of imperialism achieved in fictional form. But it is clear to most critics that it is much more than that, for it is primarily a conventional, and satisfyingly executed, *novel*.[4]

John Flory is a 35-year old Englishman, manager of the local operation of a timber company at 'Kyauktada' in Burma. He is set aside from the other whites by his liberal attitudes towards the local people, who are simply 'niggers' to the others; his alienation is symbolised by a disfiguring birthmark on his face. The whites are confronted with a decree that tells them to admit a 'native' member to the Club, and Flory is in favour of his friend Dr Veraswami while the others are adamantly, and obscenely, opposed to any native membership. In a second strand of the narrative, Flory falls for Elizabeth Lackersteen, niece of one of the other whites, who has come to stay at Kyauktada; he is temporarily displaced by a rival, Verrall, but seems to be reinstated toward the end of the novel when Verrall departs leaving debts, and after Flory has heroically saved the whites from a native attack on the Club. But the English are not in control of their own affairs. The engine of the narrative is U Po Kyin, the corrupt and revolting Subdivisional Magistrate of the region, who is constantly plotting for his own ends (which include membership of the Club) by means of slander, incitement of riots and other machinations and manipulations. When Flory foils the assault on the Club, U Po Kyin fears that Flory's standing after this will guarantee the election of Dr Veraswami, rather than himself, to the Club. U Po Kyin pays Flory's Burmese mistress to disgrace Flory, in church and in front of Elizabeth; Flory's reaction to this disgrace is to shoot himself.

Orwell need not have been ashamed of this narrative, which is ingenious, full of unexpected turns, and produces many impressive incidents and scenes: the riot, the ballot for a 'native' member, interrupted by the return of Maxwell's body, Elizabeth's encounter with the buffalo, the *pwe*-dance, the hunting expedition, the bazaar, Flory's fall from Verrall's horse, and others. The incidents impinge primarily on Flory. Told in the third person, not in the first person as was the earlier 'John Flory' manuscript, the novel nevertheless maintains Flory as the main experiencer or *focaliser* of the action:[5] it is almost always his attitudes, reactions and feelings that count.

If we recall Orwell's comments quoted at the beginning of this section, in his letter to Henry Miller he was pleased with his

'descriptions of scenery', while in 'Why I write', though not con-
demning them, he seems to have regarded 'detailed descriptions' as
an immature artistic aim. Note that Orwell in both cases refers to
'descriptions' rather than 'description': the plural reference suggests
stand-alone set pieces rather than the technique of description more
diffusely distributed in the novel. It is indeed set pieces, passages
which stand out as if he has suddenly changed gear, with which we
are faced – and set pieces tend to be unfashionable in the modern
novel. However, a crucial consideration is whether they are simply
offered for their own sake, as pieces of pretty writing, or are justified in terms of the narrative or characterisation needs of the novel.
In the case of *Burmese Days*, it can be argued that the descriptions
are not merely 'purple passages', but are justified or motivated in
their context. They function to symbolise the mood of a scene, or
the state of mind of a character: features of a landscape, flora and
fauna, light and heat and rain, are evoked as symbols of emotions
and atmosphere, in the manner of what T. S. Eliot called the 'objective correlative' – emotions are not described, but symbolised by
objects.[6] Although Orwell does not hesitate to tell us about the thoughts
and emotions of his characters in *Burmese Days*, he also uses the
device of the objective correlative frequently. Immediately after the
riot against the Club has been quelled, the rains begin, bringing
relief after the tropical heat and blinding sunlight that have oppressed
and irritated the whites throughout the novel so far; and at this point
of the narrative the rains symbolise relief and calm for the moment,
in the tension between the Burmans and the whites; and then the
rains symbolise a change of atmosphere to menace, betrayal and
machination in the succession of scenes which lead to Flory's downfall
(p. 266 and the following chapters, beginning ch. 23). Here is another
brief, obvious and conventional example. Flory has just met Elizabeth
Lackersteen, has rescued her from a menacing buffalo and accom-
panied her to the Club. Flory's instant and intense desire for Elizabeth is conveyed in two pages (pp. 79–80) of references to the luxuriant
flowers around the Club, and their strong scents: 'a wave of black-
currant scent flowed from the petunias beside the path . . .' and the
like; Flory (who speaks too much in Elizabeth's presence) is given
a long speech on the luxuriance of the flowers there; then he gazes
at her sitting at the Club:

The girl had sat down in the wicker chair that Ko S'la had set out for her at the end of the veranda. The dark-leaved orchids hung behind her head, with gold trusses of blossom, breathing out warm honey-scent. Flory was standing against the veranda rail, half-facing the girl, but keeping his birthmarked cheek hidden. (*Burmese Days*, p. 80)

The eroticism of Flory's vision of Elizabeth, with its conventional symbolism of orchids, gold trusses/tresses, breathing, warmth, honey and its scent, is clear.

Let us return briefly to a passage from the novel quoted in Chapter 5, in which a realistic account of Flory's spartan bedroom switches to more exotic imagery:

The bedroom was a large square room with white plaster walls, open doorways and no ceiling, but only rafters in which sparrows nested. There was no furniture except the big four-poster bed, with its furled mosquito net like a canopy, and a wicker table and chair and a small mirror; also some rough bookshelves containing several hundred books, all mildewed by many rainy seasons and riddled by silver fish. A *tuktoo* clung to the wall, flat and motionless like a heraldic dragon. Beyond the veranda eaves the light rained down like glistening white oil. Some doves in a bamboo thicket kept up a dull droning noise, curiously appropriate to the heat – a sleepy sound, but with the sleepiness of chloroform rather than a lullaby. (*Burmese Days*, pp. 47–8)

A transition from realistic to atmospheric writing is cued by the silver fish and the *tuktoo* – insects, birds and small animals are a recurrent element in Orwell's evocation of the climate of Kyauktada. The *tuktoo* is presumably a kind of lizard; it reappears stalking a moth a few pages later. Orwell uses the word in a characteristic way: the novel contains a scattering of Burmese words which are untranslated yet comprehensible in a vague way, giving an air of the exotic and foreign. On the same page Flory's servant Ko S'la dresses in 'his pink *gaungbaung* and muslin *ingyi*'. It does not matter if we cannot understand these words precisely, or look them up – the residual vagueness is more suggestive, more exotic.

From the *tuktoo* Orwell moves our, and Flory's, attention to the light, heat, and noise of outdoors. The light has an unnatural texture, the heat of the afternoon makes activity impossible, the sound of the doves is like an anaesthetic, and not, as in European symbolism, positive and charming. Flory is lying on his 'sweat-damp' bed, bored, idle, bad-tempered. His Burmese mistress arrives and is rudely dismissed after sex. Flory is still angry, self-disgusted and lethargic. He walks out into the jungle, and there follows a memorable descriptive sequence where the point is clearly that the strange beauty of the setting, and its solitude, help to crystallise and relieve his feelings. The descriptions change as his mood changes. The first section of jungle is described to mirror his displeasure and disgust:

> Flory went out and followed the road uphill into the jungle. It was scrub jungle at first, with dense stunted bushes, and the only trees were half-wild mangoes, bearing little turpentiny fruits the size of plums. Then the road struck among taller trees. The jungle was dried-up and lifeless at this time of year. The trees lined the road in close, dusty ranks, with leaves a dull olive-green. No birds were visible except some ragged brown creatures like disreputable thrushes, which hopped clumsily under the bushes; in the distance some other bird uttered a cry of '*Ah* ha ha! *Ah* ha ha!' – a lonely, hollow sound like the echo of a laugh. There was a poisonous, ivy-like smell of crushed leaves. It was still hot, though the sun was losing his glare and the slanting light was yellow. (ibid, pp. 53–4)

This is more or less the negative-toned descriptive style that we encountered in Chapter 5. The nouns that refer to the objects which make up the framework of the description are familiar and matter-of-fact:

> road ... jungle ... jungle ... bushes ... trees ... mangoes ... fruits ... road ... trees ... jungle ... trees ... birds ... creatures ... thrushes ... bushes ... bird ... cry ... sound ... smell ... leaves ... sun ... glare ... light.

There are no polysyllabic, learned, foreign or poetic words among them. The epithets to these nouns are negative in a dull, unexaggerated way:

scrub ... dense stunted ... the only ... half-wild ... little ... dried-up ... lifeless ... close, dusty ... dull ... No ... ragged brown ... disreputable ... clumsily ... some other ... lonely, hollow ... poisonous, ivy-like ... crushed ... hot ... slanting ... yellow.

But the style is changing even within this paragraph. In the last three sentences there is a modulation into a higher and more literary register with the mocking laugh of an unseen and unidentified bird; the 'poisonous, ivy-like' smell; the implicit violence of 'crushed'; the still-present heat, central symbol of the pressure on, and the spiritual and physical discomfort of, the whites in Burma; the un-European yellowness and slant of the sunlight; the very literary use of the pronoun 'his' instead of 'its', animating the sun and reinterpreting the word 'glare'. The glare is not only a property of the light, harsh and unrelieved, but, in the context of 'his', the look of a person, hostile and unwavering. 'Yellow' is of course a stereotype for oriental skin, and is used in that way several times in this novel. In this paragraph Flory is walking through a scrub jungle which is at first as lifeless and drab as his spirit; but as the style is heightened, the place takes on an additional dimension of menace. However, the mood lightens as Flory goes on:

After two miles the road ended at the ford of a shallow stream. The jungle grew greener here, because of the water, and the trees were taller. At the edge of the stream there was a huge dead pyinkado tree festooned with spidery orchids, and there were some wild lime bushes with white, waxen flowers. They had a sharp scent like bergamot ... [T]he sight of this stream always heartened him; its water was quite clear, rarest of sights in a miry country ... [A] narrow track ... led to a pool fifty yards upstream. Here a peepul tree grew, a great buttressed thing six feet thick, woven of innumerable strands of wood, like a wooden cable twisted by a giant. The roots of the tree made a natural cavern, under which the clear greenish water bubbled. Above and all around dense foliage shut out the light, turning the place into a green grotto walled with leaves. (ibid, p. 54)

Flory has come to this place by a path made by cattle, which 'few human beings ever followed'. It is a private, magical place where he is to experience something 'beautiful beyond all words'. He bathes in the pool, and then his attention, and ours, is returned to the peepul tree:

> There was a stirring high up in the peepul tree, and a bubbling noise like pots boiling. A flock of green pigeons were up there, eating the berries. Flory gazed up into the great green dome of the tree, trying to distinguish the birds; they were invisible, they matched the leaves so perfectly, and yet the whole tree was alive with them, shimmering, as though the ghosts of birds were shaking it . . . Then a single green pigeon fluttered down and perched on a lower branch. It did not know that it was being watched. It was a tender thing, smaller than a tame dove, with jade-green back as smooth as velvet, and neck and breast of iridescent colours. Its legs were like the pink wax that dentists use.
>
> The pigeon rocked itself backwards and forwards on the bough, swelling out its breast feathers and laying its coralline beak upon them. A pang went through Flory. (ibid, pp. 54–5)

In the series of three passages we find a sequence of picturesque writing concentrating into an intense symbolism: the drab landscape, the glaring light, then exotically named trees and flora, a wealth of colours culminating in the many-times repeated 'green', finally concentrating on the 'green pigeon', highly defamiliarising to a European reader, with its pink legs and 'coralline beak'. Besides the colours, the exotic flowers and trees and birds, there are other elements which are stock features of description in this novel, including high register poetic words such as 'iridescent', 'coralline', 'shimmering', and some similes which are very typical of Orwell:

> woven of innumerable strands of wood, like a wooden cable twisted by a giant

> a bubbling noise like pots boiling

> Its legs were like the pink wax that dentists use.

The comparisons are generally striking because slightly incongruous, even laboured: legs like dentists' wax, a tree-trunk like a cable – something natural (or, elsewhere in Orwell, something abstract) represented in terms of something manufactured or mechanical. Examples abound in the essays: the opening of 'A Hanging':

It was in Burma, a sodden morning of the rains. A sickly light, like yellow tinfoil, was slanting over the high walls into the jail yard. (*CEJL*, I, 66)

and from 'Politics and the English Language':

phrases tacked together like the sections of a prefabricated hen-house. (*CEJL*, IV, 159; cf. Chapter 3, p. above)

These picturesque similes are a stock part of the decorative technique of *Burmese Days*; dozens of examples could be cited:

The Irrawaddy flowed huge and ochreous, glittering like diamonds (p. 17)

white mists that poured through the valleys like the steam of enormous kettles (pp. 63–4)

wastes of sea like rough-beaten silver (p. 67)

morning sunlight . . . yellow as goldleaf (p. 70)

ringworm like a coat of mail (p. 72)

a white pagoda rose from the plain like the breast of a supine goddess (p. 92)

like long curved needles threading through embroidery, the two canoes . . . (p. 149)

Flaring like a white-hot coin, the moon . . . (p. 167)

black clouds were streaming eastwards like a pack of hounds (p. 242)

Such similes permeate the book; they are visually precise yet subjectively evocative, and make a major contribution to Orwell's rather romantic yet functional picturesque.

Another type of description in *Burmese Days* is the evocation, by an impressionistic technique that we find again in *Homage to Catalonia*, of heightened activity or sense-impression. Memorable examples are the renderings of the *pwe*-dance and of the bazaar.[7] Significantly, both are 'native' events to which Flory has, misguidedly, conducted Elizabeth; he is fascinated and excited, but she is oppressed, disgusted. The high point of the bazaar description is one overwhelmingly dense sentence in which the most diverse impressions scramble thick and fast. The sentence concerned ('There were vast pomelos . . .') is a breathtaking prolongation of the listing structure which is common in Orwell – see Chapter 4, p. ?? above). It is a long sequence of noun phrases which refer colourfully to the merchandise of the bazaar. The nouns are crowded close together, without main verbs, with the effect that the most disparate objects are thrust together, requiring great agility in the reader, who has to slow down the reading to separate the curiously described objects and appreciate their full force. Here is the fantastic sentence, with some surrounding context:

Elizabeth had recoiled from the stench and din, but he did not notice it, and led her deeper into the crowd, pointing to this stall and that. The merchandise was foreign-looking, queer and poor. There were vast pomelos hanging on strings like green moons, red bananas, baskets of heliotrope-coloured prawns the size of lobsters, brittle dried fish tied up in bundles, crimson chilis, ducks split open and cured like hams, green coco-nuts, the larvae of the rhinoceros beetle, sections of sugar-cane, *dahs*, lacquered sandals, check silk *longyis*, aphrodisiacs in the form of large, soap-like pills, glazen earthenware jars four feet high, Chinese sweetmeats made of garlic and sugar, green and white cigars, purple brinjals, persimmon-seed necklaces, chickens cheeping in wicker cages, brass Buddhas, heart-shaped betel leaves, bottles of Kruschen salts, switches of false hair, red clay cooking-pots, steel shoes for bullocks, papier-mâché marionettes, strips of alligator hide with magical properties. Elizabeth's head was beginning to swim. At the other end of the bazaar the sun gleamed through a priest's umbrella, blood-red, as through the ear of a giant. In front of a stall four Dravidian women were pounding turmeric with heavy stakes in a large wooden mortar. The hot-scented yellow powder flew up and tickled Elizabeth's nostrils, making her sneeze. She felt that she could not endure this place a moment longer. She touched Flory's arm. (*Burmese Days*, pp. 120–1)

This is only the most striking part of a whole chapter of crowding sensations. The style is built on the by now familiar elements of the picturesque: exotic terms for exotic objects – 'pomelos', 'turmeric' – some untranslated – '*dahs*', '*longyis*', and some unitalicised as if a translation is unnecessary, 'brinjals'; vivid colour terms – green, red, crimson, white, purple, blood-red, yellow; references to fruits, animals, fish, spices; high-register and polysyllabic terms – 'heliotrope', rhinoceros, aphrodisiac, persimmon, marionettes; similes – 'pomelos . . . like green moons', 'as through the ear of a giant', the latter a brilliant metaphorical linking of experiences: the priest in the marketplace uniting the secular and the spiritual, the umbrella defamiliarising the priest (for European eyes), the umbrella not just red but blood-red for life and death, and suddenly transformed into a mythical object, the ear of a giant.

'Defamiliarisation', as exemplified in the priest–umbrella–blood-red–giant's ear series, is a crucially important device in literary writing.[8] By techniques such as Orwell's unusual and pointed similes, unexpected vocabulary, reference to unusual objects or familiar objects in unusual settings, the reader's view of the objects represented is freshened: they become strange, more perceptible when freed from the habits of everyday perception. Orwell's list of sights and of objects which are mundane in a Burmese bazaar offers to the European eye – the reader, Flory, Elizabeth – a kaleidoscope of strange images.

HETEROGLOSSIA IN *BURMESE DAYS*

Before leaving *Burmese Days*, I want to show that the novel continues the heteroglossic technique begun in the first book, *Down and Out*, and further developed in the third, *A Clergyman's Daughter*. There is a difference, however, in the narrator's orientation toward the voices of the other in this colonial novel. In the two early books discussed in Chapter 6, Cockney is represented by an unexaggerated use of existing literary conventions; it is seen as embodying values different from those of the central characters, but it is not regarded with hostility. And other alien voices, such as those of the various foreigners who work in the Paris restaurants, are again not extreme, and are treated with amusement or even affection. In *Burmese Days*, on the other hand, caricature is often the instrument of parodic attack on the personality and the views of speakers.

Two ranges of alien voices are parodically represented in *Burmese Days*: the British at the Club, and various types of 'native'. Both represent cultural and ideological values which are distinct from those of the central consciousness, John Flory. The Asians come off best – but then, Flory is attracted to Burma, and the Burmese (apart from the villainous U Po Kyin) are in a sense victims rather than agents: they are exploited, provoked and insulted by the Europeans. When the Burmese speak to one another (presumably in Burmese), their speech is represented in ordinary English, without errors or stereotypical 'native' idioms; when they speak to the whites, their utterances are brief and formal, peppered with honorifics, but not mocked. Significantly, the bigoted and foul-mouthed Ellis expects the Burmese servants to speak broken English, and is outraged when the Club butler does not:

'How much ice have we got left?'

'Bout twenty pounds, master. Will only last today, I think. I find it very difficult to keep ice cool now.'

'Don't talk like that, damn you – "I find it very difficult!" Have you swallowed a dictionary? "Please, master, can't keeping ice cool" – that's how you ought to talk. We shall have to sack this fellow if he gets to talk English too well. I can't stick servants who talk English. D'you hear, butler?' (*Burmese Days*, p. 25)

The only extensive 'Asian' speech caricatures are of Flory's Indian friend, Dr Veraswami, and of 'Mr Francis and Mr Samuel, the two derelict Eurasians' who make a cameo appearance. As he does in *Down and Out*, Orwell sketches the speech mannerisms of characters as he introduces them, cueing the reader as to what to expect; a national stereotype is also part of the cue. Veraswami is an educated Indian, and 'His voice was eager and bubbling with a hissing of the s's'; his behaviour is hyperactive, and when he first appears he is 'exclaiming effusively' (*Burmese Days*, p. 36):

'But truly, truly, Mr Flory, you must not speak so! Why iss it that always you are abusing the pukka sahibs, ass you call them? they are the salt of the earth. Consider the great things they have done – consider the great administrators who have made British

India what it iss. Consider Clive, Warren Hastings, Dalhousie, Curzon. They were such men – I quote your immortal Shakespeare – ass, take them for all in all, we shall not look upon their like again!'

The doubled 'ss' spelling indicating presumably a voiceless /s/ sound rather than the normal voiced /z/ in words like 'is' and 'as', the unusual positioning of 'always' in the second sentence, and the unnecessary 'ing' form of 'abusing', together with a slightly formal, literary, style, are sufficient to cue a stereotype of Indian English; the effusiveness is signalled by exclamations and, in general, by a determined loquaciousness and wordiness in Veraswami's conversation. Veraswami is not mocked; the general impression is of warmth and companionability.

The mixed-race Mr Francis is a 'meagre, excitable man'; 'his life-history would pour out of him in unquenchable torrents. He was talking in a nasal, sing-song voice of incredible rapidity'; he 'burst out more effusively than ever . . . chattering in evident dread that he would be interrupted . . .' (*Burmese Days*, p. 114):

> 'Of my father, sir, I remember little, but he was very choleric man and many whackings with big bamboo stick all knobs on both for self, little half-brother and two mothers. Also how on occasion of bishop's visit little half-brother and I dress in *longyis* and sent among the Burmese people to preserve incognito. My father never rose to be bishop, sir. Four converts only in twenty-eight years, and also too great fondness for Chinese rice-spirit very fiery noised abroad and spoil sales of my father's booklet entitled *The Scourge of Alcohol*, published with the Rangoon Baptist Press, one rupee eight annas. My little half-brother die one hot weather, always coughing, coughing,' etc. etc. (ibid)

Francis's English is less correct than Veraswami's, containing consistent non-native errors including a lack of articles – '[a] very choleric man' – and other omissions and inappropriate usages – 'one hot weather'. Orwell allows him scant connectives and little punctuation, presumably indicating that (as we have been told) he speaks at breakneck speed. He moves rapidly from topic to topic, leaving his addressee to work out the significance, and packs many ideas into a single sentence – 'Four converts only . . . one rupee eight annas'. The language is comic without being cruel. Francis and Samuel are pathetic outcasts in this divided society, able to live successfully in neither racial sector; the deviant language, which tries so hard to be English, symbolises their alienation.

In content and style, the speech of the Europeans at the Club is designed to condemn them. There are, for a start, few enough of them for some memorable idiolects to be established: besides Flory, there are Ellis, Westfield, Maxwell; the local Deputy Commissioner and Secretary of the Club, Macgregor; the drunken timber-firm manager, Lackersteen, his wife, and their niece Elizabeth; Verrall, in charge of a detachment of military police, and then briefly, his replacement. The importance of speech mannerisms to the social and political meanings of *Burmese Days* can be gathered from the fact that Orwell devotes a very early chapter, Chapter 2, to a comprehensive presentation of the speech of the main European players within their most 'political' setting, the Club. As usual, he provides a comment on how individuals speak, at least in the cases where a person's speech is meant to signify personal and social attitudes.

This is the way Orwell describes Westfield, the District Superintendent of Police: 'His way of speaking was clipped and soldierly, missing out every word that well could be missed out. Nearly everything he said was intended for a joke, but the tone of his voice was hollow and melancholy.' (*Burmese Days*, pp. 18–19) Westfield's speech, like his 'prickly moustache', conforms to a military stereotype, brusque and insistent in its syntax; many of his sentences lack subjects, while others lack verbs; there are also characteristic exclamations like 'what?' and 'eh?'; mild swear words ('dammit') and slang ('pickled'):

'Hullo, Flory me lad. Bloody awful morning, what?.... Yes, dammit. Couple of months of this coming. Last year we didn't have a spot of rain till June. Look at that bloody sky, not a cloud in it. Like one of those damned great blue enamel saucepans. God! What'd you give to be in Piccadilly now, eh?.... Yes, Dear old *Punch*, *Pink'un* and *Vie Parisienne*. Makes you homesick to read 'em, what? Let's come in and have a drink before all the ice goes. Old Lackersteen's been fairly bathing in it. Half pickled already.' (ibid, p. 19)

Westfield plays no real part in the plot but is an important symbol of colonialist ideology, specifically representing the military mentality, the desire to keep the 'natives' down by force. Orwell treats Westfield's speech carefully and consistently, sustaining the clipped style when he makes small appearances much later in the book (e.g. the prelude to the Club membership ballot, pp. 216–19). The deliberateness of this speech representation as a coding of the military mind is confirmed by the fact that the clipped, impatient style is used also for the callous military police lieutenant Verrall, and for his unnamed successor (pp. 175, 251–2). This is then a sociolect, not an idiolect, carrying a definite social meaning.

Ellis has much more to say than Westfield, and plays a bigger role in the plot – his intemperate assault on a Burmese boy precipitates an uprising and an attack on the Club. 'He had a spiteful Cockney voice . . . He had a queer wounding way of speaking, hardly ever opening his mouth without insulting somebody. He deliberately exaggerated his Cockney accent, because of the sardonic tone it gave to his words' (*Burmese Days*, pp. 20, 21). No attempt is made in the spelling to represent Ellis's Cockney accent, so the reader will reconstruct it in his or her head, or not; Ellis's speech also carries none of the lexical or syntactic markers of Cockney that we found in *Down and Out*. The main characteristics of Ellis's idiolect – which figures prominently in the dialogues of the Club members – are aggression, insult and obscenity:

> 'My God, I should have thought in a case like this, when it's a question of keeping those black, stinking swine out of the only place where we can enjoy ourselves, you'd have the decency to back me up. Even if that pot-bellied, greasy little sod of a nigger doctor *is* your best pal. *I* don't care if you choose to pal up with the scum of the bazaar. If it pleases you to go to Veraswami's house and drink whisky with all his nigger pals, that's your lookout. Do what you like outside the Club. But, by God, it's a different matter when you talk of bringing niggers in here. I suppose you'd like little Veraswami for a Club member, eh? Chipping into our conversation and pawing everyone with his sweaty hands and breathing his filthy garlic breath in our faces. By God, he'd go out with my boot behind him if ever I saw his black snout inside that door. Greasy, pot-bellied little – !' etc. (*Burmese Days*, pp. 22–3)

There is a great deal of this unpleasantness from Ellis's mouth throughout the novel. Ellis is the spokesman for the racism and violence of the Club members – the others, like Macgregor, can claim to be more liberal, but Ellis's language and thoughts taint the whole of the close-knit Club.

Macgregor, the senior European, is presented as an ineffectual buffoon, and his language reflects this characterisation.

> His conversation was evidently modelled on that of some facetious schoolmaster whom he had known in early life. Any long word, any quotation, any proverbial expression figured in his mind as a joke, and was introduced with a bumbling noise like 'er' or 'ah', to make it clear that there was a joke coming. (ibid, p. 27)

His language is studiously good-natured but pedantic, pretentious and bathetic in its attempts at jokes and anecdotes. Here is how he copes with objections to the prospect of a 'native member':

> 'I gather,' he said, 'that our friend Ellis does not welcome the society of – ah – his Aryan brother?'
>
> 'No, I do not,' said Ellis tartly. 'Nor my Mongolian brother. I don't like niggers, to put it in one word.'
>
> Mr Macgregor stiffened at the word 'nigger', which is discountenanced in India. He had no prejudice against Orientals; indeed, he was deeply fond of them. Provided they were given no freedom he thought them the most charming people alive. It always pained him to see them wantonly insulted.
>
> 'Is it quite playing the game,' he said stiffly, 'to call these people niggers – a term they very naturally resent – when they are obviously nothing of the kind? The Burmese are Mongolians, the Indians are Aryans or Dravidians, and all of them are quite distinct–'
>
> 'Oh, rot that!' said Ellis, who was not at all awed by Mr Macgregor's official status. 'Call them niggers or Aryans or what you like. What I'm saying is that we don't want to see any black hides in this Club. If you put it to the vote you'll find that we're against it to a man – unless Flory wants his *dear* pal Veraswami', he added.
>
> 'Hear, hear!' repeated Mr Lackersteen. 'Count on me to blackball the lot of 'em.'

Mr Macgregor pursed his lips whimsically. He was in an awkward position, for the idea of electing a native member was not his own, but had been passed on to him by the Commissioner. However, he disliked making excuses, so he said in a more conciliatory tone:

'Shall we postpone discussing it until the next general meeting? In the meantime we can give it our mature consideration. And now,' he added, moving towards the table, 'who will join me in a little – ah – liquid refreshment?' (ibid, pp. 29–30)

Other members of the Club have speech idiosyncracies, including Mrs Lackersteen: 'She had a sighing, discontented voice.' (ibid, p. 27) 'Her accent was growing more aristocratic with every word she uttered.' (ibid, p. 182–3) She is languid, complaining, scheming; she puts on airs. Clearly she is meant to represent a certain type of selfish, frustrated, socially ambitious colonial wife. Hers is a small if objectionable voice; it is the whole motley picture of the group including her which signifies the range of unpleasant attitudes and behaviours of the English in Burma. So Orwell gathers them as a group in the Club for several scenes, giving rein to their various argumentative, complaining, insulting voices, allowing them to speak their own condemnation.

8 Point of View in Orwell's Fiction

In this chapter we will consider some techniques of style which contribute to the building of 'point of view' in Orwell's fiction. We will look at strategies for focusing point of view in *Keep the Aspidistra Flying* (1936) and *Coming Up for Air* (1939) with some comparison with the earlier novels and the non-fictional writings. In the two novels to be discussed there is a foretaste of techniques used in the last novel, *Nineteen Eighty-Four* (1949).

The familiar phrase 'point of view' is in fact a little ambiguous, is used with a variety of meanings in literary criticism and will later be replaced by some more exact modern terms.[1] A novelist creates a fictional world; it should be clear from the approach of the present study that this is not a world consisting of concrete facts objectively presented, but a world presented from a particular angle, refracted through the views and values, not to mention the imagined visual angle of viewing and the other sensory impressions, of a character or narrator. It is a person's view of the fictionally created world, filtered through and coloured by language; that person is the author, or a narrator s/he constructs as a voice to tell the story, or a character in the story through whose eyes – and mind – we are privileged to see the world of the fiction. The illusion of seeing through a character's mind may be formed through the choice of words that are given to the character – or words written *about* the character: the character does not even have to speak for us to see through his or her eyes.

Orwell's writing, fictional and other, is in a very obvious sense about the views, the vision, of an individual subject. In the essays and in the non-fictional books such as *Down and Out*, *Wigan Pier* and *Homage to Catalonia*, the 'I' is none other than Orwell himself, speaking through the personal style or idiolect which I analysed in Chapter 4. Each of these three books, as we have seen, easily breaks out from narrative to essay mode, from story-telling to the recording of fact and the voicing of opinion. From them, and from the essays themselves and the journalism, we can read off a set of opinions and preferences which are Orwell's own: opinions on colonialism, socialism, and totalitarianism, on fads and cranks, on language and literature, on the past and the projected future, on poverty, on class, on machines, on towns, suburbs and the country, and so on; Orwell's recurrent sensations and emotions are communicated too: his nostalgia for an earlier England, his aversion to dirt, confinement, and cold. Orwell's philosophy in politics and culture, his aesthetic and his linguistic views, have often been discussed and it is no business of this book to further examine them here. My point is simply that, particularly in the early writings, they receive relatively direct expression in the 'I' of the Orwellian persona.

Orwell however, through the 1930s and 1940s, developed the techniques of a novelist as well as sustaining his skills as an essayist. In a fictional narration, point of view is a much more complex structure, and involves more subtle and various linguistic strategies, than in the more monological essay or documentary modes. By 'monologism', a term taken from Bakhtin (the source of 'heteroglossia', discussed and illustrated earlier, Chapters 6 and 7), I refer to the domination of a piece of writing by a single voice, a single viewpoint and set of ideas or a whole recognisable ideology. When Orwell writes about a hanging, or boys' weekly magazines, or his experiences in the Spanish Civil War, it is explicitly to speak his ideas on the topic; other people's ideas, if referred to, are treated as objects, quoted and scrutinised not as living ideas in their own right but as specimens or evidence in relation to Orwell's own opinions. Monologism is certainly an option in narrative: it is the keynote of the great nineteenth-century novelists such as George Eliot and Dickens, who put their views on the table in a strong authoritarian tone, and present an external, uninvolved, perspective on their characters in terms of those views. In Orwell, we find monologism in *Down and Out*, in which, as we have seen, there is a single narrator's voice running all through, framing everything; within that frame, the 'voices of the other', the Paris eccentrics and the Cockneys, are displayed specimen-like, with no curiosity for or empathy with the values expressed in the speech styles. However, this kind of monologic treatment, a rough-and-ready technique in Orwell's first published narrative, would be quite inappropriate for the novels he went on to write.

All Orwell's full-length novels – and in this respect as in others, the fable *Animal Farm* is an exception – are examples of a particular kind of *psychological* novel. At the centre of each of them is the inner life of just one character, in comparison with whom the other characters in the book are given minor treatment. In *A Clergyman's Daughter* the central figure is Dorothy Hare; in *Burmese Days*, John Flory; in *Keep the Aspidistra Flying*, Gordon Comstock; in *Coming Up for Air* it is George Bowling; and in *Nineteen Eighty-Four*, Winston Smith. Each novel focuses intensely and exhaustively on the ideas and feelings of its 'hero', and in particular, on the character's reactions to and interactions with the political, social and material world conveyed by the novel. In this concentration on the feelings and the consciousness of a central character, Orwell was following one of the major trends of twentieth-century fiction. No doubt the theories of the mind put forward by Freud and Jung gave a major impetus to psychological fiction; it became the major mode for the most influential novelists in the early part of the twentieth century, including Virginia Woolf, James Joyce, and D. H. Lawrence, and in France, Marcel Proust. The mind was put in the centre as an object of fundamental interest.

It is easy to understand that the psychologically rich and dominant consciousnesses of the heroes of these novelists – Bloom in *Ulysses*, Paul Morel in *Sons and Lovers*, Swann in Proust, Mrs Ramsey in *To the Lighthouse* – present a powerful challenge to the authorial monologism of the classic nineteenth-century novel. In the earlier tradition, a novelist such as George Eliot might focus on a single protagonist and claim to know everything there was to know about her, but Eliot would, in her own voice, *tell* us about the thoughts and feelings of a Maggie Tulliver or Dorothea Brooke. The character would be seen from an *external perspective*, the disengaged outside view of the omniscient author. The shift in the twentieth century was to an *internal perspective*, the creation of an impression that we are *shown* the character's thoughts, in their personal form; not paraphrased in the words of the author's commentary.[2] The character was regarded as a free subject with a point of view independent of that of the author, rather than an object to be scrutinised and judged.[3]

This shift from the omniscient author to the free, sentient hero as central subject of the fiction could only be managed by a revolution in the ways language was used to convey the character's consciousness (and to curb the author's!). A prime endeavour of

the early twentieth-century novelists was the development of techniques of language for the representation of thoughts and feelings:
stream of consciousness and interior monologue, association of ideas,
the objective correlative, the vocabulary of emotion and reflection,
various kinds of syntactic arrangement conventionally representing
the movements of the mind in thought, and a special way of interweaving the narrator's and the character's thoughts known aptly as
the 'dual voice' or, more technically, 'Free Indirect Discourse'. Orwell
was nothing like as radical as, say, Joyce and Woolf in his use of
such techniques, but he did employ them to some extent, and he
was particularly influenced by James Joyce's treatments of characters' consciousness.[4] Illustrative extracts from *Keep the Aspidistra
Flying* and *Coming Up for Air* will be analysed shortly, with further explanation of the techniques concerned.

Before examining in more detail how Orwell handles the treatment of his heroes' thoughts and feelings, we may clarify the discussion by distinguishing two aspects of 'internal perspective', two
dimensions of 'point of view'. Both have the potential for resisting
the author's or narrator's authority by 'answering back', by challenging the monologic.

The first we will call *focalisation*, the term and the idea coming
from the French theorist Gérard Genette. It has already been mentioned (Chapter 7, p. 121 above, and note 5) in relation to *Burmese
Days*. Focalisation concerns the question: through whose eyes is
the story witnessed and told, the events and scenes described? Classically, in the 'omniscient' tradition, focalisation is managed through
the eyes of the author, or those of the narrator who stands in for
him. But the concept of focalisation allows for the possibility, increasingly common in modern fiction, of the story being told from
some other point of view – that of the central character (Stephen
Dedalus in Joyce's *Portrait of the Artist as a Young Man* [1916]),
several characters (William Faulkner, *The Sound and the Fury* [1931],
As I lay Dying [1930]), or variably, shifting to and fro between
narrator and character(s), as is generally the case with Lawrence.
Variable focalisation is typical of Orwell: although, as we have
seen, Flory is the main experiencer and viewpoint in *Burmese Days*,
the novel is told in the third person and there are sections of nar-
rator-focalisation, and also short sections of focalisation through
other characters' eyes – briefly, Elizabeth Lackersteen in the account of her voyage to Burma (pp. 91–2), and Ellis for his hysterical

reaction to the killing of Maxwell just before he assaults the Burmese boy (pp. 228–9). Broadly speaking, Orwell's fiction, as it develops, moves toward an increasing use of focalisation by central character, although the framework of external narration, and an Orwellian view of the world, persist.

The second aspect of point of view to be distinguished here is *mind-style*.[5] Focalisation relates to the question of *whose* eyes and mind witness and report the world of the fiction; mind-style concerns the individuality, the substantive (if imaginary) structure and content, of the mind that does the focalising. Mind-style is the major way in which the memorable characters of modern fiction are distinguished: Bloom, Stephen Dedalus, Paul Morel, Clarissa Harlowe, Humbert Humbert, Holden Caulfield, Winston Smith. Mind-style is a product of the way their perceptions and thoughts, as well as their speech, are presented through language; and the special stylistic techniques associated with internal perspective mentioned above (stream of consciousness, etc.) provide the foundation and the materials for the building of distinctive mind-styles.

THE MIND-STYLE OF GORDON COMSTOCK

Both *A Clergyman's Daughter* and *Burmese Days* concentrate on the experiences, thoughts and feelings of single central characters. The former has more 'telling' or external presentation than 'showing'; Dorothy is observed and discussed, we get little sense of her inner feelings. *Burmese Days*, the next novel to be written, moves a long way in the direction of focalisation by character: Flory's reactions and opinions dominate the book, as we have seen, but the reader is given little opportunity for empathy, for intimate knowledge of how Flory's mind works. But *Keep the Aspidistra Flying* takes a long stride toward a richer psychological presentation, for in this novel, as in *Coming Up for Air* of three years later, Orwell makes use of modern linguistic techniques to suggest unique mind-styles for his heroes. In a nutshell, he had read and was influenced by *Ulysses*.

In drawing on *Ulysses* as a source for these two novels, he learned not only methods for the presentation of thought-processes, but also a comic vitality which is little evident elsewhere in this severe writer. (It must be observed that most readers' impression of Orwell is drawn from the bleak last work, *Nineteen Eighty-Four*, and from the fundamentally serious *Animal Farm, Wigan Pier* and *Homage to Catalonia*. The two novels I am about to discuss are much less familiar.) The hero of *Keep the Aspidistra Flying*, Gordon Comstock, would be more appropriately called an *anti*-hero, a descendent of the introspective, alienated hero of Dostoevsky's *Notes from Under-ground* (1864), and a forerunner of the hilariously incompetent anti-heroes of British fiction of the 1960s, prototypically the bungling Jim Dixon of Kingsley Amis's *Lucky Jim* (1954). Gordon comes from a monumentally unsuccessful family which had produced few children, no money, and no memorable activity. Pressed by his family to 'do well', he defiantly rejects the 'money god', throws up his work as an advertising copy-writer (for which he has a gift), and takes a job at subsistence level, with no prospects, in a bookshop. In his own eyes he lives as a poet: he has published one instantly remaindered volume, *'Mice'*, and is ineffectually working on a long poem on the ills of urban life. He professes contempt for money, commercialism, and success, but his mind is driven by an obses-sion with his own lack of money; he claims to abhor pretentious-ness and sham, but his own behaviour displays an ill-founded cultural snobbishness. Such contradictory attitudes are a poor foundation for a relaxed or harmonious life. Part of the comedy is the specta-cle of Gordon himself, seedy, uncomfortable, frustrated, rent by anxieties caused by his 'philosophy'; part of it the outrageous scrapes he gets himself into: a romantic day with his girl-friend, with the promise of sex at last, ruined by his continuous sense of being penniless; an evening out with his friends, paid for by a windfall, which turns into a drunken nightmare. The aspidistra symbolises the life he has rejected: a 'good' job, wife, family and home, fur-niture on credit. Comically, he topples into just that life at the end of the story. The comedy is, of course, largely at Gordon's ex-pense: physically, he is a figure of fun with his weedy body and tatty clothes, but his penniless poet's 'philosophy' is pathetically inadequate and even contradictory; ultimately he is driven by an arrogant selfishness which is rewarded by social snubs and social disaster – the climax of his career as a poet is a humiliating drunken evening full of outrage and embarassment caused by him, leading to arrest, a fine and loss of his job.

Before looking at focalisation it is worth briefly recording that the novel continues to make use of the main stylistic resources which

Orwell had established in his early books. Precise 'objective' description is found, particularly in the description of interiors including the bookshop, the rooms in which Gordon lives, pubs, the police cell, and, for illustration here, his sister Julia's room:

> Julia would have died of starvation sooner than put up with such squalor as Gordon lived in. Indeed every one of her scraps of furniture, collected over intervals of years, represented a period of semi-starvation. There was a divan bed that could very nearly be mistaken for a sofa, and a little round fumed-oak table, and two 'antique' hardwood chairs, and an ornamental footstool and a chintz-covered armchair – Drage's: thirteen monthly payments – in front of the tiny gas-fire; and there were various brackets with framed photos of father and mother and Gordon and Aunt Angela, and a birchwood calendar – somebody's Christmas present – with 'It's a long lane that has no turning' done on it in pokerwork.
> (*Aspidistra*, p. 132)

(Note that this is focalisation by a detached observer rather than Gordon's or Julia's point of view.) There is also naturalism or sordid realism in pub, brothel and street scenes, verging on surrealism in the sequence of Gordon's intoxication, and very much contributing to our idea of his own squalid perceptions. And there is picturesque landscape description or pastoral, appropriately placed in the narrative of Gordon and Rosemary's romantic day out in the country (ch. 7). Finally, there is heteroglossia, a technique which figures in most of the books from *Down and Out* to *Nineteen Eighty-Four*: the novel contains many miniature appearances by incidental characters, mainly low-life, whose speech characteristics (and their dress and gestures) are highlighted. These contribute to the humour, both in themselves as grotesques in the Dickens tradition, and as objects of Gordon's judgement, despised by him and parodied in their speech – his attitude to them helps to emphasise his pettiness and sham 'superiority'. The importance of heteroglossia in *Aspidistra* is established in the first chapter, with caricatures of the speech styles of a succession of social types (represented by customers to the bookshop) seen from Gordon's distastefully snobbish point of view: an ignorant consumer of romantic fiction (strong Cockney), a pretentious middle-class woman reader (vacuous reviewer's jargon), a cultured homosexual ('R-less Nancy voice'), tramps ('base' Cockney), 'two upper-middle-class ladies' ('fruity-voice' and 'curry-voice'), and others. Using techniques discussed in Chapter 6, Orwell econ-omically notates and highlights speech styles, establishing a range of class and cultural negatives in Gordon's view of the world.

The novel is narrated in the third person, and contains many pass-ages in which Orwell's 'personal voice', as well as the Orwellian styles of realism just mentioned, is present. The narrative has a frame-work of third-person views which are external to Gordon's con-sciousness. Within that framework, often interwoven with it in quite complicated ways, there are segments which are clearly indicating Gordon's viewpoint. *Aspidistra* makes the strategy obvious at the start: it opens with two chapters in which Gordon's view of the world dominates: the places he inhabits – the bookshop, his room, the streets – are focalised through his consciousness, and from the outset Orwell builds up a distinctive style for representing Gordon's vision. The opening is not stream of consciousness (there are later passages which are closer to the *Ulysses* model) but it is clear that Orwell's narrator is showing us the character and the character's perceptions, rather than himself seeing and evaluating the world.

Orwell's basic technique, learned from the representation of Bloom's thought in *Ulysses*, is *free indirect thought*. Free indirect thought is a variant of free indirect discourse (the other is free indirect speech); it has the following characteristics:[6]

- Third-person pronouns, 'she' and 'he', are used, as opposed to the 'I' of direct speech and of free direct discourse;
- Verbs are past tense, and spatial and directional terms are distant ('there', not 'here') as in ordinary narration of action; thus the character is imagined as located in the past, and elsewhere, not in the 'I/now/here' of the ongoing experience;
- However, some deictics or orienting words, principally adverbs of present time and place, may be used which relate to the charac-ter's immediate experience: 'here', 'now', 'today', 'tomorrow'. Strictly speaking, combinations of past tense verbs and present adverbs ('He was miserable now') are ungrammatical, but in nar-rative discourse they are conventionally read as definitive sig-nals of the interweaving of the narrator's voice and the character's experience: this interweaving is 'the dual voice'.
- In vocabulary, a mixture of types of word is found, cueing two registers within the same passage. Some words will be either neutral,

or characteristic of the narrator; some will be suggestive of the character's idiolect or sociolect (stereotypical styles are available if, for example, the character is a child, a poet, a pedant, or someone with distinctive technical knowledge).

- Colloquial words and syntax are used, presupposing that the language of thought is more like speech than formal written language.
- Subjective forms and exclamations are found.

The novel opens with three short paragraphs starting with external narration but working gradually into free indirect thought; here is the very first:

> The clock struck half past two. In the little office at the back of Mr McKechnie's bookshop, Gordon – Gordon Comstock, last member of the Comstock family, aged twenty-nine and rather moth-eaten already – lounged across the table, pushing a four-penny packet of Player's Weights open and shut with his thumb. (*Aspidistra*, p. 7)

The second begins with the chime of a clock, rendered by the onomatopoeic 'ding-dong' rather than a narrative report such as 'chimed', 'struck', 'sounded': it is Gordon of course who hears it, and we start to enter his mind:

> The ding-dong of another, remoter clock – from the Prince of Wales, the other side of the street – rippled the stagnant air. Gordon made an effort, sat upright, and stowed his packet of cigarettes away in his inside pocket. He was perishing for a smoke. However, there were only four cigarettes left. Today was Wednesday and he had no money coming to him till Friday. It would be too bloody to be without tobacco tonight as well as all tomorrow.

Here we are taken slightly outside the narrator and inside the character by the colloquialisms – 'made an effort', 'stowed', 'perishing', 'bloody' which in fact get *more* colloquial as the series progresses; these are of course cues for Orwell's 'demotic style', but as this novel progresses we are led to read them as signals of Gordon's rough, negative mind-style. The passage into free indirect thought, with its character-internal segments, is clinched by the present tense deictics in the last two sentences, starting with 'today', which align the reader with the time-sphere which is Gordon's present.

By this gradual process, Orwell establishes Gordon as the focaliser, but, because the third-person frame continues, he is able to keep control of the narration, retaining the potential for comment and irony. The next few paragraphs contain an account of the inside of the shop, the street and the weather outside. The passage might be read as a narrator's scene-setting description of the kind that is commonly found at the beginning of a novel; however, the establishment of Gordon as focaliser, and frequent reminders of his presence by verbs and adjectives of perception, colloquialisms, and snatches of free indirect thought prevent this misreading. The passage has somehow to be read as the joint production of Orwell and of Gordon. Some sentences are formal and literary, and could be the narrator's; but Gordon is a poet, at least a versifier with a literary education, so they could be his; certainly the judgements are such as he would make. A simile such as the following, of a type found prolifically in Orwell (pp. 126–7 above) could as easily be formulated by his fictional would-be poet:

> On the top shelves near the ceiling the quarto volumes of extinct encyclopedias slumbered on their sides in piles like the tiered coffins in common graves. (*Aspidistra*, p. 8)

After the survey of the inside of the shop and a disapproving look at his reflection in the shop door:

> He lengthened the focus of his eyes again. He hated mirrors nowadays. Outside, all was bleak and wintry. A tram, like a raucous swan of steel, glided groaning over the cobbles, and in its wake the wind swept a debris of trampled leaves. The twigs of the elm-tree were swirling, straining eastward. The poster that advertised Q. T. Sauce was torn at the edge; a ribbon of paper fluttered fitfully like a tiny pennant. In the side street too, to the right, the naked poplars that lined the pavement bowed sharply as the wind caught them. A nasty raw wind. There was a threatening note in it as it swept over; the first growl of winter's anger. Two lines of a poem struggled for birth in Gordon's mind:
> Sharply the something wind – for instance, threatening wind? No, better, menacing wind. The menacing wind blows over – no, sweeps over, say.

The something poplars – yielding poplars? No, better, bending poplars. Assonance between bending and menacing? No matter. The bending polars, newly bare. Good.

> Sharply the menacing wind sweeps over
> The bending poplars, newly bare.

Good. 'Bare' is a sod to rhyme; however, there's always 'air', which every poet since Chaucer has been struggling to find rhymes for. But the impulse died away in Gordon's mind. He turned the money over in his pocket. Twopence halfpenny and a Joey – twopence halfpenny. His mind was sticky with boredom. He couldn't cope with rhymes and adjectives. You can't, with only twopence halfpenny in your pocket. (*Aspidistra*, p. 10)

We are reminded that it is Gordon doing the looking – i.e. focalising – by the opening sentence, but we are not quite *into* his mind: he would not think 'I am lengthening the focus of my eyes again'. However, we rapidly pass into free indirect thought with the conjunction of past tense and present adverb in 'He hated mirrors nowadays' which could easily be the rendering of a thought in third person. The next four sentences, from the metaphorical swan to the poplars bowing, could be Orwell's way of putting things, or Gordon's; more likely, Gordon's, since they are poetic in tone and imagery, and at this time he has, under the inspiration of this wintry scene, some lines of his poem coming into his head. At this point ('Sharply the something wind . . .') the style moves out of the narrative frame, from free indirect discourse to free direct discourse, direct representation of Gordon's thoughts. The style now closely resembles the stream-of-consciousness technique which Joyce uses for Leopold Bloom in *Ulysses*: fragmentary sentences, either short, or lacking some of their grammatical parts, or both ('No, better, menacing wind.'; 'Good.'); colloquialism tending to the vulgar ('sod'); a sense of dialogue within the mind of the character; association of ideas, with always, in Gordon's case, his mind drifting back towards money. Notice that the narrator is never completely absent: 'But the impulse . . .' takes us back to free indirect style, a reminder of the frame that is also typical of Joyce.[7] Here, for comparison, is a short passage from *Ulysses*:

He went out through the backdoor into the garden: stood to listen towards the next garden. No sound. Perhaps hanging clothes out to dry. The maid was in the garden. Fine morning.

He bent down to regard a lean file of spearmint growing by the wall. Make a summerhouse here. Scarlet runners. Virginia creepers. Want to manure the whole place over, scabby soil. A coat of liver of sulphur. All soil like that without dung. Household slops. Loam, what is this that is?.... (*Joyce: Ulysses*, pp. 60–1)

The pattern of free indirect thought moving into stream of consciousness is repeated, though sparingly, elsewhere in *Aspidistra*, always when Gordon is on his own, self-consciously ruminating, with the Bloomian stream of consciousness reserved for moments of emotional intensity – self-disgust, anger with the world, poetic composition. Here is just one example:

Sharply the menacing wind sweeps over. A stream of cars hummed easily up the hill. Gordon eyed them without envy. Who wants a car, anyway? The pink doll-faces of upper-class women gazed at him through the car window. Bloody nit-witted lapdogs. Pampered bitches dozing on their chains. Better the lone wolf than the cringing dog. He thought of the Tube stations at early morning. The black hordes of clerks scurrying underground like ants into a hole; swarms of little ant-like men, each with dispatch-case in right hand, newspaper in left hand, and the fear of the sack like a maggot in his heart. How it eats at them, that secret fear! Especially on winter days, when they hear the menace of the wind. Winter, the sack, the workhouse, the Embankment benches! Ah!

[Mentally quotes parts of his poem, with sarcastic reactions in stream of consciousness.]

Neatly, taking a pleasure in his neatness, with the sensation of dropping piece after piece of a jigsaw puzzle into place, he fashioned another stanza:

> They think of rent, rates, season tickets,
> Insurance, coal, the skivvy's wages,

> Boots, school bills, and the next instalment
> Upon the two twin beds from Drage's.

> Not bad, not bad at all. Finish it presently. Four or five more
> stanzas. Ravelston would print it. (*Aspidistra*, pp. 70–1)

Aspidistra uses 'Modernist' techniques of language to depict, as if
directly, the nature of a character's thoughts; to show Gordon as
egocentric, hyperconscious, as the bearer of obsessive thoughts of
money and women, as a rude and dismissive snob. (His speech, as
well as his thoughts, betrays these traits and preoccupations.) In
this early novel it is effective, but very evidently an experiment
following the example of Joyce; the mature use of free indirect
discourse is to be found in *Nineteen Eighty-Four*.

SELF-NARRATION: *COMING UP FOR AIR*

It seems that Orwell toyed with first-person narration very early in
his writing career, in the 'John Flory' text from the end of the
1920s which survives as a fragment of manuscript (see p. 120 above).
But *Coming Up for Air* (1939) is the only completed fictional work
to make thorough use of the technique; it is a brilliant comic achievement, full of wit and vitality yet still expressing serious Orwellian
preoccupations, principally the critique of commercialism and of
'progress'; nostalgia, distaste for the present and a fear of the future. The hero, George Bowling, is a fat, middle-aged insurance
salesman who lives the life that Gordon Comstock dreaded but fell
into: a meaningless business life with mediocre pay, a nagging wife
and two demanding children in a suburban housing estate. He hates
the present, fears the impending war, and longs for relief – not
escape, for he is realistic about the inevitability of the life he leads.
It is relief from the oppressions of the present that is expressed in
the metaphor 'coming up for air':

> Coming up for air! Like the big sea-turtles when they come pad-
> dling up to the surface, stick their noses out and fill their lungs
> with a great gulp before they sink down again among the sea-
> weed and the octopuses. We're all stifling at the bottom of a dustbin,
> but I'd found my way to the top. Back to Lower Binfield! (*Coming
> Up*, p. 168; cf. pp. 33–4)

Lower Binfield is the small town of his boyhood, a place and a period beautifully evoked in a long autobiographical and descriptive sequence (*Coming Up*, pp. 35–110). George Bowling seeks to draw his great gulp of air by revisiting Lower Binfield; takes a trip there on the strength of a windfall from a bet, without his wife's knowledge. Predictably, the place has been spoilt by building, commerce and outsiders; he returns home disillusioned to discover (predictably) that his wife has found out his deception, and so he is back 'at the bottom of [the] dustbin'.

Aspects of the descriptive style of *Coming Up for Air* have already been discussed and illustrated (Chapter 5, pp. 65–8): the precision of reference, and the power of sensory evocation in the reminiscing passages. These qualities, and in general the affectionate and detailed depiction of the countryside, are real strengths of the novel. The descriptions are far less affected or 'purple' than those in *Burmese Days*, and any derogatory sense of 'picturesque' would not apply to them. What is even more remarkable is how well they are incorporated within a totally different style of narration, the vulgar, bantering and self-centred style in which George Bowling tells his story. This first-person narrative discourse is unique in Orwell, but is as individual and vital as the voices of such famous I-narrators as Huckleberry Finn, Nick Carraway and Holden Caulfield.[8] It is a very substantial technical achievement.

From the very opening (and the opening attack and tone are very important in this sort of dramatic fiction), Orwell creates an energetic and personal style for narration which is sustained throughout the whole book – but, as I have said, the story-telling style frames some very different manners of descriptive language which nevertheless seem entirely natural to George Bowling's mind-style. George is a complex character (as he tells us!), and we can start to understand how this stylistic diversity can exist within the mind-style of one psychologically plausible character if we draw an elementary distinction between two senses of my term 'self-narration' in this section heading. He is both the *speaker* of the narrative and the *subject* of the narrative. Some aspects of the language build an image of a certain kind of act of narration, a certain kind of relationship with an implied audience (the *speaker* dimension); others depict the self he is discussing (the *subject* dimension) as opposed to the one he is projecting by his speech.

If we look first at the speaker dimension, we are struck by the fact that the novel begins abruptly and tantalisingly:

> The idea really came to me the day I got my new false teeth. (*Coming Up*, p. 9)

What idea? George knows, the reader does not know, but the implication of the definite article in '*the* idea' is that this idea has already been identified for someone else: an audience who are already listening (or imagined by George to be listening) to this oral story. (The idea is presumably to spend his £17 racing win on a return to Lower Binfield; on p. 143 he is 'still in doubt as to what I'd spend my seventeen quid on' and the specific intention does not surface until p. 166.) One of the principal strategies of this speaker is to convey the illusion that he is working with an audience in front of him, sharing his ideas, to whom he is telling his story (the technique was perfected by the poet Robert Browning in his 'dramatic monologues'): this dramatises and energises the act of narration by allowing us to imagine it happening in a real situation of face-to-face communication. This impression of interaction with an audience is a version of *dialogism*. This concept was introduced in Chapter 4 as one aspect of Orwell's personal style, and illustrated from his essay 'The Art of Donald McGill' (p. 45).

Dialogism is one of three features of language that contribute to the narrating style of this novel; the other two are *oral mode* and the *demotic*. Let us see how these features develop by examining some more text from the beginning of the novel, supplemented by briefer quotations from elsewhere in the book: a more extended extract from the opening will give a flavour of the style:

> The idea really came to me the day I got my new false teeth.
>
> I remember the morning well. At about a quarter to eight I'd nipped out of bed and got into the bathroom just in time to shut the kids out. It was a beastly January morning, with a dirty yellowish-grey sky. Down below, out of the little square of bathroom window, I could see the ten yards by five of grass, with a privet hedge round it and a bare patch in the middle, that we call the back garden. There's the same back garden, same privets, and same grass, behind every house in Ellesmere Road. Only difference – where there are no kids there's no bare patch in the middle.
>
> I was trying to shave with a bluntish razor-blade while the water ran into the bath. My face looked back at me out of the

mirror, and underneath, in a tumbler of water on the little shelf over the washbasin, the teeth that belonged in the face. It was a temporary set that Warner, my dentist, had given me to wear while the new ones were being made. I haven't such a bad face, really. It's one of those bricky-red faces that go with butter-coloured hair and pale-blue eyes. I've never gone grey or bald, thank God, and when I've got my teeth in I probably don't look my age, which is forty-five.

Making a mental note to buy razor-blades, I got into the bath and started soaping. I soaped my arms (I've got those kind of pudgy arms that are freckled up to the elbow) and then took the back-brush and soaped my shoulder-blades, which in the ordinary way I can't reach. It's a nuisance, but there are several parts of my body that I can't reach nowadays. The truth is that I'm inclined to be a little bit on the fat side. I don't mean that I'm like something in a side-show at a fair. My weight isn't much over fourteen stone, and last time I measured round my waist it was either forty-eight or forty-nine, I forget which. And I'm not what they call 'disgustingly' fat, I haven't got one of those bellies that sag half-way down to the knees. It's merely that I'm a little bit broad in the beam, with a tendency to be barrel-shaped. Do you know the active, hearty kind of fat man, the athletic bouncing type that's nicknamed Fatty or Tubby and is always the life and soul of the party? I'm that type. 'Fatty' they mostly call me. Fatty Bowling. George Bowling is my real name. (*Coming Up*, pp. 7–8)

'Oral mode' is a manner of writing which simulates the habits of the speaking voice.[9] We have seen that orality, the impression of a man speaking, is an important tendency in Orwell's personal voice. In this novel it is highlighted, and maintained throughout (though containing markers of other styles in places). Oral mode is achieved by a combination of quite simple features. There are throughout contractions of auxiliary verbs: 'I'd', 'There's', 'haven't', 'it's', etc. We find also ellipsis, the omission of part of a sentence – grammatically complete sentences being an insistent school requirement for written prose:

'Only difference...', 'Fatty Bowling', 'Only petty disasters, of course' (p. 11)

'Always the same. Long rows of little semi-detached houses . . .'
(p. 13)

A related oral cue (anathema in formal prose) is the starting of a
sentence with a conjunction: 'And I'm not what they call . . .', 'And
I was fat as well as forty-five' (p. 8),

'And besides . . .' (p. 9)

'But in every one of those little stucco boxes . . .' (p. 14)

Elliptical sentences are sparing, perhaps one every two or three pages,
but sometimes they cluster when George gets worked up:

There's a kind of atmosphere about these places [milk bars] that
gets me down. Everything slick and shiny. . . . Everything spent
on the decorations and nothing on the food. No real food at all.
Just lists of stuff with American names . . . No comfort, no priv-
acy. Tall stools to sit on, a kind of narrow ledge to eat off, mirrors all around you. (*Coming Up*, p. 25)

There are also minor ungrammaticalities which pass unnoticed in
speech but would be criticised in writing: 'those kind of pudgy arms'.
There are exclamations throughout the book: 'No use!' (p. 10), 'No!'
(p. 23), 'Christ!' (p. 26), 'It was *fish*! A sausage, a thing calling
itself a frankfurter, filled with fish!' (pp. 26–7), 'King Zog! What
a name!' (p. 30), 'How I could smell it! (p. 31), 'Jesus!' (p. 176).
There are some conversational markers which are difficult to clas-
sify, for example 'really' in the first sentence,

'forty-eight or forty-nine' ('inches' implied)

'what *they* call'

'*they* mostly call me'

Finally, there are syntactic organisations which are conventionally
read as markers of oral mode: parataxis and short information units
(see Chapter 4, p. 26 above):

I've never gone grey or bald,/ thank God,/ and when I've got my teeth in/ I probably don't look my age,/ which is forty-five.

Tall stools/ to sit on,/ a kind of narrow ledge/ to eat off,/ mirrors all around you.

Turning now to the markers of *demotic* style, there is throughout the book a stream of colloquial and vulgar words and idioms; the demotic has been amply discussed above, and can simply be illustrated by a sample list from the early pages of this novel:

false teeth, nipped out, got into, shut the kids out, beastly, kids, thank God, got into, pudgy, on the fat side, bellies that sag, broad in the beam, bloody, in dock, several quid, ten bob, poky, cheese it, some poor bastard, bunked, wallop, whizzed, bloody fool, ugly little devil, wetting our bags.

There are also many homely or vulgar similes:

'Two kids in a house the size of ours is like a quart of beer in a pint mug' (p. 10)

'a voice like a circular saw' (p. 17)

'The girl flinched like a dog that sees the whip' (p. 18)

people 'like turkeys in November . . . Not a notion of what's coming to them' (p. 29)

'middle-aged woman that has a face just like a bulldog' (p. 205)

Returning now to the overall rhetoric of *dialogism* which was noticed from the very first sentence, there are innumerable striking direct addresses to an audience all the way through: .

Just imagine a fat Hamlet, for instance! (p. 22)

No! Don't mistake me (p. 23)

Let me try and describe it to you (p. 26)

I'll tell you about that later (p. 23)

I've tried to tell you something about the world before the war (p. 90)

Sometimes George anticipates his audience's response and enters into argument:

Why did you marry her? you say. But why did you marry yours? (p. 135)

Oh, yes, I know *you* knew what was coming. But *I* didn't. You can say I was a bloody fool not to expect it, and so I was (p. 176)

Very often these imaginary conversational interactions are cued by questions of the kind represented by 'Do you know the active, hearty kind of fat man...?' in our extract. There is one astonishingly direct question which, pretending to seek specific 'real' information from very 'real' listeners, stands out from the printed page:

Do you know the road I live in – Ellesmere Road, West Bletchley? (p. 13)

More usually the questions seem to be about general knowledge:

Do you notice how often they have undersized men for these bullying jobs? (p. 18)

Do you know these Anglo-Indian families? (p. 133)

Do you know that type of middle-aged woman... (p. 205)

Or in declarative form:

You know the kind of kitchen people had in those days (p. 48)

You know the kind of day... (p. 161)

You know those very cheap small houses ... (p. 177)

You know that god-awful feeling ... (p. 195)

These are appeals to the audience or reader to bring shared social knowledge to the interpretation of what the narrator is saying. Usually this is *stereotypical* knowledge: George is asking his audience to agree on a range of pre-packaged cultural prejudices, 'kinds' and 'types' of people, places and experiences. The direct enquiry addressed to 'you', though foregrounded in this narrative, is not essential, for a lot of the work can be done less noticeably by phrases with 'that' and 'those': 'those brick-red faces that ...', 'those kind of pudgy arms ...', 'those bellies that ...'. By these means, George works on his audience to build a common ground, a set of values for interpreting and judging the story he tells.[10] At the same time, we as readers, who know we are reading a printed fiction rather than sitting in the saloon bar being told a tale, have the detachment to see that *he* is being constructed by Orwell's discourse as a character with prejudices and partial knowledge. These prejudices are part of the assumed character of George Bowling the speaker-narrator. The subject, George Bowling, leans on them to cope with his everyday interactions with the world, but inside him he has an almost contradictory set of values.

In *Coming Up for Air* Orwell has created a narrative voice which is, in his own work, quite distinctive; but it belongs to a specific literary type. George is given a style of narration which the Russian Formalists (quite unknown to Orwell, I am sure) called *skaz*.[11] Skaz is a style of dramatic narration in written prose; the speaker appears to be play-acting, putting on a part. The Russian Formalist critic who identified this genre, Boris Eichenbaum, remarks that 'it is often as if an actor is concealed in back'. The character assumed by the actor affects a highly oral narrative style, as if telling a tale to his listeners; the features of speech, verbal play, techniques of language rather than theme, are strongly foregrounded. The *skaz* narrator is strongly delineated socially, adds Bakhtin, usually a low-class character – in the world of Russian literature, the actor in back simulates a folk story-teller rather than a high literary narrator. All this seems precisely to convey what is being done through George Bowling. In terms of the speaker/subject distinction, the speaker is characterised as a garrulous, vulgar, fat, middle-aged insurance salesman, fond of the pleasures of the flesh (he considers spending his £17 win on cigars, whisky and a woman), highly conscious of the impression he makes, loudly dressed and cynically and coarsely spoken. In the first three chapters of the novel, George meticulously builds up this image; but he lets us know that the speaker is not the whole subject:

> [I]nternally, mentally, I'm not altogether fat . . . I'm vulgar, I'm insensitive, and I fit in with my environment . . . But also I've got something else inside me, chiefly a hangover from the past. I'll tell you about that later. I'm fat, but I'm thin inside. Has it ever struck you that there's a thin man inside every fat man, just as they say there's a statue inside every block of stone? (p. 23)

The inner feelings and attitudes of George Bowling are aligned with those positives and critiques which were always on the agenda for Orwell from the later 1930s. Lower Binfield before the First World War is a symbol of 'the old English order of life' (p. 108), a stable and happy world with straightforward family relationships and political organisation, a comprehensible economic system of production, supply and purchase; a world with comfortable traditional houses, real food, real sweets and real beer. George Bowling was formed in that world, and retains its values as the core of his being; from it stem the powerful passages of recollection triggered by sensory association, and the idyllic descriptions of the countryside:

> [I]t was Sunday morning, and I could smell the church. How I could smell it! You know the smell churches have, a peculiar, dank, dusty, decaying, sweetish sort of smell. There's a touch of candle-grease in it, and perhaps a whiff of incense and a suspicion of mice, and on Sunday mornings it's a bit overlaid by yellow soap and serge dresses, but predominantly it's that sweet, dusty, musty smell that's like the smell of death and life mixed up together. It's powdered corpses, really. (p. 31)

> It was astonishing, and even at that age it astonished me, that there, a dozen miles from Reading and not fifty from London, you could have such solitude. You felt as much alone as if you'd been on the banks of the Amazon. The pool was ringed completely round by the enormous beech trees, which in one place

came down to the edge and were reflected in the water. On the other side there was a patch of grass where there was a hollow with beds of wild peppermint, and up at one end of the pool an old wooden boathouse was rotting among the bulrushes.

The pool was swarming with bream, small ones, about four to six inches long. Every now and again you'd see one of them turn half over and gleam reddy-brown under the water. There were pike there too . . . (p. 76)

The first passage comes from the opening of a long reminiscent section, a daydream of his childhood triggered by the association of a name he hears as he is walking along the Strand: a 'King Zog' who is in the news reminds him of 'Og the king of Bashan' heard in church when he was a boy. The *skaz* style of oral display gives way to a quieter style of sense and feeling which is sustained for many pages. The fishing passage – fishing as a boy is an experience he yearns to recapture – is typical of many parts in which the inner consciousness of the character is fixed on the details of a countryside scene which is delineated precisely, technically and colourfully. The styles of both of these extracts, emanating from the 'thin man' inside George, contrast strongly with the language of the loud-mouthed narrator, but each variety of language represents a part of him.

Other parts of the inner George which periodically erupt through the brash exterior of banter and bluff express anger and panic. Aspects of modern life cause him to rant in rage: the milk bar (pp. 25–6), the arty back-to-nature community which has felled the woods and built houses around Binfield House (pp. 211–12), the swindle through which housing estates like George's are financed and their occupiers enslaved; on these occasions George produces a style of rant close to Orwell's own in, say, *Wigan Pier*:

We're all respectable householders – that's to say Tories, yes-men, and bumsuckers. Daren't kill the goose that lays the gilded eggs! And the fact that actually we aren't householders, that we're all in the middle of paying for our houses and eaten up with the ghastly fear that something might happen before we've made the last payment, merely increases the effect. We're all bought, and what's more bought with our own money. Every one of those poor downtrodden bastards, sweating his guts out to pay twice the proper price for a brick doll's house that's called Belle Vue because there's no view and the bell doesn't ring – every one of those poor suckers would die on the field of battle to save his country from Bolshevism. (*Coming Up*, pp. 16–17)

George's panic surfaces repeatedly in fantasies of the imminent war, though as he explains, 'I'm not frightened of the war, only of the after-war'; in hysterical style, he expresses a vision of a totalitarian future which foreshadows the world of *Nineteen Eighty-Four*:

And the next war coming over the horizon. 1941, they say. Three more circles of the sun, and then we whizz straight into it. The bombs diving down on you like black cigars, and the stream-lined bullets streaming from the Bren machine guns . . . [The after-war] frightens me. The barbed wire! The slogans! The enormous faces! The cork-lined cellars where the executioner plugs you from behind! [I]t means good-bye to this thing I've been telling you about, this special feeling inside you. Call it peace, if you like. But when I say peace I don't mean absence of war, I mean peace, a feeling in your guts. And it's gone forever if the rubber trun-cheon boys get hold of us. (*Coming Up*, p. 165)

Other styles represented in George's consciousness could be il-lustrated: his caricature of the 'anti-fascist' speaker at the political meeting he attends, his report of the arty type at Upper Binfield, his rendering of working-class speakers. The hearty and vulgar *skaz* of the speaking persona contains a whole range of linguistic styles and ideologies – as if the technique of heteroglossia has been dis-placed to *within* the first-person narrator. We will meet some of these styles again, particularly the political parodies, in the third-person *Nineteen Eighty-Four*, in which Winston Smith lives to his own destruction the anxieties and the regressive escapism of George Bowling.

9 *Animal Farm*

Coming Up for Air, written in Morocco where Orwell and Eileen spent the winter of 1938–9, was published on 12 June 1939, just before the outbreak of the world war which its hero awaits; Orwell's next work of fiction, *Animal Farm*, was not written until November, 1943–February, 1944. The gap between the two books was unusual for Orwell. He had been publishing a book a year: the seven novels and documentary works which appeared between 1933 and 1939 (listed with dates on p. 61 above) and a volume of essays, *Inside the Whale*, in April 1940. There seems to have been a conscious pause for reflection and planning in the early 1940s: in April, 1940, he wrote to Geoffrey Gorer that 'at present I am very anxious to slow off and not to hurry on with my next book, as I have now published 8 in 8 years which is too much'.[1] He said he was planning 'a long novel in three parts', of which the first was to be called either *'The Lion and the Unicorn'* or *'The Quick and the Dead'*.

Orwell and Eileen moved to London in May 1940: Eileen was working in the Censorship Department at Whitehall, Orwell was to work at the BBC from August 1941 to November 1943. He wrote reviews and journalism for *Time and Tide*, *Horizon*, *Partisan Review* and *Tribune*, of which he became Literary Editor on leaving the BBC.

The larger project no doubt continued to mature during this period of journalism and broadcasting, but the details of his thoughts and plans are, as usual with Orwell, not clearly available to us. In the autumn of 1940 he wrote three political essays, 'England your England', 'Shopkeepers at War' and 'The English Revolution' which were published in 1941, under the title *The Lion and the Unicorn: Socialism and the English Genius*, in the series 'Searchlight Books' edited by Tosco Fyvel and Orwell for Secker & Warburg. This is not the first volume of the fictional trilogy which he mentioned earlier as in prospect, but it could be considered the political preface in a series of three different books, of which the second volume was to be *Animal Farm* (a fable of the Russian Revolution) and the third *Nineteen Eighty-Four* (a dystopian vision of post-revolutionary totalitarianism in an imaginary future Britain).[2] Certainly he was planning *Nineteen Eighty-Four* long before he actually wrote it in 1946 – as early as 1943, he said, and indeed an outline called 'The Last Man in Europe' exists in manuscript, probably from 1943.[3] (And as I have pointed out (p. 158 above), George Bowling's panic about the 'after-war' in *Coming Up for Air* (written 1938–9) presages themes of *Nineteen Eighty-Four* much earlier still.)

As Orwell took stock of his political ideas and his writing future after completion of *Coming Up for Air*, so we may at this point very briefly review his stylistic situation at the time. By the end of the 1930s, Orwell had established a voice of his own as a down-to-earth, serious yet witty essayist; he had also practised and mastered a range of more literary techniques appropriate to a certain kind of novel. His novels focus on the mind, feelings and development of the individual; always an individual whose relationship with the surrounding social, cultural and political world is problematic. Orwell has a variety of 'realistic' descriptive techniques for communicating the substance of the world in which the hero lives – Dorothy's Suffolk, Gordon Comstock's London, the battlefield in Spain – all requiring different techniques. He also, drawing much from Joyce, developed styles for the rendering of modes of thought and feeling, the mind-styles of these alienated individuals faced with the anxieties and guilts of colonialism, sex, modernity, technology. Orwell could be said to have developed a modernist style of novel in the spirit of Joyce and Lawrence, and a heightened language for the consciousness of his central characters. The characters also live and think in a language-rich world, realised by Orwell through the techniques of heteroglossia.

Orwell's last fiction, *Nineteen Eighty-Four*, continues with the modernist and heteroglossic strategies of his earlier work – *Aspidistra* and *Coming Up for Air* are particularly close to the last novel both thematically and linguistically. Before that, however, there comes *Animal Farm*, a beast fable of the Russian Revolution and its betrayal, written in the sparest linguistic style and more reminiscent of Swift than of Joyce. It is a radical stylistic departure for Orwell: to only a slight extent prepared for by his earlier linguistic experiments, and unique in the lucid simplicity of its prose.

Animal Farm is one of the most familiar books in world literature. It tells how the livestock and working animals at Manor Farm are given an account of a dream by Old Major, a prize Middle White Boar: 'a dream of the earth as it will be when Man has vanished' (p. 12). Major predicts an uprising of the animals against their owner, Mr Jones, and this happens three months later. Meanwhile the leading pigs, Napoleon and Snowball, and their spokesman Squealer, elaborate Major's ideas into a system of thought which they call 'Animalism', based on the principles of equality among the animals, and avoidance of the vices of humankind. After the overthrow of Jones, the animals run the farm cooperatively, but gradually the pigs take more and more tyrannical control and assume the vices of humanity; they deprive the other animals of proper sustenance, and of a say in the running of the farm; they engage in foolish grandiose projects, principally the building of a windmill;[4] they trade and consort with human beings; they kill. At the end the pigs have become men, the other animals are in their customary state of oppressed deprivation. The wheel has come full circle.

The fable exists quite clearly and coherently on two beautifully matched levels, and in this clarity and system lies the secret of its success. At the first level, it is a story about the fabulous humanlike deeds of farm animals, their triumphs and their ultimate betrayal and failure: this is the level at which the story's charm has been enjoyed by generations of young readers. Orwell's principal source was surely the section of Swift's *Gulliver's Travels* (1726) in which Gulliver travels to the land of the Houyhnhms, a race of benevolent horses who rule their own society with the humans or Yahoos in a role of servitude. But the beast fable is in fact much older, a classical genre dating at least from the Greek fables of 'Aesop' of the fifth century BC,[5] in which the sayings and deeds of animals represent human moral dilemmas. Orwell's animal 'fairy story' (as he subtitled it) encompasses the whole range of farm animals. Some are individualised, others treated *en masse*. Characterisation is slight, but focused and consistent, and draws more on our existing stereotypes of types of beast than on elaborate portayal in the book. For example, rightly or wrongly, pigs have a bad name for selfishness and gluttony, and that is their image in this text; similarly, the dogs are vicious but fawning, the cat self-centred and crafty, the donkey bad-tempered; the two carthorses Boxer and Clover are slow-witted, strong, gentle and loyal; the sheep are brainless and behave as a flock without any individual initiative. Although the farm animals think and talk, do the work of humans and to some extent use tools, nothing really outrageous or fantastic, nothing out of the nature of their species, is attributed to them. The narrator is at pains to describe the difficulties encountered by the animals in farming and building: they cannot use any tool which requires standing on two legs, and therefore have to break up the stone for the windmill by dropping it; a pig climbs a ladder with difficulty; a brush or chalk is held between the knuckles of the trotters, cows are milked in the same way, and so on. That which is natural or easy for the animals is also mentioned, e.g. weeding is much more efficient under their regime than when done by humans, because the animals are naturally equipped to browse; grains of corn and scraps of hay are collected without waste by the hens and ducks with their sharp eyes and well-adapted beaks. At the animal-story level of reading, the reader will be curious about how such practicalities are accomplished, and the text encourages and gratifies this curiosity. What is more, the text secures the reader's empathy with the animals by techniques of focalisation which stick close to their interests and expectations, as we will see.

The above should be expressed, however, not in terms of *all* the animals, but of 'animals-except-pigs'; the thoughts, speech and behaviour of the pigs are treated in an alienated, grossly human, manner (cf. Swift's distasteful portrayal of the Yahoos). In the case of the pigs, who appropriate the leadership and exploit their power against the interests of the other animals, their nature is humanly perverted as they speak in the voice of political rhetoric and duplicity, and are gradually transformed into a grotesque parody of human beings as they take to selling and buying, drinking alcohol, wearing clothes and walking on their hind legs. At the level of the text as animal story, then, the reader's engagement in the account of a gradual division between oppressors and oppressed is guided by appropriate language for the two groups, with, as we will see, a narrator's style very close to that of the group of the majority, the betrayed innocents, the horses, sheep, fowl, etc.

The story of oppression, betrayal and suffering is carried in parallel on the second level, the level of political allegory. Everyone except the child reader knows that the beast fable is also a satire on a real, historical, narrative of revolution betrayed. Orwell uses the animals to present an evaluation of the events and personalities of the Soviet Union from the 1917 Revolution to the Stalinist purges of the 1930s and the Teheran Conference of 1943, with a condemnation of the techniques of Soviet totalitarianism, particularly the falsification of history and reality by a wilful perversion of language. There is a close correspondence of the characters and incidents in *Animal Farm* with Soviet communism and its sources: thus, 'Major' represents Marx, 'Napoleon' Stalin, 'Snowball' Trotsky, the windmill represents the first Five-Year Plan of 1928, the meeting of pigs and humans at the end represents the Teheran Conference – the meeting between Stalin, Roosevelt and Churchill – and so on. These correspondences have been recovered and charted in detail by previous commentators on *Animal Farm*.[6] The satire on the Soviet Union was too direct for several publishers to whom Orwell first offered the book – after all, Russia was still at that time a wartime ally. Moreover, hostile critics of the political Left objected that in attacking Soviet Communism Orwell was abandoning his apparently firmly established socialist beliefs. These objections miss Orwell's intentions – although it must be admitted that the book itself does not make these intentions clear. In his preface to the Ukranian edition of *Animal Farm*, written in 1947, Orwell explains that he was attacking Soviet Communism not simply for itself, but because he wanted to attack the Soviet *myth* as received in Britain, where it was harmful to the Socialist movement (*CEJL*, III, pp. 455–9). He also wrote that the book 'is intended as a satire on dictatorship in general'.[7] Misinterpretation of *Animal Farm* has arisen largely because of the simplicity of its language, in particular, the extreme lightness of touch of the narrative style, its refusal to offer any strong direct evaluation of the events of the fable. As William Empson, poet and expert on ambiguity, advised Orwell, 'the danger of this kind of perfection is that it means very different things to different readers'.[8] One pertinent fact about the book is that, because of its imaginative coherence, it can impart pleasure and moral significance to readers who do not recognise the Soviet references: the story and its values exist independent of the historical allegory. But it is equally obvious that the politically naive reading will miss Orwell's essential purpose and its satirical expression. It is not just an animal story, but a fiction which, indirectly and by literary techniques, makes a political statement about dictatorship. As Orwell noted in 'Why I Write,' '*Animal Farm* was the first book in which I tried, with full consciousness of what I was doing, to fuse political purpose and artistic purpose into one whole' (*CEJL*, I, p. 29).

NARRATIVE STYLE IN *ANIMAL FARM*

All the critics agree on the simplicity of the language in *Animal Farm*, and that it is unique in the canon of Orwell's writing. If we take George Woodcock (Orwell's friend, and author of a fine critical study) as representative, we find him speaking of 'this crystalline little book', 'conciseness of form and simplicity of language', 'a bare English, uncluttered by metaphor,' a style 'direct, exact and sharply concrete,' 'a series of lively visual images held together by a membrane of almost transparent prose'.[9] Woodcock and other critics also stress how different the spare, neutral prose is from the styles achieved in Orwell's other fiction. As we saw, Orwell had developed a 'demotic' idiolect which, while vernacular in vocabulary, is hardly cool or neutral, rising often to heights of rhetoric and stridency. When we looked at descriptive aspects of Orwell's writing, we found that his prose is less often as clear 'as a window pane', more often decorative and emotive or symbolic. And as far as fictional narration is concerned, we have seen that the narrator's voice is strongly foregrounded in the other books, so much so that one compositional problem which Orwell had to solve in the 1930s was the toning-down of the Orwellian narrative persona and its replacement by a character's focalisation. *Animal Farm* represents the ultimate reduction in the status of the narrative voice, which is extremely impersonal, but in this book it is not displaced by the viewpoint of a *single* character, as with John Flory, Gordon Comstock or George Bowling; in *Animal Farm* Orwell creates a sort of *collective* focalisation, as we will see in the next section.

It is vital to relate the linguistic simplicity of *Animal Farm* to a second context. Not only is it a technical departure from Orwell's stylish and experimental earlier fiction and from his more exuberant essay writing, the style of *Animal Farm* is also an outcome of a new phase of his thinking about the politics and morality of language usage. In Chapter 3 I gave an account of Orwell's views on language, detailing in particular the position which emerged in the first half of the 1940s. He analysed the ills of political speech and writing, which in his view resulted in the self-deception and lying which were the intellectual preconditions for totalitarianism. The period of gestation and writing of *Animal Farm* coincides with the development of his new focus on the morality of public language; and a major theme of the book is the perversion of language by an oppressive dictatorship. The simplification, one might even say purification, of his own language in *Animal Farm* no doubt reflects his desire for linguistic honesty in political writing, and is the foil against which the degradation of language by the pigs is presented. His six-point programme for good usage (reproduced on p. 34 above) goes a long way to describing the practical measures which he followed in simplifying and clarifying the narrative voice in *Animal Farm*.[10]

As a basis for understanding the language of *Animal Farm*, let us first try to make sense of the usual observations that its narrative style is 'impersonal' and 'simple'. Note that to some extent this will involve saying that certain linguistic features are *not* present. Since linguistic absences, even though stylistically significant, are not easy to grasp, readers are advised to sharpen their sense of what is distinctive in *Animal Farm* by reviewing some contrasting extracts quoted and analysed earlier in this book, for example the three examples of the personal voice quoted in Chapter 4, the garrulous George Bowling in Chapter 8, and the naturalistic, surrealistic and picturesque descriptions in Chapters 5 and 7.

The opening pages of *Animal Farm*, like all good fictional openings, set the tone and therefore illustrate many of the points that need to be made:

Mr Jones, of the Manor Farm, had locked the hen-houses for the night, but was too drunk to remember to shut the pop-holes. With the ring of light from his lantern dancing from side to side, he lurched across the yard, kicking off his boots at the back door, drew himself a last glass of beer from the barrel in the scullery, and made his way up to bed, where Mrs Jones was already snoring.

As soon as the light in the bedroom went out there was a stirring and a fluttering all through the farm buildings. Word had gone round during the day that old Major, the prize Middle White boar, had had a strange dream on the previous night and wished to communicate it to the other animals. It had been agreed that they should all meet in the big barn as soon as Mr Jones was safely out of the way. Old Major (so he was always called, though the name under which he had been exhibited was Willingdon Beauty) was so highly regarded on the farm that everyone was quite ready to lose an hour's sleep in order to hear what he had to say.

At one end of the big barn, on a sort of raised platform, Major was already ensconced on his bed of straw, under a lantern which hung from a beam. He was twelve years old and had lately grown rather stout, but he was still a majestic-looking pig, with a wise and benevolent appearance in spite of the fact that his tushes had never been cut. Before long the other animals began to arrive and make themselves comfortable after their different fashions. First came the three dogs, Bluebell, Jessie, and Pincher, and then the pigs who settled down in the straw immediately in front of the platform. The hens perched themselves on the window-sills, the pigeons fluttered up to the rafters, the sheep and cows lay down behind the pigs and began to chew the cud. The two cart-horses, Boxer and Clover, came in together, walking very slowly and setting down their vast hairy hoofs with great care lest there should be some small animal concealed in the straw. Clover was a stout motherly mare approaching middle life, who had never quite got her figure back after her fourth foal. Boxer was an enormous beast, nearly eighteen hands high, and as strong as any two ordinary horses put together. A white stripe down his nose gave him a somewhat stupid appearance, and in fact he was not of first-rate intelligence, but he was universally respected for his steadiness of character and tremendous powers of work. After the horses came Muriel, the white goat, and Benjamin, the donkey. Benjamin was the oldest animal on the farm, and the worst tempered. He seldom talked, and when he did it was usually to make some cynical remark – for instance, he would say that God had given him a tail to keep the flies off, but he would sooner have had no tail and no flies. Alone among the animals on the farm he never laughed. If asked why, he would say that he saw nothing to laugh at. Nevertheless, without openly admitting it, he was devoted to Boxer; the two of them usually spent their Sundays together in the small paddock beyond the orchard, grazing side by side and never speaking. (*Animal Farm*, pp. 5–7)

Let us begin with syntactic simplicity. Sentences are never very short (thus avoiding an oral, clipped effect) nor very long (avoiding bookishness). Their typical syntax is a sequence of short phrases and clauses paratactically strung together, with meaning packaged in short information units:

With the ring of light/ from his lantern/ dancing from side to side,// he lurched across the yard,// kicking off his boots/ at the back door,// drew himself a last glass of beer/ from the barrel/ in the scullery,// and made his way up to bed,// where Mrs Jones was already snoring.

Clauses are typically active, transitive, with a human or animal subject performing a simple action in a location or on an object:

Subject	Verb	Object or location
Mr Jones	had locked	the hen-houses
	shut	the pop-holes
he	lurched	across the yard
	kicking off	his boots
	drew	a last glass of beer
	made his way	up to bed
Mrs Jones	snoring	
other animals	began to arrive	
pigs	settled down	in the straw
hens	perched	on the window-sills
pigeons	fluttered	up to the rafters
sheep and cows	lay down	behind the pigs
	chew the cud	
cart-horses	came in	
	walking	
	setting down	hoofs

and so on. The active, transitive pattern of Subject, Verb, Object (SVO) is particularly noticeable in passages describing sequences of actions such as the 'battle of the cowshed'.

There is a noticeable lack of adjectives throughout the whole text, with the exception of single, simple descriptive and identifying adjectives: 'strange dream', 'big barn', 'raised platform', 'enormous beast', etc. There is a related avoidance of complex noun phrases: 'vast hairy hoofs' with two adjectives is as complex as we get in this opening passage. Complex noun phrases, particularly those with adjectives and qualifying phrases both before and after the central noun, take a lot of processing, and, like hypotaxis, connote an intellectual complexity which is inappropriate to the focalisers of this story.

Turning to the idea that *Animal Farm* is 'impersonal' in manner, it is obvious that this effect is achieved by eliminating those linguistic markers which suggest the presence of 'a personal voice' (Chapter 4) or a dominating narrator (Chapter 8). One effect of this abstinence is that the book's narrative discourse contains no first-person pronouns, neither singular ('I', 'me', 'my') referring to a narrative persona, nor plural ('we', 'us', 'our') appealing to a community of views or experiences among readers or any other group external to the text. There are no stereotypical generalisations, no references to 'those kinds of . . .' (Chapter 8, pp. 154–5). The few present-tense general statements are extremely modest in their claims: 'it is not easy for a pig to balance himself on a ladder', p. 23). There is no invocation of a reader, no dialogism. Moreover, the text is absolutely parsimonious as far as modality is concerned, avoiding terms which typically signal judgement or evaluation (see p. 49 above) – 'may', 'should', etc., and making very few comments of any kind. The remark on the carthorse, Boxer, is very typical of what Orwell's narrator permits himself in this respect:

> A white stripe down his nose gave him a somewhat stupid appearance, and in fact he was not of first-rate intelligence, but he was universally respected for his steadiness of character and tremendous powers of work.

To whom did he appear stupid, and by whom was he universally respected? The judgement does not go beyond what the other animals might think of their colleague. Orwell generally avoids any claim of knowledge or opinion which might be felt to be external to the animals' world. The following aside is about as far as he strays outside the bounds of what they would know; Snowball tells the animals that electricity produced by the windmill will drive various machines:

> The animals had never heard of anything of this kind before (for the farm was an old-fashioned one and had only the most primitive machinery), and they listened in astonishment while Snowball conjured up pictures of fantastic machines . . . (p. 44)

The animals would not know that the farm was 'old-fashioned' and its machinery 'primitive', because they have no comparison: here then is a very slight hint of a viewpoint different from and more knowledgeable than theirs.

We turn now to the character of the vocabulary and its contribution to the narrative style. The basic vocabulary register is plain and simple, concrete and domestic: 'drunk', 'lurched', 'kicking off his boots', 'glass of beer', 'scullery', 'snoring'. There are plenty of colloquial idiomatic phrases such as 'safely out of the way', 'got her figure back'. Understandably, there are many ordinary words relating to farm equipment and procedures, and to animals: 'henhouses', 'pop-holes', 'tushes', 'perched', 'fluttered' 'chew the cud'; 'harness-room', 'stables', 'bits', 'nose-rings', 'dog-chains', 'knives', 'castrate', 'reins', 'halters', 'blinkers', etc. (p. 20). The prevalence of this type of vocabulary gives the text an old-fashioned pastoral air which accords well with Orwell's nostalgia for an older rural England. Some words seem to be deliberately archaic, typically the word 'muted' (p. 37) which has been noticed by other commentators: it refers to pigeons defecating on the heads of the humans in the battle of the cowshed. Other traditional terms, less noticeable, are found here and there: 'cartage' (p. 43), 'governess-cart' (p. 54), 'clamps', 'chaff', 'mangels' (p. 65).

The ordinariness of the dominant vocabulary links the narrative style of *Animal Farm* with Orwell's earlier 'demotic' register, but there are important differences. Orwell's demotic in the essays, *Down and Out*, and the second part of *Wigan Pier*, for example, is heightened into an instrument of personal rhetoric or naturalistic description by sordid references, by vulgarisms and swear words, by emotive, negative and hyperbolic adjectives. *Animal Farm* avoids these populist and expressive gestures, but remains resolutely controlled, mundane and low-key in its lexical register. It is also virtually free of any obvious metaphor: the dancing light in the opening paragraph (which is entirely functional) is exceptional. And there are no elaborate, laboured similes, foreign words or jargon. Orwell was clearly following the programme for linguistic plainness and conceptual clarity which he was to set out in 'Politics and the English Language'.

We will shortly consider how the everyday vocabulary of *Animal Farm* relates to focalisation in the fable. There is one further observation to make on vocabulary, however, and that concerns the rather conspicuous use throughout the text of a slightly 'higher' level of vocabulary than the mundane lexis of farmyard affairs. 'Ensconced' in the opening sequence is more striking than most words in this register, to which I would add the more typical 'communicate', 'highly regarded', 'wise and benevolent', 'not of first-rate intelligence', 'universally respected'. The vocabulary in question is somewhat elevated, a bit formal and staid; not showy or literary, but slightly more proper and educated than one would associate with the animals. Some more examples: 'vivacious', 'inventive', 'degrading', 'positive pleasure', 'parasitical', 'light skirmishing manoeuvre', 'impromptu celebration', 'under the superintendence', 'a conciliatory message', 'point of honour'.

FOCALISATION, EMPATHY AND DISTANCE

From whose point of view is the story told? What has been said in the previous section about the impersonality of the narrator's voice, and the plainness of the narrative's diction, suggests that Orwell subdues any appearance of a separate story-teller with his own knowledge and opinions. He knows as much as the animals know – perhaps, in terms of farming and building technique, a bit more – but there is no privileged, God-like knowledge which would set the narrator above or apart from the animals. There is no version of the Orwell-figure (either narrator or character) that appears in every other book by our author. Basically, focalisation is from the point of view of the animals; but this statement needs to be made a little more precise.

The distinction between *internal perspective* and *external perspective*, introduced in the previous chapter, applies to the present book; and the distinction is used to express a division of empathy. The villains in the moral scheme – principally the pigs, but also the dogs, Moses the raven, and Mollie the vain horse who defects – are externally presented. (The same applies to the humans.) Their physical appearance and reputation are stressed, their motives are never explored. They are how they appear to others, and they are potentially grotesque from the outset:

The best known among them was a small fat pig named Squealer, with very round cheeks, twinkling eyes, nimble movements, and a shrill voice. He was a brilliant talker, and when he was arguing some difficult point he had a way of skipping from side to side and whisking his tail which was somehow very persuasive. The others said of Squealer that he could turn black into white. (*Animal Farm,* pp. 15–16)

Napoleon, the pig who takes control after the expulsion of Snowball, is never seen from the inside, though his dictatorial decisions run the greater part of the plot. A good example would be his role in the sale of some timber, in which he produces a highly confusing, rumour-filled atmosphere eventuating in his betrayal by Frederick (the allegorical representative of Hitler): we are never shown his motives and reasons, though his actions, assumed titles and appearance are presented in a number of ludicrous images in the same chapter (Chapter 8). Later, when the pigs take to drinking, further comic images are generated:

At about half past nine Napoleon, wearing an old bowler hat of Mr Jones's, was distinctly seen to emerge from the back door, gallop rapidly round the yard, and disappear indoors again. (p. 92)

The grotesque treatment of the pigs is progressive. Their physical traits are at the outset individuating, but the grotesquerie of the bodies is more and more emphasised until finally, standing on their hind legs and wearing clothes, they have become men-monsters. And all the time we hear nothing of their thoughts – though, as we will see, we hear a lot of their speech.

Orwell's way of referring to the actors in this beast-drama constantly insists on a distinction between 'the pigs' and 'the animals'. 'The animals' are basically horses, cows, sheep, hens and ducks, and they are described, as Hammond puts it 'as if from the inside'.[11] Four are named, and of these only two, the horses Boxer and Clover, are assigned anything in the way of individual thought and feeling. That they are animals, rather than human characters in a novel, makes it seem natural that they receive no depth or complexity of psychological presentation, but the horses are allowed feelings and motives. Boxer's reactions to events are communicated throughout:

'His answer to every problem, every setback, was "I will work harder!" – which he had adopted as his personal motto'

'he decided to be content with the first four letters' of the alphabet

'He is dead. . . . I have no wish to take life'

'Boxer, who had now had time to think things over, voiced the general feeling'

'Boxer would never listen to her'

and so on. He is a stereotype of faithful loyalty and hard work; his 'motherly' colleague Clover embodies care and pathos, and is treated to an extended account of deep, sorrowful feeling after the murderous purges begin (pp. 75–6).

Boxer and Clover are to a large extent representatives of the primary focalisation of the animals, which is *collective*: the horses 'voice the general feeling'. Scores of clauses throughout the book give their actions, reactions and feelings as a group; the following are typical:

The singing of this song threw the animals into the wildest excitement.

they were so delighted with the song

the animals hated Moses

the animals could hardly believe in their good fortune

all the animals capered with joy

[the animals] gazed round them

All the animals nodded in complete agreement

Now if there was one thing that the animals were completely certain of

The animals had their breakfast

the animals trooped down to the hayfield

The animals were happy

the animals were completely certain.

The animals had now reassembled in the wildest excitement

the animals decided unanimously

the animals crept back into the barn

the animals were dismayed

the animals did not want Jones back

the animals were somewhat surprised

There are countless other examples of this sort of structure. Three things may be noticed about them. First, they are generally in the simple active syntax which was observed in the style of the narrative frame (of course they are technically part of that frame); the simplicity, it seems to me, reflects on the psychological and moral straightforwardness of the members of this category 'animals-except-pigs'. Second, the vocabulary displays the kind of domestic, rural, modesty which we have noticed; it is very rare that the slightly more elevated diction is associated with the animals' experiences – 'every mouthful of food was an acute positive pleasure' (p. 26) is an exceptional instance of incongruity of register. Third, these formulaic clauses between them hold the content of the animals' world of experience and behaviour: they encode animal actions, sensations, emotions, knowledge and doubts. In fact, they establish the primary focalisation of the tale: they ensure that the story is told from the viewpoint of the animals. And because these focalisation-clauses are conveyed in the basic style of the narration itself, empathy between the narrator and the animals-except-pigs is established.

There is also, of course, the slightly elevated register which we have noticed, which is proper to the narrator and not to the animals: the function of this hint of a more experienced and literate perspective is to keep open the possibility of detachment. Though Orwell sympathises with the animals and their suffering under the tyranny of the pigs, he maintains a slight distance. They are naive and gullible, too ready to blame themselves when the pigs tell them that their memory is defective. Orwell allows us to perceive these realities and not be dominated by the 'reality' which is falsely experienced by the animals. This distance is helped by an affectionately humorous tone in which the animals are presented. There are comic scenes to lighten this dark narrative: the Battle of the Cowshed is a choreography of animal antics; the bleating sheep are comic and so is the silliness of Mollie the vain horse.

THE RHETORIC OF DOMINANCE AND THE PERVERSION OF LANGUAGE

One feature of this disastrous animal utopia is a marked disproportion in the allocation of language to the various classes of animal. Success in language relates directly to the amount of power enjoyed by the different species: power to understand the processes of farming and of government, power to control the fates of other species. The pigs learn to read and write fluently, the others learn less well, their success diminishing according to the conventional stereotypes of their intelligence: Orwell analyses their relative attainments in detail (pp. 29–30), constructing the descending hierarchy pigs–donkey–goat–dogs–horses–sheep–hens–ducks. Their different commands of language correspond roughly to their degrees of control over their lives in this new regime.

There is a marked difference in the amounts of *speech* assigned to the different animals. Except for one small oration by Pilkington at the end, humans do not speak, though their rumours and plots are to some small extent reported. All the rest of the animals are imagined to have speech, though as far as the lower orders go, this seems to be limited to confessing crimes, and these confessions are reported, not direct. In the early days the animals participate in debates, but their contributions (other than those of the pigs) are reported rather than direct speech. Only the horses, the goat and the donkey hold conversations, and then in a very limited way, and – scanning the text as a whole – surprisingly rarely, at least in direct speech (pp. 16, 39, 41, 60, 70, 71–2, 74–5, 77 (one word!), 88, 90, 101, 103–4, 114).

Not surprisingly, dominance by speech is exercised by the pigs. There are four speakers among them: Major, who delivers a long Marxist exhortation on exploitation and rebellion; Napoleon, the Stalin-like leader for most of the narrative; Snowball, who is expelled by Napoleon; and Squealer, who is the intermediary and spokesman for Napoleon's regime and has by far the most speech in the book. Language as deployed by these speakers has different roles, but together their speech makes up *Animal Farm*'s version of the 'voices of the other' which appear regularly in Orwell's writing. Against the mundane, familiar language in which the story and the animals' experiences are narrated, the pigs' speech stands out as an alien linguistic world, half laughable but ultimately chilling. It exemplifies the 'swindles and perversions' of English which Orwell analysed in 'Politics and the English Language', and which are a constant butt for parodic attack in his later writings – there is a sketch of political speech in *Coming Up for Air* (Part Three, chapter 1), parodies of the writings of the intelligentsia in 'Politics and the English Language', and of course this mode of linguistic satire is fully developed in *Nineteen Eighty-Four*.

Major's long speech (pp. 7–12) is a set-piece parody of, in general terms, political demagoguery, and specifically, the discourse of theoretical Marxism. It is not, however, excessive in its manner – jargon is rare, sentences are not over-elaborate, emotive terms are controlled. As the mainspring of the story, presented as the intervention which encourages the animals to rebellion when opportunity arises, this speech must be experienced as if it was persuasive at the time: not outrageous, comic, or incomprehensible through extreme distance from the animals' register. It begins in a plain serious mode, with the experienced public speaker's careful signposting of the way he is going to organise his oration, and a calculated note of pathos:

> 'Comrades, you have heard already about the strange dream that I had last night. But I will come to the dream later. I have something else to say first. I do not think, comrades, that I shall be with you for many months longer, and before I die, I feel it my duty to pass on to you such wisdom as I have acquired.'

Although initially subdued, the speech is immediately dialogic: Major foregrounds himself as the authoritative 'I', and gathers his audience as 'Comrades': he is going to maintain a controlled focus on and appeal to his listeners, because his intention is to implicate them in his reasoning and persuade them to action. 'Comrades' and 'you' recur throughout the speech. After the preliminaries, the rhetoric shifts up a gear:

> 'Now, comrades, what is the nature of this life of ours? Let us face it: our lives are miserable, laborious, and short. We are born, we are given just so much food as will keep the breath in our bodies, and those of us who are capable of it are forced to work to the last atom of our strength; and the very instant that our usefulness has come to an end we are slaughtered with hideous cruelty.'

The dialogic dimension continues to be prominent, designed to carry the audience along by preempting their responses. Note the rhetorical question 'what is . . .?', used throughout the speech: 'But is this simply part of the order of nature?', 'Why then do we continue in this miserable condition?' etc. Also contributing to the dialogic rhetoric is the pronoun 'we', used here as in political discourse generally to imply community of interest and consensus of belief.[12] As Major heightens the rhetoric after the calm opening, the style becomes rhythmic, estranged from ordinary speech by organisation of the syntax into three-part structures (triads) which are typical of political oratory: 'miserable, laborious, and short'; 'born . . . food . . . work'. Vocabulary becomes emotive: 'slaughtered with hideous cruelty'. Major begins to work with generalisations which suggest absolute certainty: 'No animal in England is free. The life of an animal is misery and slavery: that is the plain truth.' Slogans follow naturally: 'All men are enemies. All animals are comrades.' For all the dignity of his style, and his scholastic analysis of production and consumption, Major is basically playing on the animals' feelings, and laying down the law: the law consists of a set of declarations towards the end of his speech, the basis of 'The Seven Commandments' which are later inscribed on the wall of the barn (p. 23).

After the death of Major, and after the Rebellion, the law is determined principally by Napoleon and Snowball, and then by Napoleon after Snowball's expulsion. Napoleon uses language very differently from Major. He addresses the animals rarely, and when he does, his speeches are 'short and to the point' (p. 118). His decisions are communicated to the animals, along with other announcements and opinions which are necessary to regulating the animals' view of the world, by his garrulous spokesman Squealer. But although Napoleon has little direct speech in this narrative, his utterances are repeatedly summarised in forms which present them as instruments of great power. He is the source of a stream of what are called in linguistics *speech acts*:[13] utterances which, in being spoken, do not simply refer to some state of affairs in the world, but actually perform an action – in this case, Napoleon performs speech acts which coerce and control the animals. Some of the verbs which name these speech acts are:

> announced, read out the orders, abolished, dismissed, ordered, decreed, forbidden, pronounced a solemn decree, instructed, gave orders, delivering orders, laid down as a rule, commanded, pronounced a short oration, pronounce the death sentence, pronounced, issued his orders, accepted a contract, called upon, demanded

Napoleon decrees a state of affairs, Squealer announces it, 'explains' it, and the world of the animals is thereby changed – a procedure in which language is clearly both source and instrument of power.

It can be seen that language is of fundamental significance in *Animal Farm*, and in a number of respects. It is first of all the medium for narration, the telling of the tale, and in that role it has a specific stylistic character, which both models the mind-style of the animals (in its underlying mundane, pastoral simplicity) and slightly distances them (by the somewhat elevated narrator's register). When we look at the language of the pigs, comparing it both in quantity and in style with that associated with the other animals, we realise that language is also part of the *action of the book, and that* the relationship of language and power symbolised by linguistic actions is a theme examined by this fable. This theme becomes more specifically focused as the pigs' regime gets indefensibly brutal and selfish: language can be used in a perverted way in order to support a distorted, untruthful, version of reality. There is a hint of this in the first presentation of Squealer (quoted above) as a brilliant talker who 'could turn black into white'. This is precisely Squealer's role throughout the narrative, a role which he takes over from the banished Snowball. The Seven Commandments, initial moral code of Animalism, are by Snowball reduced for ease of memorisation by the animals (also to blur its details) to the maxim 'Four legs good, two legs bad' which even the dim-witted sheep can bleat enthusiastically. The text continues:

> The birds at first objected, since it seemed to them that they also had two legs, but Snowball proved to them that this was not so.
>
> 'A bird's wing, comrades,' he said, 'is an organ of propulsion and not of manipulation. It should therefore be regarded as a leg. The distinguishing mark of Man is the *hand*, the instrument with which he does all his mischief.'
>
> The birds did not understand Snowball's long words, but they accepted his explanation, and all the humbler animals set to work to learn the new maxim by heart. (*Animal Farm*, p. 31)

The long words stand out against the simpler language of the narrative, and are a patent grotesquerie of language by which Orwell mocks the lying logic of Snowball as Snowball squares the world with the maxim by redefining wings as legs. The animals, though handled sympathetically rather than patronisingly, are naive, and take in Snowball's explanation. It is Squealer who performs this function of redefining black as white for the animals for most of the story. When the pigs greedily claim the apple harvest for themselves, 'Squealer was sent to make the necessary explanation to the others': this is not done in a spirit of selfishness, but it has been proved by Science that apples are necessary to the pigs if they are to manage the farm and keep Jones from returning . . . (p. 32). Similarly he 'explains' many other deviations from the Commandments, and other illogicalities: for example, pp. 49–50, 52, 57 – he 'set the animals' minds at rest. He assured them that the resolution against engaging in trade had never been passed'; p. 60 'he put the whole matter in its proper perspective'; when it is learned that the pigs are sleeping in beds, contrary to Commandment 4: 'The rule was against *sheets*'. At this point the alteration of language to falsify history, a great theme of *Nineteen Eighty-Four*, becomes explicit, for the Commandment is repainted on the barn wall: 'No animal shall sleep in a bed *with sheets*'. The horror and the historical revisions escalate: Commandment 6, 'No animal shall kill any other animal' is soon negated by the addition of 'without cause' after the murderous purges (p. 78). The narrator comments, with gentle irony, 'Somehow or other, the last two words had slipped out of the animals' memory.' Finally, all the Commandments, and thus the principles

of the Rebellion, are erased, and replaced by a single Commandment which voices a self-contradictory 'justification' for the superiority of the pigs:

> ALL ANIMALS ARE EQUAL
> BUT SOME ANIMALS ARE MORE
> EQUAL THAN OTHERS (p. 114)

The insane logic of this slogan is clearly within the domain of what
Orwell was later to call 'doublethink', simultaneous belief in two
contradictory propositions (see Winston Smith's account in *Nineteen Eighty-Four*, p. 35). Voiced in language, doublethink produces
a stylistic shock – here, the blatant perversion of the meaning of
the word 'equal', a key logical and ethical term. Semantic contradiction is found elsewhere in orders which are issued by the pigs to
manage the other animals:

> Napoleon announced that there would be work on Sunday after-
> noons as well. This work was strictly voluntary, but any animal
> who absented himself from it would have his rations reduced by
> half. (p. 53)

> Napoleon had commanded that once a week there should be held
> something called a Spontaneous Demonstration. (pp. 97–8)

Forced spontaneity is part of Orwell's vision of the totalitarian future in *Nineteen Eighty-Four* (see p. 23) Also attacked in that novel
are false announcements of productivity and rations, a topic which
figures in *Animal Farm* too. Squealer's Sunday morning readings
of trumped-up production figures may be noted (p. 79), but his announcement of a reduction in rations is more significant for language
and doublethink:

> Once again all rations were reduced, except those of the pigs and
> dogs. A too rigid equality in rations, Squealer explained, would
> have been contrary to the principles of Animalism.

Note how the meaning of 'equality' is here eroded in preparation
for the debasement of 'equal' in the final version of the Commandments. Squealer continues:

> For the time being, certainly, it had been found necessary to make a readjustment of rations (Squealer always spoke of it as a 'readjustment', never as a 'reduction'), but in comparison with the days of Jones, the improvement was enormous. (p. 95)

'Readjustment' for 'reduction' is, as narrated here, a pointed euphemism, precisely the kind of verbal dishonesty to which Orwell has sensitised us in a memorable paragraph of 'Politics and the English Language':

> In our time, political speech and writing are largely the defence of the indefensible . . . Thus political language has to consist largely of euphemism, question-begging and sheer cloudy vagueness. Defenceless villages are bombarded from the air, the inhabitants driven out into the countryside, the cattle machine-gunned, the huts set on fire with incendiary bullets: this is called *pacification*. (*CEJL*, IV, p. 166)

10 *Nineteen Eighty-Four*

Orwell's last novel, *Nineteen Eighty-Four*, is so well-known, and has achieved such a powerful impact on the imagination of generations of readers, that one begins by despairing of saying anything fresh about it. Its sources, its satirical elements, its political content, the ambiguous or complex nature of its critique of totalitarianism and socialism, its psychological meanings, and the nature of Orwell's views on 'Newspeak', have been extensively discussed. However, as is usual in Orwell criticism, there has been little attention to the linguistic strategies by which the novel is constructed. In this chapter I will try to assist an understanding of the structure and rhetoric of *Nineteen Eighty-Four* through a study of its linguistic varieties and their relationships. I will be concentrating on aspects of form and style that I have already identified in his earlier works, and thus reinforcing the thesis that has been implicit in my book, namely that there is an overall unity to Orwell's writings despite their superficial technical diversity.

Nineteen Eighty-Four has an individual creativity, is still a force in public political imagination fifty years after it was written: 'newspeak', 'doublethink' and its paradoxical mathematical expression '2 + 2 = 5', 'Room 101', 'War is peace' and the other slogans, 'Big Brother', even the title and the date 1984, are still referred to frequently in talk, and, particularly, in the media.[1] The memorable ideas and phrases of the novel are still part of the way we represent contemporary political life. The atmosphere of the book, its powerful mixture of squalor, violence and grim humour, haunts the imagination of readers. It is certainly the greatest of Orwell's books in terms of its reception and impact, but its effects are produced by techniques which we have already studied in his earlier works. To say this is not to belittle *Nineteen Eighty-Four*, but to see it as the product of a stage in his career as a novelist – sadly, the last stage, for *Nineteen Eighty-Four* was published only six months before his untimely death.

'The last stage' does not imply a final perfection in Orwell's imagination and novelistic technique. *Animal Farm* is a more perfect

work of art, and even the self-critical Orwell seems to have recognised the merit of that little 'fairy tale': recall his comment in 'Why
I Write', quoted above, Chapter 9, p. 163. *Nineteen Eighty-Four*
lacks the consistency and clarity of *Animal Farm*, in fact it reverts
to the 'mixed' or 'open' genre of fiction writing that he practised
early in his career. The most obvious sign of this is the inclusion of
many pages of quotation from 'the book', supposedly Goldstein's
critique of the ruling oligarchy, possession of which contributes to
Winston Smith's downfall. Then there is an Appendix on 'The Principles of Newspeak', again extraneous to the main narrative structure of the novel. As we have seen, such insertions are a characteristic
Orwellian departure from conventional narration, but it cannot be
denied that they complicate the process of reading, and even the
most patient reader would find the extracts from 'the book' a little
tedious; Orwell's attempt to break up the quoted text and integrate
chunks of it in the narrative by having Winston read sections of it
first to himself and then to Julia while they lie in bed is, frankly,
ludicrous. Other faults have been noted by critics: the woodenness
of much of the dialogue, the tendency towards melodrama, stylistic
indulgence (but see *heteroglossia*, below). There is some evidence
of slapdash writing – after all, the novel was written (as usual) quickly,
and while Orwell was very ill indeed – but clearly the novel has
triumphed over its minor faults.

In *Nineteen Eighty-Four* the world has been divided into three
blocs, Oceania, Eurasia and Eastasia, constantly at war but with no
hope or indeed intention of victory. The function of war is to use
up surplus production and to focus the emotions of the population.
Oceania is like 'Animal Farm' in suffering a totalitarian government which maintains a social system which is hierarchical in power
and privilege: the 'Inner Party' at the top, next the 'Outer Party',
and at the bottom the 'proles'. Control is exercised by constant surveillance using normal police-state mechanisms and, most memora-
bly, the 'telescreen' in every room which both transmits propaganda
and watches over individuals. (Note that this is Orwell's sole 'scientific' innovation – this is not science fiction, not a futuristic novel
of some remote machine age.) The object of the Inner Party is thought
control, the prevention of unorthodox thoughts both by coercion and
by the curtailed form of English 'Newspeak'. A major concern is
the elimination of history through the destruction and falsification
of records. The totalitarian state recalls the Stalinist USSR in its

broad outline and in details (Big Brother recalls Stalin, Goldstein Trotsky, the torture, confessions and executions the Soviet purges). But, like *Animal Farm*, this novel is not simply a satire on the Soviets, for it also refers to Nazi Germany, and its setting is plainly postwar London. Many of the practices of censorship and information control were commonplace in wartime Britain and were, as W. J. West has shown, directly experienced by Orwell in his work for the BBC, and through his wife's work for the Censorship Department.[2] *Nineteen Eighty-Four* is a satire on existing practices, drawing them out to absurd extensions. As happened in the case of *Animal Farm*, Orwell's political critique in *Nineteen Eighty-Four* was misinterpreted, and he had to explain that the novel is neither a straight attack on socialism nor a prediction of what *would* happen:

[A]llowing for the book being after all a parody, something like NINETEEN EIGHTY-FOUR *could* happen. This is the direction in which the world is going at the present time, and the trend lies deep in the political, social and economic foundations of the contemporary world situation.

Specifically, the danger lies in the structure imposed on Socialist and on Liberal capitalist communities by the necessity to prepare for total war with the USSR and the new weapons, of which of course the atomic bomb is the most powerful and the most publicized. But danger lies also in the acceptance of a totalitarian outlook by intellectuals of all colours.[3]

And in a letter to Francis A. Henson, an American trade union leader:

My recent novel is NOT intended as an attack on Socialism or on the British Labour Party (of which I am a supporter) but as a show-up of the perversions to which a centralised economy is liable and which have been partly realised in Communism and Fascism.[4]

Much more could be written on the political and historical context and references of *Nineteen Eighty-Four* and on Orwell's polemical intentions in the novel, but the present linguistic study is not the place to take the discussion further. Another important topic which is beyond my scope is the whole question of Orwell's literary sources: his debt to works such as H. G. Wells's futuristic novels (e.g. *When the Sleeper Awakes*, 1899), Yevgeny Zamyatin's political satire *We* (1923), Aldous Huxley's utopian *Brave New World* (1932), not to mention the classic utopian satire, Swift's *Gulliver's Travels* (1726). Orwell also drew on and parodied the views of the American economist James Burnham, whose influential book *The Managerial Revolution* (1941) he had reviewed and responded to. Fortunately the sources of *Nineteen Eighty-Four* have been identified and discussed by other critics, with an authoritative account by William Steinhoff.[5] None of his sources provides a close model for the kind of book that *Nineteen Eighty-Four* is, and we can come to more of an understanding of its form and style by relating it to his own earlier writings. *Gulliver's Travels*, however, will be discussed as an influence on the content and style of the 'Newspeak Appendix'.

FOCALISATION: THE HYPERCONSCIOUS ANTI-HERO

Orwell conveys what he calls the 'dangerous nightmare situation' of *Nineteen Eighty-Four* through the experience of one individual, Winston Smith, an Outer Party worker in the Ministry of Truth whose job is to falsify – 'rectify' – the historical record by rewriting reports in *The Times*. Winston defies the regime by a series of unorthodox acts: starting a diary, having a sexual relationship with Julia, a member of the Junior Anti-Sex League, renting a room in the prole quarter. He is approached by a member of the Inner Party, O'Brien, who entraps him by lending him 'the book' and (in farcical disguise) providing the illicit rented room, has him arrested and finally acts as his interrogator and torturer. Under torture, Winston is brainwashed and finally destroyed.

Winston Smith has ancestors: John Flory in *Burmese Days*, Gordon Comstock in *Keep the Aspidistra Flying*, George Bowling in *Coming Up for Air*. All are 'little men', petty clerk-like figures of no worldly success and of unenviable physique; somewhat educated, either readers or, in different ways, writers; no longer young, sexually frustrated; self-conscious and self-pitying. Each of these pathetic characters is charged with bearing some part of Orwell's political and aesthetic 'message' as it develops over the years: Flory shoulders the argument against colonialism, Comstock and Bowling set themselves up against commercialism, Bowling has an intense hatred of modern life and politics with a great nostalgia for the past, Winston sees through the power-hunger of the intellectuals and the sham of collectivism. Noble resistance is ineptly performed by absurd and inadequate characters, all of whom are destroyed – such is the depth of Orwell's pessimism.

The warning in *Nineteen Eighty-Four* was that if politicians and the intelligentsia were allowed to continue developing the tendencies towards totalitarianism which Orwell saw in the 1930s and 1940s – in 1938 as he imagined the monstrous predicament of the decent and helpless George Bowling, and in 1948 as he revised his creation of Winston Smith – individual human life with its drives, its intellectual independence and its sense of a situation in time and in culture would be prevented. This warning, this message, is communicated not by author's statement in the mode of the essays and journalism, but by dramatic presentation of the experience of the doomed Winston Smith; and by irony.

The concepts of *mind-style* and *focalisation* introduced in Chapter Eight are central to the question of how, technically, Orwell uses Winston's eyes and thoughts to convey political ideas through art. In the following sections, which deal loosely with mind-style, we will discuss Winston's overwhelmingly negative experience of the world of Airstrip One. In this section it will be shown briefly that the focalisation of the novel is Winston's.

Orwell's fiction throughout his career has dual characteristics: it is both 'realistic' and 'psychological'. There is always a solidity of reference to material objects and settings which produces the feel of realism; though as we have seen, the writing is rarely purely documentary but tends toward an emotive naturalism and even surrealism. But the novels are also, conforming to the modern mode of fiction of the first part of this century, psychological: they concentrate on the inner processes and reactions of central characters. Each of the novels except *Animal Farm* has one character much more prominent than any of the others, his thoughts and feelings given freer and freer rein with each successive book. We have seen that this strategy involves two areas of linguistic technique: the suppression of an independent narrating or 'authorial' voice commenting on the world and on the character's ideas; and the use of conventions such as stream of consciousness, free direct and free indirect thought, verbs of perception and of mental process, to highlight the character as source of experience and of thought.

These conditions are found in *Nineteen Eighty-Four*. Everything that Orwell wants to say about totalitarianism is communicated through the sensations and thoughts of Winston Smith, without any authorial commentary. The basic conception of Winston is extremely effective for Orwell's purpose: he is an intelligent, observant man with some fight and strategy in him – by no means a passive victim of state oppression; he is very physical, his unadmirable body constantly registering feelings and pain; he is acutely self-conscious, always reflecting on his situation and the system in which he exists.

Many of the material elements of the world of *Nineteen Eighty-Four* are introduced in the first few pages, not by narrative passages setting the scene, but through Winston's eyes and thoughts:

It was a bright cold day in April, and the clocks were striking thirteen. Winston Smith, his chin nuzzled into his breast in an effort to escape the vile wind, slipped quickly through the glass doors of Victory Mansions, though not quickly enough to prevent a swirl of gritty dust from entering along with him.

The hallway smelt of boiled cabbage and old rag mats. At one end of it a coloured poster, too large for indoor display, had been tacked to the wall. It depicted simply an enormous face, more than a metre wide: the face of a man of about forty-five, with a heavy black moustache and ruggedly handsome features. Winston made for the stairs. It was no use trying the lift. Even at the best of times it was seldom working, and at present the electric current was cut off during daylight hours. It was part of the economy drive in preparation for Hate Week. The flat was seven flights up, and Winston, who was thirty-nine and had a varicose ulcer above his right ankle, went slowly, resting several times on the way. On each landing, opposite the lift-shaft, the poster with the enormous face gazed from the wall. It was one of those posters which are so contrived that the eyes follow you about when you move. BIG BROTHER IS WATCHING YOU, the caption beneath it ran.

Inside the flat a fruity voice was reading out a list of figures which had something to do with the production of pig-iron. The voice came from an oblong metal plaque like a dulled mirror which formed part of the surface of the right-hand wall. (p. 7)

Sight, hearing, feeling and smell are immediately engaged, and they are Winston's senses; it is his fatigue as he climbs the stairs.

The sensations are all unpleasant: a picture of life in the London of the novel is being built up, wholly through Winston's immediate experience. We are not told directly about the telescreen: Winston hears it as he enters the flat, goes to turn down the volume, positions himself so that he cannot be seen by it. We next learn about the devastated London landscape, and about the four Ministries in their vast buildings, the slogans on the wall of the Ministry of Truth, as if seeing the whole of this through Winston's eyes at the windows of his high flat. The reader is told things that s/he did not know, but nothing that Winston could not have known. There is, it is true, an 'omniscient author' who knows everything about Winston, but there is no claim to know *more* than Winston could have known. Valerie Meyers alleges that Winston 'makes cultural references inconsistent with his ahistorical education', citing references to Charlemagne and Julius Caesar.[6] In fact, such references are extremely rare, one such being Winston's fantasy that he would 'shoot [Julia] full of arrows like Saint Sebastian' (p. 18), two others the references to nineteenth-century houses (p. 8) and a Norman pillar (p. 123) – Winston seems otherwise very confused about the history of architecture. These are passing references. There is none of the sort of cultivated gesture that is found in George Eliot's *Middlemarch*:

> Miss Brooke had that kind of beauty which seems to be thrown into relief by poor dress. Her hand and wrist were so finely formed that she could wear sleeves not less bare of style than those in which the Blessed Virgin appeared to Italian painters . . .[7]

In her very first sentence, George Eliot sets herself above her heroine and establishes a knowing bond with the reader. Orwell positively avoids the 'omniscient' strategy, and the style that goes with it. The authoritarian relative clause which we noticed in *Coming Up for Air* (p. 155) and which dominates Eliot's voice – 'that kind of beauty . . .' – is virtually non-existent. Where it occurs, as in our quotation ('one of those pictures . . .'), it is a formulation which might have entered Winston's mind, concerning some trivial knowledge.[8] Related to the lack of generalisations and of external cultural reference is an avoidance of judgemental modality stemming from the narrator, and specifically, of comment upon Winston. When some comment is made on Winston, it usually turns out to be the product of his own self-consciousness; for example, when Winston prepares to begin writing in his diary:

> For some time he sat gazing stupidly at the paper. (*Nineteen Eighty-Four*, p. 12)

There is nothing in the novel which would suggest that the narrator regards Winston as 'stupid'; this is in fact a self-judgement, a half-comic demotic word through which he expresses his inability to write. The rest of the paragraph, to be quoted below, evidences an acute consciousness of himself and of his failure to put thoughts on paper. Another curious example of linguistic self-consciousness opens Part 2, Chapter 9:

> Winston was gelatinous with fatigue. (p. 159)

At first glance, the high-register, semi-technical term 'gelatinous' looks like an authorial intrusion: as we have seen, Orwell was wont to drop in the odd learned word to check the alertness of the reader or to hint at an authorial presence (p. 75 above). But the passage continues:

> Gelatinous was the right word. It had come into his head sponta-
> neously. His body seemed to have not only the weakness of a
> jelly, but its translucency. (ibid)

Like Gordon Comstock or George Bowling, Winston is constantly thinking about himself, and, being at least a kind of writer, enjoys his words.

Mental activity is continuous with Winston, and physical sensitivity is never far away. The continuation of the paragraph in which he sees himself 'gazing stupidly at the paper' is typical:

> For some time he sat gazing stupidly at the paper. The telescreen
> had changed over to strident military music. It was curious that
> he seemed not merely to have lost the power of expressing him-
> self, but even to have forgotten what it was that he had originally
> intended to say. For weeks past he had been making ready for
> this moment, and it had never crossed his mind that anything
> would be needed except courage. The actual writing would be

easy. All he had to do was to transfer to paper the interminable restless monologue that had been running inside his head, literally for years. At this moment, however, even the monologue had dried up. Moreover his varicose ulcer had begun itching unbearably. He dared not scratch it, because if he did so it always became inflamed. The seconds were ticking by. He was conscious of nothing except the blankness of the page in front of him, the itching of the skin above his ankle, the blaring of the music, and a slight booziness caused by the gin. (ibid, p. 12)

The passage is full of verbs and other elements indicating mental processes and physical sensations:

gazing, expressing himself, forgotten, intended making ready, crossed his mind. courage, running inside his head, dried up, itching, dared not, conscious, itching, blaring, booziness.

This is entirely typical of Winston's basic mind-style as it is expressed throughout the novel: he is continuously reacting, reflecting, making plans, conscious all the time of physical sensations including noise, cold, the state of his own body. The physical side of his consciousness is so prominent that examples can easily be found, without the need for quotation here; of course the scenes of his captivity and torture are a major source, not only for the extreme pain of torture but also for the more continuous sensations of discomfort, stench, hunger and fatigue: Chapter 1 of Part 3, where he is in a cell awaiting 'treatment' in the Ministry of Love, is particularly marked in the area of sensory reaction, see for example p. 205, 'The pain of sitting on the narrow bench . . . Whenever his physical sensations were a little under control the terror returned' (as if they are largely *out* of control, as the text continuously indicates). Note that the constant pressures of Winston's body are particularly galling for a person of Winston's intellectual self-consciousness: they prevent him thinking – 'Even now, in spite of the gin, the dull ache in his belly made consecutive thought impossible' (ibid, p. 91).

The expression 'the interminable restless monologue that had been running inside his head, literally for years' neatly captures the nature of Winston's thought processes. He is one of those self-conscious people who experience their thoughts as a voice inside the head, speaking in articulate language. The heroes of the modern psychological novel are of this nature; the novelist constructs his or her novel as a representation on paper of these thoughts, using the conventions which we noted in Chapter 8. *Nineteen Eighty-Four* is consistently interior, but could not be called avant-garde in its techniques. Orwell does not use interior monologue or stream of consciousness as he does in places in *Keep the Aspidistra Flying* and *Coming Up for Air*. However, he uses free indirect discourse, but not for the 'dual voice' which interweaves character's thoughts and narrator's comment, since the narrative voice is, as we have seen, suppressed as a separate identity. Free indirect thought is used to make Winston's thoughts immediate to the reader, to avoid fixing them in a past-tense narrative frame. The tell-tale present tense deictics in past tense sentences occur often enough to cue FID: 'the thing that he was now about to do' (*Nineteen Eighty-Four*, p. 10), 'Even now, in spite of the gin . . .' (ibid, p. 91), 'To this day he did not know with any certainty that his mother was dead' (ibid, p. 145), 'the cell, or room, in which he now was' (ibid, p. 210). Near-range demonstratives, which are the spatial equivalent of temporal 'now', are also found: see 'this' and 'these' in the passage beginning 'whether London had always been like this' quoted on p. 197, below. More generally, free indirect thought is signalled by a high degree of subjectivity in the discourse representing Winston's thoughts, many verbs and adjectives of mental state and process, a vocabulary that is demotic and emotional, the colloquial general pronouns 'we' and 'you', exclamations, and rhetorical questions and hypotheses addressed to and pondered by himself:

> He picked up the children's history book and looked at the portrait of Big Brother which formed its frontispiece. The hypnotic eyes gazed into his own. It was as though some huge force were pressing down upon you – something which penetrated inside your skull, battering against your brain, frightening you out of your beliefs, persuading you, almost, to deny the evidence of your senses. In the end the Party would announce that two and two made five, and you would have to believe it. It was inevitable that they should make that claim sooner or later: the logic of their position demanded it. Not merely the validity of experience, but the very existence of external reality, was tacitly denied by their philosophy. The heresy of heresies was common sense. And what was terrifying was not that they would kill you for thinking other-

wise, but that they might be right. For, after all, how do we know that two and two make four? Or that the force of gravity works? Or that the past is unchangeable? If both the past and the external world exist only in the mind, and if the mind itself is controllable – what then?

But no! His courage seemed suddenly to stiffen of its own accord. The face of O'Brien, not called up by any obvious association, had floated into his mind . . . (pp. 72–3)

MEMORY, DREAM AND HALLUCINATIONS

Winston's thought is not simply constant and reflective, it also moves frequently to high levels of mental activity, showing imagination, strenuous attempts to reconstruct memories; panic and hysteria. As with George Bowling, panic and hysteria concern his pessimistic vision of the future – his future personal fate and in more general terms that of the citizens of Oceania. Memory is his chief weapon against the Party's programme of obliterating the past. Imagination releases him from the horrors of the present. (The main character in Zamyatin's novel *We* suffers from the 'illness' of imagination, which causes him to think heretical thoughts.)[9] Winston's thoughts easily move into a poetic or emotive mode. His prized glass and coral paperweight, a 'solid object' from the past,[10] triggers an elaborate and attractive fantasy:

The room was darkening. He turned over towards the light and lay gazing into the glass paperweight. The inexhaustibly interesting thing was not the fragment of coral but the interior of the glass itself. There was such a depth of it, and yet it was almost as transparent as air. It was as though the surface of the glass had been the arch of the sky, enclosing a tiny world with its atmosphere complete. He had the feeling that he could get inside it, and that in fact he was inside it, along with the mahogany bed and the gateleg table, and the clock and the steel engraving and the paperweight itself. The paperweight was the room he was in, and the coral was Julia's life and his own, fixed in a sort of eternity at the heart of the crystal. (*Nineteen Eighty-Four*, p. 130; cf. p. 142)

In crude terms, this is escapism; the point is that the styles associated with Winston have the resources to take his consciousness away from the present to another, more certain and more attractive world, often his childhood: the style contrasts strongly with others that prey on his consciousness, for example the 'voices of the other' which crowd on him in heteroglossia, the style of violence, and the style of squalor – examples are quoted in the following sections.

Memories and dreams pervade his experience throughout the book. Both categories of mental experience are fundamental to his resistance to Big Brother and the Party: if he can reconstruct the past, he can assure himself that the past and the present as continuously reshaped by the Party are not reality but 'swindles and perversions'. From the beginning of the novel he is, in a happy phrase, 'struggling to think his way backward' (ibid, p. 32), and the memories come in powerful scenes: Chapters 6 and 7 of Part 1 contain notable examples: going with a whore, his wife Katharine, the crowd of prole women fighting over saucepans, the story of Aaronson, Jones and Rutherford. Often memories come unbidden, often by association: the smell of coffee takes him 'back in the half-forgotten world of his childhood' (p. 74, also p. 125); scent on Julia reminds him of the whore (pp. 126–7). Such involuntary processes also occur in the many dreams which he experiences, dreams which introduce the language of hallucination. He dreams of his mother in language packed with dream imagery:

> At this moment his mother was sitting in some place deep down beneath him, with his young sister in her arms. He did not remember his sister at all, except as a tiny, feeble baby, always silent, with large, watchful eyes. Both of them were looking up at him. They were down in some subterranean place – the bottom of a well, for instance, or a very deep grave – but it was a place which, already far below him, was itself moving downwards. They were in the saloon of a sinking ship, looking up at him through the darkening water. (ibid, p. 30)

The imagery of vortex and abyss continues for several lines. (It is superseded by the Golden Country; see next section.) The dream-work is difficult to interpret, perhaps, but it is enough to establish 'the last man' as the dangerous creature recognised by the Party, a man whose imagination transcends the controls of the present and who, through imagination, can construct a past, however fragmentary.

Winston not only dreams and experiences involuntary memories, he also hallucinates, and the dream style is the foundation for surreal moments when his mind drifts out of his body and his physical situation. He hallucinates literally – and it is called 'hallucination', (pp. 240, 241) – after torture, but it is a feature of his mind, and starts quite early in the novel: while doing physical jerks to the order of the telescreen, 'his mind slid away into the labyrinthine world of doublethink' (p. 35); 'the face of O'Brien, not called up by any obvious association, had floated into his mind' (p. 73); 'he was inside [the paperweight]' (p. 130). Later, vivid surrealistic passages occur:

> He was rolling down a mighty corridor, a kilometre wide, full of glorious, golden light, roaring with laughter and shouting out confessions at the top of his voice . . . With him were the guards, the other questioners, the men in white coats, O'Brien, Julia, Mr Charrington, all rolling down the corridor together and shouting with laughter. (p. 210)

For much of the torture section of the story, Winston is 'high', disoriented by constant light, loss of a sense of time and place, shot with drugs and electric shocks, shattered with beatings. Orwell is capable of producing a full-blown hallucinogenic style, and on reflection the seeds of this are found in his earliest work which contains passages verging on surrealism (see Chapter 5 above).

THE GOLDEN COUNTRY

We are beginning to see here the range of styles within *Nineteen Eighty-Four* becoming quite extensive; and the point is that we are encountering not mere display of stylistic virtuosity on Orwell's part, but the evocation of the mind-style of a complex, imaginative, yet mentally disorganised individual. The metaphor of the 'Golden Country' extends the range by taking in a *pastoral* mode of writing in which Orwell was already experienced: the evocation of landscape, and particularly by the mention of small rural details. As we have seen, pastoral is a strong feature of *Coming Up for Air*: it is prominent in George Bowling's affectionate reminiscences of his boyhood, and communicates unproblematically his yearning for a departed, more innocent age which has been destroyed by 'progress', industrialisation and modernist sham. The symbolism is virtually identical in *Nineteen Eighty-Four*: the Golden Country is an imagined landscape of Winston's youth, glowing with positive value against the cold squalor of contemporary London. There is a major and clever difference, however, in that the Golden Country is, though precisely recalled, just a fragment that Winston cannot fully place or understand. Unlike Bowling, he has no complete sense of his past, and such fragments essentially contribute to his disorientation.

The Golden Country appears to Winston in dreams; a precise landscape is grafted onto the looser consciousness of the dream form:

> Suddenly he was standing on short springy turf, on a summer evening when the slanting rays of the sun gilded the ground. The landscape that he was looking at recurred so often in his dreams that he was never fully certain whether or not he had seen it in the real world. In his waking thoughts he called it the Golden Country. It was an old, rabbit-bitten pasture, with a foot-track wandering across it and a molehill here and there. In the ragged hedge on the opposite side of the field the boughs of the elm trees were swaying very faintly in the breeze, their leaves just stirring in dense masses like women's hair. Somewhere near at hand, though out of sight, there was a clear, slow-moving stream where dace were swimming in the pools under the willow trees. (*Nineteen Eighty-Four*, p. 30)

At this point the dream introduces Julia – whom at this stage he only knows by sight – into the field in an erotic dream fantasy which foreshadows what really is to happen later.

This description recurs twice more in the novel, at critical moments, and in almost identical wording. Towards the end of the novel, in the hallucinating period between his torture/interrogation and his submission in Room 101,

> he was in the enormous sunlit passage, a kilometre wide, down which he had seemed to walk in the delirium induced by drugs. He was in the Golden Country, following the foot-track across the old rabbit-cropped pasture. He could feel the short springy turf under his feet and the gentle sunshine on his face ... (ibid, p. 241)

This is delusion, an irony against Winston, who is being pampe
by his tormenters to give him the strength and sense of well-beii
necessary for him to submit to, and survive, the final torture.

The other recollection of the Golden Country, and the attendant
pastoral style, occurs much earlier, when Winston and Julia go out
into the country to make love (Part 2, Chapter 2). (The pastoral
style offers romantic associations in a very similar situation in *Keep
the Aspidistra Flying*, ch. 7.) On page 105 the text bursts out into a
bucolic style unprecedented so far, the atmosphere being unrelievedly
grim and chilling (see next section):

> Winston picked his way up the lane through dappled light and
> shade, stepping out into pools of gold wherever the boughs parted.
> Under the trees to the left of him the ground was misty with
> bluebells. The air seemed to kiss one's skin. It was the second of
> May. From somewhere deeper in the heart of the wood came the
> droning of ring doves. (*Nineteen Eighty-Four,* p. 105)

How romantic! Fragments of this style, brief but so different from
the gloomy context of descriptions of London as to be strongly
foregrounded and obviously significant in an objective–correlative
way, are dotted through the chapter of love-making. At one point
Winston seems literally to see the old pasture of the Golden Country, described in the same words as on its initial introduction as a
dream image: 'An old, close-bitten pasture, with a footpath wander-
ing across it and a molehill here and there' etc. (p. 110) Is Winston
literally looking at a place he knew in his youth? We cannot be
sure; nor can he, since he does not know whether the dream landscape was one he had seen in actuality. He had earlier dreamed of
Julia in that landscape; and he had earlier believed her to be a spy
following him on his visits to the prole quarter. If the pastoral seems
romantic, it is also deeply ambiguous.

SORDID REALISM

The grim atmosphere of the London of this novel is extremely memorable and has been widely acclaimed by critics. There is nothing
futuristic about this vision, nothing of the clean glass, steel and
concrete, the efficient technology, of science fiction or of the ideal-
ised socialist future which Orwell mocked elsewhere. It is precisely

the London of the immediate post-War years: bomb-damaged, grimy, cold, marked by shortages of food (and by synthetic food), of fuel, clothing and other supplies (razor blades were a handy symbol used frequently by Orwell, in *Aspidistra, Coming Up for Air* and pp. 7. 46 and 56 of *Nineteen Eighty-Four*); by failures in basic services such as electricity. The immediately relevant realism of the atmosphere of *Nineteen-Eighty-Four*'s London would have been instantly obvious to contemporary readers; it was just about visible to myself going up to London as a student in 1956, but is no doubt quite difficult for young readers of today to appreciate. The fact of the matter is that Orwell, in the urban scenes and the depiction of everyday life, is deploying a kind of straightforward realism in a novel which requires in other respects to be read as a satirical fantasy. The political implication of this strategy, at the time, is clear. The deprivations and discomforts of urban England in the late 1940s appeared to be the result of the damage to the economy and to manpower exacted by six years of war; but Orwell blames these same conditions, occurring in the fictional year 1984, on the cynicism and self-interest of a totalitarian regime. The atmosphere constitutes part of his critique of the governing of contemporary Britain, just as his account of censorship, surveillance and bureaucratic repression reflects his perception of the oppressive, intrusive way in which people were actually managed during and after the war.

The technique of description of this dimension of *Nineteen Eighty-Four* is a combination of documentary realism and naturalism or, more aptly here, sordid realism. Orwell conveys the run-down, uncomfortable feel of Winston's London by a few selected details, and the atmospheric indications have been completed within the first few chapters of the novel, with memorable details even in the first few pages. The opening pages, quoted on p. 186 above for focalisation, offer immediate cues, in the form of brief phrases, with absolutely no exaggeration or over-writing, to the prevailing squalor and discomfort:

> bright cold day, vile wind, swirl of gritty dust, boiled cabbage and old rag mats, no use trying the lift, the electric current was cut off.

Each of these details, simple in itself, is given greater impact by being linked to a response by the focaliser: Winston struggles to escape the wind, to prevent dust blowing in the door; the lack of electricity, and of a lift, is worsened by the effect on Winston, who is unfit and lives seven flights up. The idea of shortages is next introduced, artfully worked in with the first physical description of the hero:

> His hair was very fair, his face naturally sanguine, his skin roughened by coarse soap and blunt razor blades and the cold of the winter that had just ended. (p. 7)

Typically Orwellian is the ordinary, and usually negative, vocabulary, generally demotic in register, used to characterise the discomforts; in the passages so far quoted, 'cold', 'vile', 'gritty', 'old', 'coarse', 'blunt', but also typically Orwellian is the one arcane word 'sanguine',[11] a slight reminder that this is literary writing. Next in this sequence, Winston moves to look out of the window of his flat, and a few more sentences develop a quite adequately specified picture of the outside world:

> Outside, even through the shut window-pane, the world looked cold. Down in the street little eddies of wind were whirling dust and torn paper into spirals, and though the sun was shining and the sky a harsh blue, there seemed to be no colour in anything, except the posters that were plastered everywhere. (pp. 7–8)

Winston surveys the war-ravaged city, wondering:

> whether London had always been quite like this. Were there always these vistas of rotting nineteenth-century houses, their sides shored up with baulks of timber, their windows patched with cardboard and their roofs with corrugated iron, their crazy garden walls sagging in all directions? And the bombed sites where the plaster dust swirled in the air and the willow-herb straggled over the heaps of rubble; and the places where the bombs had cleared a larger patch and there had sprung up sordid colonies of wooden dwellings like chicken-houses? (pp. 8–9)

Within the first two pages, enough detail has been given, in precise references and simple vocabulary, to communicate a world which primarily depresses Winston by 'its bareness, its dinginess': see pp. 67–8 for his general reflections on the miserable ordinary life of a Party member:

> 'slogging through dreary jobs, fighting for a place on the Tube, darning a worn-out sock, cadging a saccharine tablet, saving a cigarette end',

and note the basic vernacular vocabulary employed. In the same later passage, London is 'vast and ruinous, city of a million dustbins'.

'Dustbins' are presumably an image of squalor for the sensitive Winston, and the squalid side of life in 1984 is developed with equal economy in two ensuing scenes, the first in the flat of Winston's neighbours where he is called by Mrs Parsons to help in the loathsome business of unblocking a sink (Part 1, Chapter 2). The Parsons episode develops the sordid side of domestic life, the aura of boiled cabbage, old rag mats, and sweat. Interestingly, Winston recalls the incident later, repeating an image that Orwell had used twelve years earlier to encapsulate the pathos and hopelessness of the poor in Wigan (see Chapter 5, p. 84, above): mixed up with his vision of London as 'city of a million dustbins' is 'a picture of Mrs Parsons, a woman with lined face and wispy hair, fiddling helplessly with a blocked drain-pipe' (p. 68).

The second scene which is framed by an atmosphere of sordid realism occurs in the canteen at Winston's place of work (Part 1, Chapter 5):

> In the low-ceilinged canteen, deep underground, the lunch queue jerked slowly forward. The room was already very full and deafeningly noisy. From the grille at the counter the steam of stew came pouring forth, with a sour metallic smell which did not quite overcome the fumes of Victory Gin. (p. 46)

Orwell's early writings show that he disliked confinement, noise and bad smells, and he communicates Winston's fastidiousness feelingly in this chapter. As Winston and his colleague Syme take their meal to a table, they are confronted by a strikingly disgusting sight: 'on one corner [of the metal-topped table] someone had left a pool of stew, a filthy liquid mess that had the appearance of vomit'. As for the food itself, Winston 'began swallowing spoonfuls of the stew, which, in among its general sloppiness, had cubes of spongy pinkish stuff which was probably a preparation of meat' (p. 47). The chapter then records some conversations about Newspeak, to which we will return, but the stew/vomit reference persists, first Syme and then Winston absent-mindedly drawing patterns with their spoons in the puddle of stew on the table (pp. 51, 55). As Winston plays with the puddle, he 'meditate[s] resentfully on the physical texture of life', looks around the room and communicates his disgust in list-structure sentences which are pure Orwellian sordid realism:

> A low-ceilinged room, its walls grimy from the contact of innumerable bodies; battered metal tables and chairs, placed so close together that you sat with elbows touching; bent spoons, dented trays, coarse white mugs; all surfaces greasy, grime in every crack; and a sourish, composite smell of bad gin and bad coffee and metallic stew and dirty clothes . . . In any time that he could accurately remember, there had never been quite enough to eat, one had never had socks or underclothes that were not full of holes, furniture had always been battered and rickety, rooms underheated, tube trains crowded, houses falling to pieces, bread dark-coloured, tea a rarity, coffee filthy-tasting, cigarettes insufficient – nothing cheap and plentiful except synthetic gin. (p. 55)

There is no elaboration, no hyperbole – this is in a way a purer version of the style of sordid realism that Orwell had devised in his earliest books. But the negativity and the reliance for evaluation on plain, vernacular adjectives ('grimy', 'battered', 'bent', 'dented', 'coarse', etc.) are features of Orwell's basic naturalistic style that he had mastered years before, and now, in what was to be his final novel, deployed to powerful effect.

VIOLENCE

Although Winston says that he minds the 'cruelty' of life in Oceania less than 'its bareness, its dinginess' (p. 67), there is no doubt that violence is never far from his mind. In the very first chapter of the novel he recalls violent feelings in the Two Minutes' Hate, 'an ecstasy of fear and vindictiveness, a desire to kill, to torture, to smash faces in with a sledge-hammer' (p. 17); as he feels this, Winston is kicking his heel against the rung of his chair. There is a recurrent image of boots and kicking, crystallised by O'Brien during Winston's interrogation: 'imagine a boot stamping on a human face – for ever' (p. 230).[12]

In the violent and frustrating world which he inhabits, Winston's panicky imagination often leads him to the threshold of losing control:

> He had an almost overwhelming temptation to shout a string of filthy words at the top of his voice. Or to bang his head against the wall, to kick over the table, and hurl the inkpot through the window – to do any violent or noisy or painful thing that might black out the memory that was tormenting him. (p. 59)

He imagines doing violence to others, notably when he suspects Julia of following and spying on him:

> He could keep on her track until they were in some quiet place, and then smash her skull in with a cobblestone. The piece of glass in his pocket [the paperweight] would be heavy enough for the job. (p. 90)

Over and over again, knowing that his acts of resistance are bound to be punished by torture and death, he imagines the violence of his own end. His physical squeamishness and sensitivity produce extreme images worded with typical Orwellian economy and directness:

> the grovelling on the floor and screaming for mercy, the crack of broken bones, the smashed teeth, and bloody clots of hair. (p. 91)

> There were moments when he foresaw the things that would happen to him with such actuality that his heart galloped and his breath stopped. He felt the smash of truncheons on his elbows and iron-shod boots on his shins; he saw himself grovelling on the floor, screaming for mercy through broken teeth. (pp. 197–8)

The latter quotation comes from the chapter in which Winston, having been arrested, waits with others in a cell to be called to his personal fate (Part 3, Chapter 1). It is one of the most powerful scenes in the book, full of grotesque vitality as a motley selection of prisoners are thrown in and dragged out. Two surreal figures, a 'chinless man' and a 'skull-faced man' are brutally assaulted; the treatment of the first may be quoted as typical of the other beatings that occur in the last part of the book, including the torture of Winston himself, although we will see that Winston's torture is not only externally presented, but also involves activities of mind:

> [A] short stumpy guard . . . let free a frightful blow, with all the weight of his body behind it, full in the chinless man's mouth. The force of it almost seemed to knock him clear of the floor. His body was flung across the cell and fetched up against the base of the lavatory seat. For a moment he lay as though stunned, with dark blood oozing from his mouth and nose. A very faint whimpering or squeaking, which seemed unconscious, came out of him. Then he rolled over and raised himself unsteadily on hands and knees. Amid a stream of blood and saliva, the two halves of a dental plate fell out of his mouth.
>
> The prisoners sat very still, their hands crossed on their knees. The chinless man climbed back into his place. Down one side of his face the flesh was darkening. His mouth had swollen into a shapeless cherry-coloured mass with a black hole in the middle of it. From time to time a little blood dripped on to the breast of his overalls. His grey eyes flitted from face to face, more guiltily than ever, as though he were trying to discover how much the others despised him for his humiliation. (pp. 203–4)

Note that this violence is presented in *external perspective*: Winston and the other prisoners are watching, and there is an element of voyeurism in this presentation of the chinless man's suffering as it is observed rather than as it is felt. Even at the end of the extract, his feelings are merely the object of another person's speculation: it was '*as though he were* trying to discover . . .'.[13] As the inner reactions and pain of the man are suppressed, there is an emphasis on specific external body parts and signs of injury; the focus is highly intense, and the things that are referred to are named simply:

> mouth, nose, blood, saliva, the two halves of a dental plate, one side of his face, flesh, mouth, black hole, the breast [note the exactness] of his overalls.

The chinless man is by these devices depersonalised, almost an animal with his 'whimpering or squeaking'. The depersonalisation or dehumanisation of the sufferer lends power and terror to violence in language: it is the foundation for an obscenity of violence which will be found in pornographic writing and which Orwell must approach in his evocation of the total inhumanity of the regime of Oceania.

The dramatic point in the story, of course, is that Winston sees this assault, and that his turn is next. He had correctly predicted the elbow, on which he is struck violently before being taken from the cell (p. 206). His torture begins in earnest on the next page. At first it is externally presented and total, a list of affected body parts reeled off all in a rush:

> Always there were five or six men in black uniforms at him simultaneously. Sometimes it was fists, sometimes it was truncheons, sometimes it was boots. There were times when he rolled about the floor, as shameless as an animal, writhing his body this way and that in an endless, hopeless effort to dodge the kicks, and simply inviting more and yet more kicks, in his ribs, in his belly, on his elbows, on his shins, in his groin, in his testicles, on the bone at the base of his spine. (p. 207)

Here the beating is externally presented to stress its severity and Winston's helplessness. But it cannot continue wholly external, because the process and outcome of his treatment is intellectual: he has to remain conscious and to retain motives, otherwise he cannot change mentally under the interrogation by O'Brien. So his feelings and thoughts are immediately worked in, to be developed extensively in the final chapters of the book:

> There were times when it went on and on until the cruel, wicked, unforgivable thing seemed to him not that the guards continued to beat him but that he could not force himself into losing consciousness. There were times when his nerve so forsook him that he began shouting for mercy even before the beating began, when the mere sight of a fist drawn back for a blow was enough to make him pour forth a confession of real and imaginary crimes. (pp. 207–8)

HETEROGLOSSIA AND THE GROTESQUE

So far we have examined the plethora of styles that are generated by Winston's own consciousness: his own ruminative and reflective thought-processes, his physical reactions, his imaginative flights, his romantic fantasies in the deceptive language of pastoral, his feel for the atmosphere of the city in which he dwells, the way he represents his own violent emotions, the way he sees violence to others, and experiences violence by others upon himself.[14] In addition to these modes of language and thought which come from within him, there is in *Nineteen Eighty-Four* a considerable range of voices which come from the dreadful society he inhabits – 'voices of the other', which bombard Winston's consciousness and are objects of Orwell's parody. This is such an extensive subject that I can do little more than indicate and illustrate its scope and variety.

I said that Winston was 'bombarded' with other voices. The world of *Nineteen Eighty-Four* is an oppressively noisy world. But there is a structure here which Orwell had used elsewhere in his fictional writings, notably *Down and Out* and *Burmese Days* (see Chapters 6 and 7 above). Like Winston, the narrator in the former and the central character in the latter are surrounded by minor characters that are presented eccentrically or even grotesquely, and who speak in peculiar voices. Grotesque appearances or mannerisms are presented by Orwell in thumbnail sketches, and the peculiarities of voice briefly described or illustrated. As a context for the heteroglossia that afflicts Winston in *Nineteen Eighty-Four*, we may first note the vast menagerie of grotesque caricatures that Orwell places around him. I have space only to list them and to quote some striking phrases that characterise some of them.

Goldstein (p. 15) 'a lean Jewish face, with a great fuzzy aureole of white hair and a small goatee beard ... It resembled the face of a sheep, and the voice, too, had a sheep-like quality'.

Mrs Parsons (p. 22) 'A colourless, crushed-looking woman, with wispy hair and a lined face ... a dreary, whining sort of voice'.

Tillotson (p. 40) 'a small, precise-looking, dark-chinned man'.

Ampleforth (p. 41) 'a mild, ineffectual, dreamy creature ... with very hairy ears'.

Syme (p. 46) 'a tiny creature ... with dark hair and large, protuberant eyes, at once mournful and derisive'.

Parsons (p. 52) 'a tubby, middle-aged man with fair hair and a froglike face'.

Colleagues (p. 56) 'small, dark, and ill-favoured ... little dumpy men, growing stout very early in life, with short legs, swift scuttling movements, and fat inscrutable faces with very small eyes'.

Rutherford (p. 70) 'a monstrous man, with a mane of greasy grey hair, his face pouched and seamed, with thick negroid lips'.

Two prole women (p. 75) 'two monstrous women with brick-red forearms'

Prole man (p. 78) 'a very old man, bent but active, with white moustaches that bristled forward like those of a prawn'.

Charrington (p. 84) 'frail and bowed, with a long benevolent nose, and mild eyes distorted by thick spectacles'.

Wilsher (p. 100) 'a blond-headed, silly-faced young man'.

anon (p. 100) 'a small, swiftly-moving, beetle-like man with a flat face and tiny, suspicious eyes'.

Eurasian prisoners (p. 104) 'round Mongol faces', 'scrubby cheekbones', 'nests of hair'.

Washerwoman (pp. 122–3) 'a monstrous woman, solid as a Norman pillar, with brawny red forearms'.

O'Brien's servant (p. 149) 'a small, dark-haired man in a white jacket, with a diamond-shaped, completely expressionless face which might have been that of a Chinese'.

Political speaker (p. 160) 'a small lean man with disproportionately long arms and a large bald skull over which a few lank locks straggled'.

Chinless man (p. 202) 'a chinless, toothy face exactly like that of some large, harmless rodent'.

Skull-like man (p. 202) 'the emaciation of his face. It was like a skull'.

O'Brien (p. 227) 'pouches under the eyes, the skin sagged from the cheekbones'.

Finally:

Winston seeing himself in a mirror, that is as if externally, after his torturing (pp. 233–4) 'A bowed, grey-coloured, skeleton-like thing was coming towards him' – and further extensive grotesque description.

In these grotesque miniatures, some recurrent features may be noticed: comparison with animals, small stature, thinness or fatness, eccentric hair or eyes or other facial features. They are all in their various ways 'estranged', alien, often inhuman. They enliven and diversify the texture of the novel, but more than that, cumulatively they add up to an impression that Winston (it is always he who sees these people) lives in a world peopled by a variety of strange monsters. In their estrangement and their diversity, they are the physiognomical equivalent of heteroglossia.

The most palpable assault by alien voices comes from the ever-present telescreen, which emits a cacophony of noises and speech styles. The voices, noises and music which come from it are generally harsh and bullying, and often politically charged. The basic bullying voice is found, for example, in the chapter where prisoners are assembled in the cell in the Ministry of Love (Part 3, Chapter 1): the telescreen constantly 'yells' (five times), 'roars', and emits a 'furious, deafening roar' whenever the prisoners do something out of order. Often the voices (like the grotesque faces) are coloured with animal metaphors: the gym instructress, who has a 'piercing female voice' (p. 32), 'yapped' and 'barked' as well as 'rapped out' and 'screamed'; 'screamed out the shrewish voice' (p. 36). The telescreen at the Chestnut Tree Cafe mocks the 'traitors' with a 'cracked, braying, jeering note, a yellow note' (pp. 70 and 253). Goldstein on the telescreen 'bleats' (p. 18). At the end of the novel 'an excited voice was gabbling from the telescreen' (p. 255). The animals respectively are dog, shrew, donkey, sheep and goose: none is a compliment, applied to a human. If 'roar' is not a dead metaphor, a lion is evoked as well. Trumpets, metal, glass and machines are used to suggest the harsh, inhuman quality of the telescreen voices. Besides the numerous trumpet calls and the military music, we find 'a brassy female voice was squalling a patriotic song' (p. 91) and of the same voice it is said 'her voice seemed to stick into his brain like jagged splinters of glass'. The voice from the hidden telescreen in Winston's rented room is 'the iron voice' (pp. 189, 258). 'Raspingly' (p. 26) suggests the grating noise of a file on metal. Once the machine metaphor is developed into what is, for this novel a rare Orwellian simile: 'a hideous, grinding speech, as of some monstrous machine running without oil' (p. 15) – thus the Penguin edition, but Crick's edition substitutes 'screech' for 'speech', thus intensifying the machine metaphor.[15]

The very first description of a telescreen voice should alert us to the fact that these utterances are not only noxious, they are also coloured by Orwell's political and social views. A 'fruity voice was reading out a list of figures which had something to do with the production of pig-iron' (p. 7). 'Fruity' recalls both 'fruity-voice', an upper middle-class woman customer sneered at by Gordon Comstock in *Keep the Aspidistra Flying* (p. 23) and 'the plummy voice from the radio' which Orwell found so distasteful (Chapter 3 above, p. 22). The plummy voice is the voice of upper-class privilege assuming the role of official spokesman, giving the received governmental view of the world in broadcasts on the BBC. The fruity voice is reading out production figures which, the novel implies, are lies: an affected official voice is a sign of dissimulation and manipulation. Other accents from the telescreen seem to be chosen deliberately to fit the messages which they are putting across (just as newsreaders on radio and television change the tone of their voice to interpret the character, grave, inspiring or comical, of different news stories). An 'eager, youthful voice' attempts to stir up enthusiasm for some more production figures (p. 54). At the end of the book, 'an excited voice' (the gabbling voice) announces a victory; Winston hears it as fragments of 'duckspeak':

> vast strategic manoeuvre – perfect coordination – utter rout – half a million prisoners – complete demoralisation – control of the whole of Africa – bring the war within measurable distance of its end – victory – greatest victory in human history – victory, victory, victory! (pp. 255–6)

Much earlier than page 255, we have learned that the victories claimed by the Inner Party, like all their other claims, are spurious. The duplicity of official discourse had already been analysed by Orwell in 'Politics and the English language' and in the figure of Squealer in *Animal Farm*. The parodic voices from the telescreen are part of a heteroglossic pattern in *Nineteen Eighty-Four* which continues Orwell's critique of the perversion of language which is a condition of totalitarianism.

The larger heteroglossic range includes not only official telescreen voices such as the victory announcement just noticed and the proceedings of the Two Minutes' Hate as recreated by Winston in the first chapter of the novel, but also written publications, the children's history book and the subversive 'Book'. There are also the abbreviated instructions which Winston receives at work (Part 1, Chapter 4), and O'Brien's 'hybrid jargon of the Ministries' (p. 150). Speeches of political demagoguery are never far away, though they are not reported, but rather described: a notable instance is the orator on the sixth day of Hate Week, pp. 160–1. As for 'ordinary' speech between people – if it can be called ordinary in the world of this novel – there is a wide variety of samples of different ways of speaking, too great to be analysed here: Mrs Parsons and her appalling children (Part 1, Chapter 2); various colleagues whose speech has eccentric or political connotations (Part 1, Chapter 5); the Cockney of the proles, to be examined shortly, Charrington (pp. 84–8), O'Brien in the scenes at his flat (Part 2, Chapter 8), and in the interrogations (Part 3, Chapters 2–5). The characteristics of all these types of language are exaggerated, parodied, resulting in utterances which are strident and threatening, and grate upon Winston.

In his home and at his work, Winston is assailed by alien voices that come directly from the regime, by the foolish and vacuous speech of his neighbours and the taunts and threats of their children, and by the Newspeak-tainted language of his more orthodox colleagues. Another variety to which he is exposed, on his excursions out of Party territory, is the Cockney of the proles.

We have seen in earlier chapters that Orwell gives a good deal of attention to Cockney: he discusses it in his essays (see Chapter 3, pp. 20–2) as a despised form which seems to offer no alternative to Standard English as a medium of public discourse; and he includes copious representations of the dialect in his fiction, particularly in *Down and Out* and *A Clergyman's Daughter* (to a lesser extent, in *Aspidistra*). Usually Cockney is presented in the novels as a sociolinguistic experience which is alien to the more educated central focaliser of the book, but without any particular positive values. In discussing Dorothy's encounter with the two East End lads in *A Clergyman's Daughter*, however, I entertained the possibility that Cockney, because of its unique historical relationship to Standard English, might assume an 'oppositional' role as an 'antilanguage', challenging the norms of the dominant society (Chapter 6, pp. 105–6). This possibility is relevant to *Nineteen Eighty-Four*, because Winston seems to believe that, as he writes in his diary. 'If there is hope, it lies in the proles' (p. 64): they constitute 85 percent of the population, and if only they could become conscious of their own strength, [they] would have no need to conspire. They needed only to rise up and shake themselves like a horse shaking off flies. (p. 64)[16]

The proles, and Cockney speech, figure half-a-dozen times in *Nineteen Eighty-Four*, but in striking incidents. In Chapter 3 of Part 1, Winston, dreaming of his mother, recalls an encounter with an old man (p. 33). In Chapter 7, just after the 'if . . .' just quoted, he recalls a scene of a mass of women fighting over saucepans, which he first mistook for a riot. Chapter 8 of Part 1 is an excursion into prole territory in which he hears two prole women talking, and some men arguing over the Lottery, and tries to question an old man about his memories. From his hide-out above Charrington's shop he views a washer-woman singing (pp. 123 and 126; 186). When he is held in a cell at the Ministry of Love, a drunken old woman is dumped on him (p. 197). Most of these scenes, and especially in Part 1, Chapter 8, include passages in literary Cockney rendered according to the linguistic conventions which we analysed earlier (Chapter 6, pp. 95ff). Here for example is the old man with moustaches like a prawn recounting a contretemps with a toff:

'One of 'em pushed me once,' said the old man. 'I recollect it as if it was yesterday. It was Boat Race night – terribly rowdy they use to get on Boat Race night – and I bumps into a young bloke on Shaftesbury Avenue. Quite a gent, 'e was – dress shirt, top 'at, black overcoat. 'E was kind of zig-zagging across the pavement, and I bumps into 'im accidental-like. 'E says, "Why can't you look where you're going?" 'e says. I say, "Ju think you've bought the bleeding pavement?" 'E says, "I'll twist your bloody 'ead off if you get fresh with me." I says, "You're drunk. I'll give you in charge in 'alf a minute", I says. An' if you'll believe me, 'e puts 'is 'and on my chest and gives me a shove as pretty near sent me under the wheels of a bus. Well, I was young in them days, and I was going to 'ave fetched 'im one, only – (p. 82)

At this point Winston gives up his attempt to dredge the old man's memory, and reflects poignantly:

They remembered a million useless things, a quarrel with a workmate, a hunt for a lost bicycle pump, the expression on a long-dead sister's face, the swirls of dust on a windy morning seventy years ago: but all the relevant facts were outside the range of their vision. They were like the ant, which can see small objects, but not large ones. (p. 83)

'The larger evils invariably escaped their notice' (p. 66). Winston knows that the proles will not in fact rebel, because they are unable to see the nature of their servitude, and its causes. And as far as the rhetoric of the novel is concerned, his attempt to quiz the old man is undermined, not only by his narrow horizons, but also by the inherently comical nature of the scene – the old man's grotesque appearance, his banter with the barman, the absurd style of the dialogue, in which Winston asks his questions in a verbose and wooden style and the old man offers inconsequential replies. There is nothing dignified, energetic or even inquisitive about the man's speech, so Cockney in this incident remains pathetically humorous.

Despite drawing a blank in his attempt to interview the old man, however, Winston seems to remain optimistic about the revolutionary potential of the proles. When he is established in his rented room, he hears a woman singing a popular song as she pegs out washing in the yard. She has the typical physical grotesqueness of the minor characters, but she sings tunefully, if in Cockney, and the scene is entirely pleasant and optimistic:

Under the window somebody was singing. Winston peeped out, secure in the protection of the muslin curtain. The June sun was still high in the sky, and in the sun-filled court below, a monstrous woman, solid as a Norman pillar, with brawny red forearms and a sacking apron strapped about her middle, was stumping to and fro between a washtub and a clothes line, pegging out a series of square white things which Winston recognised as babies' diapers. Whenever her mouth was not corked with clothes pegs she was singing in a powerful contralto:

It was only an 'opeless fancy,
It passed like an Ipril dye,
But a look an' a word an' the dreams they stirred!
They 'ave stolen my 'eart awye! (pp. 122–3)

She goes on singing for some time, and is the object of Winston's attention again three pages later (by which time Julia is in the room, and is applying make-up while his back is turned), where a second verse of the song is quoted. Winston responds in a quite lyrical paragraph: 'Her voice floated upward with the sweet summer air, very tuneful, charged with a sort of happy melancholy . . .' and so on in that vein. The prole woman has been sentimentalised by the apparent security of his hide-away, and the presence of Julia. The language is so exceptionally sentimental (in the context of this novel) that it is pointedly suspect, a sign of self-deception: we have witnessed this phenomenon earlier, in the pastoral style associated with their first sexual assignation. The irony is brought home violently when the washerwoman reappears, sixty pages later, when Winston and Julia enjoy their last meeting at the rented room. She sings the same song; the lovers watch her, and Winston waxes even more lyrical: '"She's beautiful", he murmured . . . The mystical reverence that he felt for her was somehow mixed up with the aspect of the pale, cloudless sky, stretching away behind the chimney-pots into interminable distance . . .' etc. – nearly two pages of Lawrentian excess. Winston is moved to reaffirm his faith in the proles:

> Sooner or later it would happen, strength would turn into consciousness. The proles were immortal, you could not doubt it when you looked at that valiant figure in the yard. In the end their awakening would come. (p. 188)

The next moment, the 'iron voice' from the concealed telescreen starts mocking them, police burst into the room, they are assaulted and arrested. The illusion is shattered.

The next time Orwell gives a full representation to a Cockney voice, and the last direct prole experience for Winston, is in the common cell before his torture (pp. 196–7). 'An enormous wreck of a woman, aged about sixty, with great tumbling breasts and thick coils of white hair', very drunk, is dumped in his lap. There is no lyricism about the immortal proles this time; just disgust, and for Winston, guilt: she might have been his mother.

> 'Beg pardon, dearie,' she said. I wouldn't 'a sat on you, only the buggers put me there. They dono 'ow to treat a lady, do they?' She paused, patted her breast, and belched. 'Pardon,' she said, 'I ain't meself, quite.'

She leant forward and vomited copiously on the floor.

'Thass better,' she said, leaning back with closed eyes. 'Never keep it down, thass what I say. Get it up while it's fresh on your stomach, like.'

She revived, turned to have another look at Winston and seemed immediately to take a fancy to him. She put a vast arm round his shoulder and drew him towards her, breathing beer and vomit into his face.

'Wass your name, dearie?' she said.

'Smith,' said Winston.

'Smith?' said the woman. 'Thass funny. My name's Smith too. Why,' she added sentimentally, 'I might be your mother!'

She might, thought Winston, be his mother. She was about the right age and physique, and it was probable that people changed somewhat after twenty years in a forced-labour camp.

An ironic understatement, pompously worded; Winston withdraws into his cynical self.

NEWSPEAK AND THE LANGUAGE OF THE PARTY

Newspeak is a fallacy, and Orwell knows it. There is a myth about *Nineteen Eighty-Four* to the effect that Orwell predicts a future in which thought can be controlled by an artificial language. Although, as we have seen, Orwell does understand that there are vital relationships between language and thought, and he does believe that clear thought can be helped or hindered by language choices, he does not suggest that orthodoxy can be imposed by a government-controlled invented language. In fact, the tone of the Newspeak Appendix – which I suspect is rarely read carefully, or not in the context of the other styles of the novel – is quite clearly satirical, more reminiscent of Swift than anything else in the book. Newspeak seems rather to be presented as the implausible fantasy of an overconfident regime. We will return to these issues, but first let us examine the critique of the political and bureaucratic language usages that are actually represented in the book.

What might be called the language of the Party is manifested in a number of interrelated varieties which are described, referred to briefly, or quoted; as usual in this novel (cf. Cockney), the actual amount of speech in the category is small, but the samples are strikingly exaggerated parodies, hence memorable. There is political oratory, for instance Goldstein (pp. 15–17), the style of Big Brother (p. 44), and the orator in Hate Week (pp. 160, 161). There is what Orwell calls 'Duckspeak', evidenced not only in public announcements such as the victory announcement on the telescreen, pp. 255–6, but also in the canteen 'conversation' of an anonymous Party member (pp. 48, 50–1). There is the lying optimism of the 'News' (p. 54). There is the 'hybrid jargon of the Ministries' illustrated in the instructions Winston receives at work (pp. 37, 42) and in a memorandum dictated by O'Brien (p. 150). Finally there is Newspeak itself, said not yet to be spoken by Party members as a whole language (as opposed to the use of Newspeak words within English), but used for editorials in *The Times*. Winston can write Newspeak, but it is not illustrated as such in the main body of the novel, though the 'jargon' consists almost entirely of Newspeak words.

At this point it is worth recalling the list of faults which Orwell found in official English (Chapter 3, pp. 29–30): *dead metaphors, borrowings, archaisms, jargon, meaningless words*, and *ready-made phrases*. All will be seen in the extracts quoted below, though there is no space for a complete analysis here. Of Orwell's six types, the last, 'ready-made phrases', is of immediate relevance to *Nineteen Eighty-Four*:

> 'long strips of words which have already been set in order by someone else' (*CEJL*, IV, p. 163).

The stylistic effect of this prefabricated language is conveyed in the account of Goldstein's 'rapid polysyllabic speech which was a sort of parody of the habitual style of the orators of the Party' (*Nineteen Eighty-Four* p. 16), or the speaker in the canteen, 'someone was talking rapidly and continuously, a harsh gabble almost like the quacking of a duck' (p. 48), whose phrases 'jerked out very rapidly and, as it seemed, all in one piece, like a line of type cast solid' (p. 51). The rapidity and fluency are made possible by the fact that the speaker is simply uttering strings of orthodox jargon and is in no sense *choosing* words in relation to intended meanings or to some state of affairs in the world. Thus language neither springs from consciousness (the speaker is not thinking), nor has any relation to truth. A striking example of the dissociation of language from thought and from facts is the speech of the orator on the sixth day of Hate Week:

His voice, made metallic by the amplifiers, boomed forth an end-less catalogue of [Eurasian] atrocities, massacres, deportations, lootings, rapings, torture of prisoners, bombing of civilians, lying propaganda, unjust aggressions, broken treaties.

In mid-speech he is handed a piece of paper which informs him that the enemy is now not Eurasia, but Eastasia; Eurasia is now an ally:

He unrolled and read it without pausing in his speech. Nothing altered in his voice or manner, or in the content of what he was saying, but suddenly the names were different. (p. 160)

Winston later reflects that:

'the speaker had switched from one line to the other actually in mid-sentence, not only without a pause, but without even break-ing the syntax' (p. 161).

In a sense then it does not matter what the speaker is saying: his utterances are just an orthodox gesture and in no sense an account of a real state of affairs. It is just automated speech, the utterance of a machine. Orwell analyses the process in 'Politics and the Eng-lish Language':

When one watches some tired hack on the platform mechanically repeating the familiar phrases – *bestial atrocities, iron heel, blood-stained tyranny, free peoples of the world, stand shoulder to shoulder* – one often has a curious feeling that one is not watching a live human being but some kind of dummy: a feeling which suddenly becomes stronger at moments when the light catches the speaker's spectacles and turns them into blank discs which seem to have no eyes behind them . . . A speaker who uses that kind of phraseology has gone some distance towards turning himself into a machine. The appropriate noises are coming out of his larynx, but his brain is not involved as it would be if he were choosing his words for himself. If the speech he is making is one that he is accustomed to make over and over again, he may be almost unconscious of what he is saying, as when one utters the responses in church. And this reduced state of consciousness, if not indispensable, is at any rate favourable to political conformity. (*CEJL*, IV, pp. 166–7)

Orwell had parodied this kind of speaker some years earlier, in *Coming Up for Air*, when George Bowling listens to a 'well-known anti-Fascist' at a Left Book Club meeting:

> his voice came across to me as a kind of burr-burr-burr, with now and again a phrase that caught my attention.
>
> 'Bestial atrocities. . . . Hideous outburst of sadism. . . . Rubber truncheons. . . . Concentration camps. . . . Iniquitous persecution of the Jews. . . . Back to the Dark Ages. . . . European civilization. . . . Act before it is too late. . . . Indignation of all decent peoples . . .' [etc.]
>
> You know the line of talk. These chaps can churn it out by the hour. Just like a gramophone. Turn the handle, press the button, and it starts. (p. 145)

Here we have the same idea of the political speaker as a machine working without consciousness, and, interestingly, the phrases George catches are excellent examples of the jargon, stock phrases and meaningless words which Orwell attacks in the essay, including one, 'bestial atrocities' which is actually used in the essay. The 'gramophone' metaphor for political speaking is earlier found in *Wigan Pier*, p. 190.

Returning to *Nineteen Eighty-Four*, Orwell follows the passage from the essay in describing Winston's perception of the speaker in the canteen, even to the metaphor of 'two blank discs instead of eyes'.

> it was almost impossible to distinguish a single word . . . And yet, though you could not actually hear what the man was saying, you could not be in any doubt about its general nature . . . Whatever it was, you could be certain that every word of it was pure orthodoxy, pure Ingsoc . . . Winston had a curious feeling that this was not a real human being but some kind of dummy. It was not the man's brain that was speaking, it was his larynx . . . it was a noise uttered in unconsciousness, like the quacking of a duck. (pp. 50–1)

'Duckspeak' may be a suitable Newspeak word for describing the gabbling style (though too humorous and metaphorical for Newspeak really), but the real evil being attacked is conceptual, the idea of speech which issues mechanically without reference to thought or to truth. When, at the end of the novel, the telescreen announces, in Duckspeak, 'the greatest victory in human history' (passage quoted on p. 206 above), or when 'an eager, youthful voice' claims that 'We have won the battle for production!' (p. 54; passage quoted above, Ch. 2, p. 17), the reader knows that it is immaterial to wonder whether this is true or not, and we know that the telescreen announcer is not even thinking about what he says. Orthodox feelings are being communicated and invoked, and that is about all one can say.

A second version of the language of the Party which appears briefly but strikingly in the novel is a clipped bureaucratic jargon, 'the hybrid jargon of the Ministries'. Winston's working instructions are written in this mode:

> times 17.3.84 bb speech malreported africa rectify
> times 19.12.83 forecasts 3 yp 4th quarter 83 misprints verify current issue
> times 14.2.84 miniplenty malquoted chocolate rectify
> times 3.12.83 reporting bb dayorder doubleplusungood refs unpersons rewrite fullwise upsub antefiling (p. 37; Oldspeak translation of the fourth order on p. 42)

O'Brien dictates into his 'speakwrite' a memo phrased in a variant of this style:

> 'Items one comma five comma seven approved fullwise stop suggestion contained item six doubleplus ridiculous verging crimethink cancel stop unproceed constructionwise antegetting plusfull estimates machinery overheads stop end message.' (p. 150)

What we have here are exaggerations of a clipped, bureaucratic style which (ignoring for a moment the Newspeak vocabulary) is familiar in office or institutional practice and also resembles telegrams. There is an absence of capitalisation and punctuation; a fondness for shortening words – '4th', 'refs' – and phrases – 'bb' (= Big Brother), 'yp' (= year plan); omission of inflections on the ends of words – 'bb's' – and of articles, linking verbs, auxiliaries and prepositions – '*the* suggestion *is* ridiculous', 'refs *to* unpersons'. The style has affinities to the language of telegrams, which is stripped

of low-information words to save cost. More specifically, the elliptical style of Newspeak and of the memoranda in *Nineteen Eighty-
Four* has been linked to what was known as 'cablese', the abbreviated
style in which reporters used to send in their stories to the newspapers and radio.[17] The media associations of cablese would have
been significant to Orwell given his concern in the novel with the
suspect veracity of public accounts of events; and we should note
in this connection the notoriously compressed conventional style of
newspaper headlines. Insofar as media language is a deformation of
language, a deviation from ordinary or demotic speech, it becomes
an unclear, unanalytical, representation of reality: the compression
of headlines, for example, has an inherent potential for ambiguity
or double meaning.[18]

It might be claimed that these clippings and ellipses are done for
speed and efficiency, or to save space when fitting headlines in
narrow newspaper columns, but it is more likely that their function
is to *symbolise* speed and efficiency, and power (note that Winston's
instructions, and O'Brien's memo, are packed with verbs of command), on the part of the person who communicates in this abbreviated mode. Let us for a moment pursue the office or institutional
association, rather than the media connection, since the texts quoted
above are more like office memoranda than news stories. (It should
be noted that we need to think about the traditional, pre-informa-
tion technology, institutional practices which would have been known
to Orwell. These have only recently been revolutionalised – but by
no means completely – by word-processing, the storage of massive
amounts of data on small computers and its ready accessibility –
even to managers – , networking, electronic mail, fax, etc. No doubt
these facilities have transformed the structure and style of institutional and media communications.) If a manager or head of department scribbles 'refs pse asap' on some candidate's application form
before passing it down to the secretary who has to send out for the
references, he (more likely a man) is communicating busy-ness and
authority. I do not think this style can be used 'upwards': a secretary (most likely a woman) would be more likely to address her
boss in polite, full sentences on one of those ubiquitous sticky note-
lets: 'Mr Brown: would you please confirm that this candidate's
qualifications are appropriate before I send out for her references'.
The manager using the brusque abbreviations is requiring the addressee to work out, by reference to institutional conventions, what

the full form of the shortened message would be: putting the onus on the inferior addressee. It is the use of a code, and of a code symbolising membership of an élite in-group.

Jargon, in institutional settings, works in the same way; Orwell had already recognised that jargon is a property of (intellectual) élites:

> English is peculiarly subject to jargons. Doctors, scientists, businessmen, officials, sportsmen, economists, and political theorists all have their characteristic perversion of the language, which can be studied in the appropriate magazines from the *Lancet* to the *Labour Monthly*. ('The English People,' written 1944, *CEJL*, III, p. 43)

The Newspeak words in the orders quoted above are themselves a form of jargon – specialised words in technical contexts, emanating from the powerful who somehow own the register and have the power to make judgement through it: 'malreported', 'malquoted', 'doubleplusungood'. There are also ordinary technical jargon phrases in these messages, for example 'machinery overheads'. If jargon symbolises privilege through specialised knowledge, it also tends to prefabrication: the jargon of a profession is a vocabulary of stock words known in advance of utterance; in 'The English People' Orwell connects it with ready-made phrases, which as we have seen are an enemy of thought. Similarly, jargon can lead to euphemism and lying; and to doublethink. A nice example is 'verify' in Winston's second instruction: he is told to check a 'misprint' in an old edition of the *Times* by referring to the current issue, and restore the truth by correcting the misprint. Reading between the lines, we realise that the December 1983 production forecasts were not fulfilled, so the predictions have to be changed after the event to conform with what was (perhaps) actually produced. Winston's job is 'rectification' (p. 42), a virtuous-sounding jargon word which in fact means the falsification of the official record of the historical past in line with the needs of the political present.

In 'Politics and the English Language' Orwell said that his concern was with language 'merely as an instrument for expressing and not for concealing or preventing thought' (*CEJL*, IV, p. 169, cf. above, p. 33). *Nineteen Eighty-Four* parodies certain varieties of political and managerial language, encouraged by the rulers of

Oceania, criticising them on the grounds that – through jargon, euphemism, prefabrication, dead metaphors, stock phrases and the like – they dissociate thought and language, turning the speaker into an unconscious machine that is not expressing thought, and indeed, through the deadness and the purely symbolic character of his language, is prevented from thinking. The skills of doublethink, and the power of Inner Party status, bestow upon O'Brien and on the anonymous source of Winston's instructions a further dimension of language, a manipulative authority which can cause subordinates to assist in the concealment of material reality. So far in these processes, Newspeak figures as an élite jargon symbolising privilege and orthodoxy. But the rulers of the totalitarian society intend Newspeak to have an even more powerful role. It will not simply cloud the truth on the occasions when it is used. When, by 2050, it becomes the sole medium known by members of the Inner and Outer Parties, it will totally shape what they can say and therefore what they can think.

Orwell puts into the minds of the regime an extreme version of the theory which is known in modern linguistics as *linguistic determinism*.[19] Let me say at once that the extreme version, not only as expressed in Newspeak but in any context, is discountenanced by any sensible person and is in any case neither provable nor disprovable; and the extreme version is not proposed by the American anthropological linguists who first discussed the arguments about language determining thought. The theory is usually credited to Edward Sapir and Benjamin Lee Whorf, and is more popularly expressed in the writings of the latter. Whorf, a student of native American ('Indian') languages, which seem to be strikingly different from the European tongues, believed that languages could differ radically in their basic structures, and that these differences could have the effect of 'packaging' reality differently for speakers. Thus, for example, speakers of languages which have different tense systems might possess different mental pictures of the way time is organised. Whorf's arguments are provocatively phrased – he was an amateur enthusiast for language rather than an academic whose way of expressing claims would have to be more formal and cautious. His evidence is anecdotal, and he paraphrases his examples from indigenous American languages to make the point accessible to English readers. The fact that he can translate the exotic, other-reality, material shows that the different world-views are not accessible only to the speakers of the languages concerned. If an English speaker can, through translation, understand the concepts of time encoded in Hopi, and presumably vice-versa, then thought or world-view is not absolutely constrained by the language one speaks. The likelihood is – and this is supported by modern cognitive psychology – that different forms of linguistic organisation (for example different styles or vocabularies) will *dispose* a language user to chop up experience differently, will encourage a *tendency* to see the world in a specifically-slanted way. There is no suggestion that a deliberate organisation of language, like Newspeak, can produce a diminished, fixed and inescapable world-view in its speakers. However, the Newspeak proposal, though extreme and certainly unachievable, is quite closely related to the more plausible claim that language *encourages* a certain view of the world; closely enough to produce a bit of a chill even in readers who see through Newspeak. One has to think twice, and suppress a gut reaction that there is something plausible about Newspeak. This double-take reaction is the effect of the deadpan style of the Newspeak Appendix; the technique resembles the satirical strategy of Swift, whom Orwell much admired (he first read *Gulliver's Travels* at the age of eight).

The reader of *Nineteen Eighty-Four* can know a good deal about Newspeak even before encountering the Appendix, through the examples of its vocabulary which occur in the text and through the enthusiastic description given in Part 1, Chapter 5 by Syme, a Newspeak expert working on the Dictionary. Newspeak is a reduced version of English with a small, carefully controlled vocabulary including a number of invented compound words such as 'Minitrue', 'Minipax', 'Newspeak' itself, 'doublethink', 'unperson'; similar compounds in the novel appear to be Newspeak but in the Appendix are not: 'thoughtcrime' appears in the text but is replaced by 'crimethink' in the Appendix. At any rate, the habit of compounding appears to be a structural preference of this variety of English. Neither Duckspeak nor cablese is actually to be equated with Newspeak, though the Duckspeak *effect* is provided for in the Newspeak programme; in the novel Duckspeak is built on the ordinary political jargons which Orwell criticised in his essays, but in the future it will ideally be produced by polysyllabic Newspeak words. It is important to grasp that no 'pure' example of Newspeak is given in the text of the novel: this absence is covered by the admission that the language will not be completed until 2050, no one speaks it and so far it is used solely for *Times* editiorials. The official varieties of English used by bureaucrats and politicians in 1984 are far indeed from Newspeak, though their language is peppered with bits of the vocabulary, even the odd term producing a very alienating effect. The point being made is surely that Newspeak is a long way short of completion.

Syme's account of Newspeak gives an informative succinct account of Newspeak: he stresses the central principle of reduction of vocabulary, the production by compounding of systems of related terms based on the same root – 'good', 'ungood', 'plusgood' and 'doubleplusgood' in his example – and the central function of Newspeak, to control thought:

> 'Don't you see that the whole aim of Newspeak is to narrow the range of thought? In the end we shall make thoughtcrime literally impossible, because there will be no words to express it. Every concept that can ever be needed will be expressed by exactly *one* word, with its meaning rigidly defined and all its subsidiary meanings rubbed out and forgotten ... the Revolution will be complete when the language is perfect.' (*Nineteen Eighty-Four*, pp. 48–9)

The Appendix's way of putting this is quoted below, pp. 223–4.

Although the general idea of Newspeak can be gleaned from the text of the novel (with also an indication of its essential absurdity, as we shall see), it is only through the Appendix that we fully realise that Newspeak is designed to be a self-contained linguistic system replacing, not grafted on, the English language. It is organised into three vocabulary categories: the 'A vocabulary' which consists of ordinary words such as 'hit', 'run', 'dog'; the 'B vocabulary' which comprises the political compounds which have already been illustrated from the text; and the 'C vocabulary' which is a supplementary list of scientific terms. The language has its own simplified grammar, its rules for inflection, compounding and suffixing (pp. 259–60). When set out in a 'grammar' in the Appendix, Newspeak has much more the appearance of a complete constructed system than that of a variety of English. It would have been clear to contemporary educated readers with linguistic interests that Orwell's model was the system of *Basic English* proposed by C. K. Ogden in 1930, which drew a lot of attention in the 1930s and 1940s.[20]

Basic ('British American Scientific International Commercial') English was designed as an easy-to-learn international English, its simplicity achieved by reduction of vocabulary to an amazing 850 words which, Odgen claimed, could serve to render most meanings communicated normally in the full vocabulary. Like Newspeak, the Basic vocabulary is classified into three categories, two of them with two sub-categories. The classification systems do not of course coincide. Orwell seems to have been well informed about Basic, and to have favoured its chance of becoming an international language higher than the artificial languages such as Esperanto and Interglossa. He attributed to it nothing of the negative ideological role which characterises Newspeak, quite the reverse: in one approving comment he suggests that translation into Basic could deflate 'the oratory of statesmen and publicists', 'high-sounding phrases' (*CEJL*, III, p. 244; see also pp. 107–8). So Orwell is not attacking Basic through Newspeak; Basic is used rather as an analogy, an aid to readers to imagine what kind of a linguistic system Newspeak might be.

Note that there is one further major difference between Basic and Newspeak. Basic was designed as a supplementary language existing alongside natural English and with specific international functions; Newspeak is intended to *replace* English as the sole language of Party members, the complete resource they could draw on for all communicative functions. The absurdity of carrying out all our discourse in a very restricted language is palpable.

Orwell almost certainly had in mind a famous parallel absurdity in *Gulliver's Travels*.[21] In Chapter 5 of Part 3, Gulliver visits the Academy of Lagado, the capital of Balnibarbi. The city and its inhabitants are, like London and the proles in *Nineteen Eighty-Four*, in a sorry state:

The next Morning after my Arrival he took me in his Chariot to see the Town, which is about half the Bigness of *London*; but the Houses very strangely built, and most of them out of Repair. The People in the Streets walked fast, looked wild, their eyes fixed, and were generally in Rags. (*Gulliver's Travels*, p. 149)

The buildings and agriculture are ruinous because they are awaiting improved methods of construction and farming to be devised by members of the Academy (a satirical portrait of the Royal Society). The examples of the projects of the academicians which are presented to Gulliver are without exception preposterous and unworkable, such as could be devised only by an intellectual elite out of touch with commonsense reality (cf. the Party in our novel): extracting sun-beams from cucumbers, building houses from the roof down, dyeing cobwebs by feeding coloured flies to spiders, etc., etc. Two of the projects are linguistic:

> The first project was to shorten Discourse by cutting Polysyl-lables into one, and leaving out Verbs and Participles; because in Reality all things imaginable are but Nouns.
> The other, was a Scheme for entirely abolishing all Words what-soever . . . [S]ince Words are only Names for *Things*, it would be more convenient for all Men to carry about them, such *Things* as were necessary to express the particular Business they are to dis-course on. And this Invention would certainly have taken place, to the great Ease as well as Health of the Subject, if the Women in Conjunction with the Vulgar and Illiterate had not threatned to raise a Rebellion, unless they might be allowed the Liberty to speak with their Tongues, after the Manner of their Forefathers: Such constant irreconcileable Enemies to Science are the com-mon People. However, many of the most Learned and Wise ad-here to the new Scheme of expressing themselves by *Things*; which hath only this Inconvenience attending it; that if a Man's Busi-ness be very great and of various Kinds, he must be obliged in Proportion to carry a greater Bundle of *Things* upon his Back, unless he can afford one or two strong Servants to attend him. (*Gulliver's Travels*, p. 158)

The reduction of language in the first scheme has some resemblance to the 'clipping' which I pointed out in the style of the 'hybrid jargon' of the Ministry of Truth, and to the merger of parts of speech in Newspeak. The uselessness of the second scheme has a closer relationship to Newspeak. Notice that, like Newspeak, this project is framed in a class distinction: only the 'most Learned and Wise', communicate through 'Things' carried on the back, as the Party members are to use Newspeak; the Lagado equivalent of the proles continue to use their tongues, as the proles retain Oldspeak. It is implied that the elite academicians, anticipating their Ingsoc descend-ants, are far from 'learned and wise', they are in fact utterly foolish to employ such an unworkable system of communication. Now the real inconveniences of Newspeak, as illuminated by this analogy, are the limitations of a finite system, and the lack of provision for flexibility of meaning. You can only carry so many 'Things' on your back and in your pockets, and these are bound to be far less than the topics you will want to talk about: real human language is infinitely creative and cannot be replaced by a restricted set of signs. Equally, meanings in natural language are flexible and abstract, quite unlike the fixity and precision of the academicians' 'Things' or the fixed concepts of Newspeak.[22]

These are just two of the fundamental problems which have not been examined by the inventors of Newspeak. If we do not read the bland academic prose of the Appendix too quickly, we will fetch up against other assumptions which have not been thought through properly. Here is the opening of the Appendix, quoted at length to give a reasonable flavour of its style, with tendentious statements about narrowing the language and thought which parallel the account by Syme quoted above:

Newspeak was the official language of Oceania and had been devised to meet the ideological needs of Ingsoc, or English socialism. In the year 1984 there was not as yet anyone who used Newspeak as his sole means of communication, either in speech or writing. The leading articles in *The Times* were written in it, but this was a *tour de force* which could only be carried out by a specialist. It was expected that Newspeak would have finally superseded Oldspeak (or Standard English, as we should call it) by about the year 2050. Meanwhile it gained ground steadily, all Party members tending to use Newspeak words and grammatical constructions more and more in their everyday speech. The version in use in 1984, and embodied in the Ninth and Tenth editions of the Newspeak Dictionary, was a provisional one, and contained many superfluous words and archaic formations which were due to be suppressed later. It is with the final, perfected version, as embodied in the Eleventh Edition of the Dictionary, that we are concerned here.

The purpose of Newspeak was not only to provide a medium of expression for the world-view and mental habits proper to the devotees of Ingsoc, but to make all other modes of thought impossible. It was intended that when Newspeak had been adopted once and for all and Oldspeak forgotten, a heretical thought –

that is, a thought diverging from the principles of Ingsoc – should be literally unthinkable, at least so far as thought is dependent on words. The vocabulary was so constructed as to give an exact and often very subtle expression to every meaning that a Party member could properly wish to express, while excluding all other meanings and also the possibility of arriving at them by indirect methods. This was done partly by the invention of new words, but chiefly by eliminating undesirable words and by stripping such words as remained of unorthodox meanings. (*Nineteen Eighty-Four*, pp. 258–9)

This kind of plain expository language is not found anywhere else in the novel, though it bears some resemblance to the style of 'the book' passed by O'Brien to Winston, though that is much more authoritarian and argumentative. This style has no affinity to the more excitable and fragmentary thoughts and speech of the main focaliser Winston, nor to the demotic rhetoric of Orwell himself, as found in his passionately critical essays. The Newspeak Appendix could not be written in the familiar Orwellian voice, for that voice could not refrain from crying that the Newspeak proposal is cynical self-delusion, humbug, swindle and perversion. And this is not an official version issuing from the Party, since it is written in Oldspeak.

Orwell seems to have created a viewpoint which is both distinct from his own persona, and quite outside the world of the fiction. To say that this is the voice of 'the narrator' would be a cop-out, for we have seen that there is no distinguishable narrator in *Nineteen Eighty-Four*, and the novel is certainly not narrated in the manner in which the Appendix is phrased. The voice of the Appendix may plausibly be attributed to a new, distinct and anonymous figure with Gulliver-like characteristics: a traveller, or in modern terms an anthropologist or a linguist, who studies a foreign society and its products and reports with apparent objectivity what he sees and hears. Cues to this role include the pronoun 'we' used twice in the first paragraph. The first 'we' (line six) refers to the writer and his readership: Oldspeak is explained in terms of what it would be called in the 'home' culture, somewhat as Gulliver makes Lagado more comprehensible by comparing it to London. This is a minimal cue, but 'we' is a demanding word, encouraging the reader to participate by preferring Newspeak to the English of the 'real' culture. The second 'we', at the end of the paragraph, has a different meaning: it is the impersonal 'we' of science, suppressing an 'I' which might seem to flag personal intervention inappropriately.

There is no 'I' in the text; contrast the writings in the mode of Orwell's persona, which use it liberally. Overt modality, or judgement from the point of view of the writer, is minimal. It would have been entirely inappropriate to the style for the sentence at the end of the above extract to speak of '*ruthlessly* stripping' words of unorthodox meanings, though that is just the sort of thing Orwell would have said if he had been writing in his own personal voice. Such modal judgements as do occur, for example 'superfluous words and archaic formations' and 'perfected' at the end of the first paragraph, or 'proper' in the first sentence of the second paragraph, or 'And rightly so' on p. 264 referring to euphony taking precedence over grammatical regularity, are to be attributed to the sources the Appendix is reporting, and are to be read ironically.

The 'objective' style of science or factual reporting is also suggested, unobtrusively, by a high proportion of passive verbs and by some nominal forms replacing full verbs; both move personal involvement into the background: 'had been devised', 'were written', 'be carried out', 'embodied', 'to be suppressed', etc., and 'communication', 'medium of expression', 'invention'. The nominal style is not taken to extremes, and there is none of the polysyllabic, Greek- and Latin-derived technical terminology which typifies the style of science: the genre of the Appendix seems to be 'objective report' rather than 'science'.

Orwell follows Swift, then, in using a non-judgemental, matter-of-fact style to report a project which to him was not only absurd (displayed in Newspeak 'examples' which are so self-evidently barbarous, fatuous and trivial that illustration is hardly necessary), but worse, philosophically and morally ill-grounded. Showing through the plain style are unanswered and unqualified questions of the most fundamental kind. Philosophically, the proponents of Newspeak take an extreme nominalist position, believing that meanings derive from words, not the other way around. They add to this an extreme determinism – that is, they believe that thoughts are controlled by words. We saw in Chapter 3 that Orwell, like Winston, held the opposite point of view: a fundamental faith in solid objects and in individual thought, and a passionate conviction that language should be used in such a way as to communicate without deception these elemental priorities. Of course, 'realist' and 'individualist' arguments do not get a look-in in the Newspeak proposal, but we would expect that gap; what does come through as irresponsible is the total failure to examine any of the sweeping nominalist and deterministic assumptions that are trotted out in the text, for example, the beginning of the second paragraph.

It is worth adding, briefly, that because the Newspeak project is theoretically ill-founded, it is inherently impracticable. We are bound to wonder how it is proposed to abolish words, how you prevent the remaining words having illicit meanings, how even a regime as powerful as that of Oceania can stop the normal processes of invention, semantic enrichment and natural change. Language is indeed a powerful weapon in the hands of the rulers of an unequal society.[23] However, as Orwell believed and as Winston wanted to believe, it is also an effective instrument of challenge, developing naturally and largely outside the reach of governmental and artificial control. That is why restrictive and prescriptive official bodies such as the French Academy have always experienced an uphill struggle, and why, fortunately, no deliberately contrived artificial language has ever been successfully established as a natural form of speech acquired spontaneously by the next generation. Planned forms of language like Basic English never catch on; unofficial developments such as the codes of CB radio[24] may be short-lived, but have their period of intense significance as yet another challenge to the official monologism of our culture. Winston need not have been so pessimistic.

I think it is characteristic of Orwell's fundamental traditionalism and romanticism that, in the Newspeak Appendix, he lets literature have the last laugh on Newspeak. The natural creativity and the semantic openness, richness and suggestivity of a real language like English are exploited to the full in literary texts. These properties, as we have seen, are quite alien to Newspeak, whose basic drive is towards closure and explicitness. Every centralised nationalist regime needs a Literature to express its ideological essence; but in 1984, the National Literature part of the project looked set to defeat Newspeak:

> Considerations of prestige made it desirable to preserve the memory of certain historical figures, while at the same time bringing their achievements into line with the philosophy of Ingsoc. Various writers, such as Shakespeare, Milton, Swift, Byron, Dickens, and some others were therefore in the process of translation . . . These

translations were a slow and difficult business, and it was not expected that they would be finished before the first decade of the twenty-first century . . . It was chiefly in order to allow time for the preliminary work of translation that the final adoption of Newspeak had been fixed for so late a date as 2050.

Notes

Chapter 1

1. I have made full use of B. Crick, *George Orwell: A Life* (London: Secker & Warburg, 1980; 2nd edn., 1992). See also M. Sheldon, *Orwell: The Authorised Biography* (London, Heinneman, 1991); P. Stansky and W. Abrahams, *The Unknown Orwell* (London: Constable, 1972) and *Orwell: The Transformation* (London: Constable,1979); J. Buddicom, *Eric and Us: A Remembrance of George Orwell* (London: Frewin, 1974). George Woodcock, *The Crystal Spirit* (London: Jonathan Cape, 1967) is an excellent critical memoir. W. J. West, *The Larger Evils* (Edinburgh: Canongate Press, 1992), discusses Orwell's later work in the light of new materials, concentrating particularly on Orwell's own experience of censorship and surveillance in England. The four-volume *Collected Essays, Journalism and Letters*, ed. Sonia Orwell and Ian Angus (Harmondsworth: Penguin, 1968) is an invaluable source, and each volume contains a biographical summary for the years it covers.
2. According to Crick, *George Orwell*, p. 7.
3. Ibid, p. 152.
4. See Crick, *George Orwell*, pp. 357ff. for an account of the reception of *Animal Farm*.

Chapter 2

1. 'Why I Write' (1946), *CEJL*, I, 30); G. Woodcock, *The Crystal Spirit* (London: Jonathan Cape, 1967) Part 4, pp. 229ff.
2. See R. Fowler, *Linguistic Criticism* (Oxford: Oxford University Press, 1986).
3. See R. Fowler, *Linguistics and the Novel* (London: Methuen, 1983) 2nd edn, on internal and external perspective. The 'personal voice' is discussed further in Chapter 4, and the compositional problems of point of view in Orwell's fiction in Chapter 8.
4. Useful critical introductions to Orwell's fiction include J. R. Hammond, *A George Orwell Companion* (London: Macmillan, 1982); R. A. Lee, *Orwell's Fiction* (Notre Dame: University of Notre Dame Press, 1969); V. Meyers, *George Orwell* (London: Macmillan, 1991). Sources for the contemporary critical reception of his books are collected in J. Meyers (ed.) *George Orwell: The Critical Heritage* (London: Routledge & Kegan Paul, 1975). Other important essays are contained in R. Williams (ed.) *George Orwell: A Collection of Critical Essays* (Englewood Cliffs, New Jersey: Prentice-Hall, 1974).
5. On Russian Formalism and on Czech and French structuralism see

T. Bennett *Formalism and Marxism* (London: Methuen, 1979); J. Culler, *Structuralist Poetics* (London: Routledge & Kegan Paul, 1975); V. Erlich, *Russian Formalism: History, Doctrine* (The Hague: Mouton, 1965); J. Ehrmann (ed.) *Structuralism* (New York: Doubleday-Anchor, 1970); T. Hawkes, *Structuralism and Semiotics* (London: Methuen, 1977); L. T. Lemon and M. J. Reis (eds) *Russian Formalist Criticism* (Lincoln, Nebraska: University of Nebraska Press, 1965).

6. R. Jakobson, 'Closing Statement: Linguistics and Poetics', in T. A. Sebeok (ed.) *Style in Language* (Cambridge, Massachusetts: MIT Press, 1960) pp. 350, 352.

7. The whole area of stylistics, its various specialisms, its history and its antecedents, and related topics and approaches in linguistics and in literary theory, is covered in K. Wales, *A Dictionary of Stylistics* (London: Longman, 1989). For a descriptive and analytical review see D. Birch, *Language, Literature, and Critical Practice* (London: Routledge, 1989). A selection of interesting books which illustrate various stylistic approaches would include R. Carter (ed.) *Language and Literature: An Introductory Reader in Stylistics* (London: Allen & Unwin, 1982); A Cluysenaar, *Introduction to Literary Stylistics* (London: Batsford Academic, 1976); D. C. Freeman (ed.) *Linguistics and Literary Style* (New York: Holt, Rinehart & Winston, 1970); G. N. Leech, *A Linguistic Guide to English Poetry* (London: Longman, 1969); H. G. Widdowson, *Stylistics and the Teaching of Literature* (London: Longman, 1975). See also the references for 'linguistic criticism', note 10.

8. M. A. K. Halliday, 'The Linguistic Study of Literary Texts' (1964), reprinted in S. Chatman and S. R. Levin (eds) *Essays on the Language of Literature* (Boston: Houghton Mifflin, 1967) p. 217.

9. The term 'literary competence' for the special knowledge which allows a reader to read literature *as literature* was coined by J. Culler, *Structuralist Poetics* (London: Routledge & Kegan Paul, 1975). For discussion of the issues, and an attempt to locate literary knowledge within social formation and history, see R. Fowler, *Literature as Social Discourse* (London: Batsford Academic, 1981).

10. 'Linguistic criticism' or 'critical linguistics' has its origin in the late 1970s with the work of a group of linguists who used a Hallidayan functional grammar to explore a theory, and a practical analytic understanding, of the way texts mediate ideology in social settings. The pioneer works were R. Fowler, R. Hodge, G. Kress and T. Trew, *Language and Control* (London: Routledge & Kegan Paul, 1979); R. Hodge and G. Kress, *Language as Ideology* ([1979], (London: Routledge, 1993) 2nd edn. For a recent application, see R. Fowler, *Language in the News* (London: Routledge, 1991). Critical linguistics was originally concerned with any texts, not specifically literary, but especially public, official texts. 'Linguistic criticism' is a rewording (parallel to 'feminist criticism', 'Marxist criticism', etc.) to signal the adaptation to literature in the 1980s. See R. Fowler, *Linguistic Criticism* (note 2 above) and *Literature as Social Discourse*

(note 9). Recent introductory books which employ this, or a closely related, approach include M. Birch and M. O'Toole, *Functions of Style* (London: Pinter, 1988); R. Carter and P. Simpson (eds) *Language, Discourse and Literature: An Introductory Reader in Discourse Stylistics* (London: Unwin Hyman, 1989); M. Toolan, *Narrative: A Critical Linguistic Introduction* (London: Routledge, 1988); M. Toolan (ed.) *Language, Text and Context: Essays in Stylistics* (London: Routledge, 1992)

11. M. A. K. Halliday, *An Introduction to Functional Grammar* (London: Edward Arnold, 2nd ed., 1994); *Language as Social Semiotic* (London: Arnold, 1978). A rare literary study by Halliday which has been very influential is 'Linguistic Function and Literary Style: An Inquiry into the Language of William Golding's *The Inheritors*', in S. Chatman (ed.) *Literary Style: A Symposium* (New York and Oxford: Oxford University Press, 1971) pp. 330–64.

12. M. A. K. Halliday, 'Language Structure and Language Function,' in J. Lyons (ed.) *New Horizons in Linguistics* (Harmondsworth: Penguin, 1970) p. 142.

Chapter 3

1. See J. Milroy and L. Milroy, *Authority in Language* (London: Routledge & Kegan Paul, 1985), Ch. 2.

2. A readable modern textbook on sociolinguistics is M. Montgomery, *An Introduction to Language and Society* (London: Routledge, 1986). A stimulating collection of essays on the social meanings of language, M. A. K. Halliday, *Language as Social Semiotic* (London: Arnold, 1978) perhaps provides a dimension missing in Orwell's argument, that specific social dialects encode their own special significances and 'package' reality in distinctive ways.

3. On dialect in fiction, see N. Page, *Speech in the English Novel* (London: Longman, 1973); G. N. Leech and M. H. Short, *Style in Fiction* (London: Longman, 1981).

4. H. Adams (ed.) *Critical Theory since Plato* (New York: Harcourt Brace Jovanovich, 1971) p. 434.

5. For extensive samples of transcribed conversational data, see J. Svartvik and R. Quirk (eds) *A Corpus of English Conversation* (Lund: C. W. K. Gleerup, 1980).

6. Orwell saw clearly the need to describe the speech/writing distinction. In 'Propaganda and Demotic Speech' he advocates collecting sample recordings of speech in order to 'formulate the rules of spoken English and find out how it differs from the written language' (*CEJL*, III, 166). For modern work on the distinction, see M. A. K. Halliday, *Spoken and Written Language* (Oxford: Oxford University Press, 1989); M. A. K. Halliday, 'Spoken and Written Modes of Meaning', in R. Horowitz and S. Jay Samuels (eds) *Comprehending Oral and Written Language* (San Diego: Academic Press, 1987) pp. 55–82 (see also other chapters in this volume). The functions of orality and

literacy in culture and history have been much more extensively studied than the grammar of oral language: see, for example, D. Tannen (ed.) *Spoken and Written Language: Exploring Orality and Literacy* (Norwood New Jersey: Ablex, 1982); also oracy in education: see M. Maclure, T. Phillips and A. Wilkinson (eds) *Oracy Matters* (Milton Keynes: Open University Press, 1988).

It is worth noting the reasons why the grammar of speech has been little studied. One was the technical difficulty of procuring good samples to study prior to the availability of portable tape-recorders in the 1960s. Far more important, though, was the bias in linguistics towards the 'grammatically correct' forms found in writing which I have mentioned. Even more so was the prestige of official and literary writings in literate societies and especially in the world of education: cf. the discussion of Orwell's views on 'Standard English'.

7. On standardisation see J. Milroy and L. Milroy, *Authority*. According to these linguists, Standard English does not exist as an identifiable linguistic variety that might be described. Standardisation is an ideological practice, a set of attitudes and proscriptions whose main characteristic is 'intolerance of optional variability in language' (ibid, p. 26).

Official attitudes to 'Standard English' in contemporary education are clearly expressed in the *Report of the Committee of Inquiry into the Teaching of English Language* (London: Her Majesty's Stationery Office, 1988) (the 'Kingman Report') and in the various curriculum documents that followed it.

8. For the concept of 'guardians' of language, see Milroy and Milroy, *Authority*, pp. 11–18. They have an appreciative account of the unusual (for the complaints tradition) 'depth, breadth and incisiveness' of Orwell's position (ibid, pp. 44–8).

9. Orwell was well aware that his 'defence of the English language' might be misread as a sentimental desire to conserve old values, and he attempted to preempt this misunderstanding in one passage in 'Politics and the English Language': e.g. 'it has nothing to do with archaism, with the salvaging of obsolete words and turns of speech, or with the setting-up of a 'standard English' which must never be departed from' (*CEJL*, IV, 168).

10. Sources for Orwell's criticisms are the essays 'The English People' and 'Propaganda and Demotic Speech' in *CJEL*, III, his column 'As I Please' also in III, and 'Politics and the English Language' in IV.

11. F. de Saussure, trans. Wade Baskin, *Course in General Linguistics* [1916], reprinted with an introduction by J. Culler (Glasgow: Fontana, 1974) pp. 71ff.

Chapter 4

1. B. Crick, *George Orwell: A Life* (London: Secker & Warburg, 1980) p. 116; cf. p. 123 on 'florid' and 'workmanlike' styles; p. 133 on 'purple' and 'plain'.
2. Ibid, pp. 151–2.

3. For an introduction to the multiplicity of meanings of the term 'style', see K. Wales, *A Dictionary of Stylistics* (London: Longman, 1989) pp. 435–7; G. Leech and M. Short, *Style in Fiction* (London: Longman, 1981) chs. 1 and 2.

4. M. A. K. Halliday, A. McIntosh and P. Strevens, *The Linguistic Sciences and Language Teaching* (London: Longman, 1964) p. 87. For an elementary account, see M. Montgomery, *An Introduction to Language and Society* (London: Methuen, 1986). Ch. 6.

5. The germ of this idea is in Halliday's earliest discussion of register: see M. A. K. Halliday, A. McIntosh and P. Strevens, *Linguistic Sciences*, p. 87: 'One sentence from any of these and many more such situation types would enable us to identify it correctly'. For development of the idea in terms of cue and model, see R. Fowler, 'Oral models in the Press', in M. Maclure, T. Phillips and A. Wilkinson (eds) *Oracy Matters* (Milton Keynes: Open University Press, 1988) pp. 135–46.

6. Respectively, W. J. West (ed.) *The War Broadcasts* (London: Duckworth, 1985) and W. J. West (ed.) *The War Commentaries* (London: Duckworth, 1985).

7. 'Dialogism', the orientation of a person's utterance toward the utterance of another person, is one of a cluster of valuable ideas drawn from the work of the Russian linguist Mikhail Bakhtin; others are 'heteroglossia' which is the basis for my Chapter 6 and later discussion in the present book, and 'polyphony' which structures the argument of the last section of Chapter 6. Cf. note 8 below for the reference to 'carnival'. Bakhtin's most influential work, first published in 1929 but not known in the West until translated into French and English in the late 1960s and early 1970s, is *Problems of Dostoevsky's Poetics*, the definitive translation of which is by Caryl Emerson (Manchester: Manchester University Press, 1984). Accounts of Bakhtin's ideas include M. Holquist, *Dialogism: Bakhtin and His World* (London: Routledge, 1990); T. Marshall, 'Dialogism' in R. E. Asher (ed.) *The Encyclopedia of Language and Linguistics* (Oxford: Pergamon Press, 1994) IV, pp. 908–14.

8. '[T]hey are a sort of saturnalia, a harmless rebellion against virtue' (*CEJL*, II, p. 194). Orwell's idea of the comic postcards as a harmless rebellion may be related to Bakhtin's notion of 'carnival': see *Rabelais and his World*, trans. H. Iswolsky (Bloomington: Indiana University Press, 1986).

9. H. Ringbom, *George Orwell as Essayist: A Stylistic Study* (Åbo: Åbo Akademi, 1973). Lists or series occur in Orwell in passages of rhetorical intensity which have different functions. With the lists in *Wigan Pier* compare the bazaar scene in *Burmese Days* (pp. 120–1 and see Ch. 7) and the account of the climax of Hate Week in *Nineteen Eighty-Four* (pp. 159–60).

10. G. Woodcock, *The Crystal Spirit* (London: Jonathan Cape, 1967).

11. R. Williams, *Orwell* (Glasgow: Fontana, 1971).

12. His views are arguably naive, oversimplified, and shallow, even if

one agrees with the broad sweep of them; but it is not the purpose of this book to evaluate his views.

13. On stereotyping through language, see R. Fowler, *Language in the News* (London: Routledge, 1991).

Chapter 5

1. See 'Why I write', *CEJL*, I, pp. 23–30; Letter to Henry Miller, *CEJL*, I, pp. 257–9.
2. Characteristic critical responses to Orwell's work are to be found in J. Meyers (ed.) *George Orwell: The Critical Heritage*, (London: Routledge and Kegan Paul, 1975). See also J. R. Hammond, *A George Orwell Companion* (London: Macmillan, 1982).
3. The photographs are not reproduced in the Penguin edition, but may be found in the Secker & Warburg edition of the complete novels, vol. 5 (1986).
4. The main influence on Orwell seems to have been the French novelist Emile Zola, whom he much admired. In 1940 he included Zola in a list of eleven 'writers I care most about and never grow tired of' (*CEJL*, II, 39). In 1932, with *Down and Out* recently finished, he tried to persuade Chatto & Windus to allow him to translate Zola (*CEJL*, I, 102). A book review of 1936 uses Zola as a standard of comparison, and produces a characteristic Orwellian simile in which the organicism of Zola is opposed to mechanical composition:

> The scenes of violence Zola describes in *Germinal* and *La Débâcle* are supposed to symbolize capitalist corruption, but they are also scenes. At his best, Zola is not synthetic. He works under a sense of compulsion, and not like an amateur cook following the instructions on a packet of Crestona cake-flour. (*CEJL*, I, 279)

5. J. R. Hammond, *A George Orwell Companion* (London: Macmillan, 1982) p. 40; cf. pp. 36–7, 99; and p. 83 for the quotation from Orwell on Dickens.
6. An illuminating, if difficult, account of the way readers produce a coherent, integrated model of the content of a text on the basis of textual cues (which give incomplete information) and their existing knowledge of the world is given in R. de Beaugrande and W. Dressler, *Introduction to Text Linguistics* (London: Longman, 1981) ch. 5.
7. The integration of separate components of a text depends on the reader bringing to bear whatever background knowledge s/he possesses from experience of the real, or other fictional, worlds. The question must be raised as to how accessible this particular world is to a modern reader. Clearly to Orwell and his narrator the shop was already old-fashioned by the late 1930s. I was born in 1938, the year before *Coming up for Air* was published, and, brought up in a rural area, can just about remember this kind of shop.
8. See B. Crick, *George Orwell: A Life* (London: Secker & Warburg,

234 NOTES

1980) ch. 6. Orwell's own account of the tramping, and of the interest
in unemployment, poverty and 'working-class conditions' which led
him to it, is well worth reading: see *Wigan Pier*, ch. See also 'The
Spike', 1931 (*CEJL*, I, pp. 58–66); and the preface to the 1935 French
edition of the *Down and Out*, translated by J. Meyers, *George Orwell:
The Critical Heritage* (London: Routledge & Kegan Paul, 1975) pp.
39–40.
9. Quoted in J. Meyers (ed.) *George Orwell: The Critical Heritage*
(London: Routledge & Kegan Paul, 1975), p. 42.
10. A simple practical suggestion: photocopies of the text and a highlighting pen are invaluable tools for revealing the kinds of lexical
pattern studied here, which are otherwise difficult to perceive in an
ordinary reading.
11. This passage, like many others in Orwell, is oppressively claustro-
phobic. Cf. the discussion of his descent of a coal-mine in chapter 2
of *Wigan Pier*, and the many references to the dimensions of small
rooms. Orwell was himself exceptionally tall and long-limbed for
his generation.
12. 'Labyrinth' recurs in Orwell; cf. *Wigan Pier*, p. 45, quoted on
p. 83, 'labyrinthine streets', *A Clergyman's Daughter*, p. 130; 'the labyrinthine world of doublethink', 'unseen labyrinth', 'the labyrinth
of London', *Nineteen Eighty-Four*, pp. 36, 39, 74.
13. This theoretical point is discussed in more detail in R. Fowler, *Linguistic Criticism* (Oxford: Oxford University Press, 1986) ch. 11.
14. 'Defamiliarisation', in the theories of the Russian formalists, is the
use of literary devices which shake readers out of automatic habits
of thought. See V. Shklovsky, 'Art as Technique' [1917] in L. T.
Lemon and M. J. Reis (eds) *Russian Formalist Criticism* (Lincoln:
University of Nebraska Press, 1965). There is considerable discussion
of the linguistics of defamiliarisation in R. Fowler, *Linguistic Criticism* (note 13).
15. Charles Dickens, *Hard Times* ed. by David Craig, (London: Penguin, 1985) p. 65.

Chapter 6

1. For reference to Bakhtin, see Chapter 4, note 7.
2. N. Page, *Speech in the English Novel* (London: Longman, 1973), Ch. 3.
3. Orwell's very distant, alienated, technique of heteroglossia would in
fact not have met with Bakhtin's approval. His discussion of
Dostoevsky makes it clear that he preferred the author to be attent-
ive to, and the reader to learn from, the novel points of view in the
alien voice; he did not approve of the use of social dialects and
idiosyncrasies to create 'objectivized', 'finalized' caricatures.
4. Page, *Speech in the English Novel*, p. 10.
5. G. N. Leech and M. H. Short, *Style in Fiction* (London: Longman,
1981) p. 163.
6. See Page, *Speech in the English Novel*, pp. 66–7, on *Wuthering Heights*.

7. J. C. Wells, *Accents of English*, vol. 2 (Cambridge: Cambridge University Press, 1982) pp. 301–2. Wells underlines the continuing importance of Cockney when he points out that this 'working-class accent is today the most influential source of phonological innovation in England and perhaps in the whole English-speaking world' (p. 301).

8. See A. C. Baugh and T. Cable, *A History of the English Language*, London: Routledge, 1993) 4th edn, pp. 187–92 for a handy succinct account of the rise of Standard English, and p. 194 for further reading.

9. See P. Wright, *Cockney Dialect and Slang* (London: Batsford, 1981), Chapter 1; Wells., *Accents* pp. 332–4; Page, *Speech*, pp. 62–4 for brief accounts. For more detail, G. L. Brook, *The Language of Dickens* (London: Deutsch, 1970); P. J. Keating, *The Working Classes in Victorian Fiction* (London: Routledge & Kegan Paul, 1971) ch. 10.

10. Page, *Speech*, ch. 3.

11. Wells, *Accents*, p. 333, points out that Dickens was using a literary stereotype representing a dialect which was 'seriously out-of-date at the time he wrote'. George Bernard Shaw's plays *Captain Brassbound's Conversion* (1899) and *Pygmalion* (1920) are famous for their treatment of Cockney. Shaw uses a quasi-phonetic notation for the dialogue.

12. For a description of the phonology of London English, see Wells, *Accents*, pp. 301–332. Handy brief descriptions of the salient features may be found in A. Hughes and P. Trudgill, *English Accents and Dialects* (London: Edward Arnold, 1987) 2nd edn, pp. 44–8, and in S. Gramley and K-M. Pätzold, *A Survey of Modern English* (London: Routledge, 1992), pp. 328–30.

13. Gramley and Pätzold, *A Survey*, pp. 308–9 discuss the diffusion of non-standard features in General English, and provide a very helpful illustrated list of ten main types of deviation. For more details, see Hughes and Trudgill, *English Accents*, ch. 2.

14. Wright, *Cockney Dialect and Slang*, ch. 4 and pp. 51–4.

15. See P. Trudgill, *The Dialects of England* (Oxford: Blackwell, 1990) pp. 14–15 for an amusing brief note on differences in conversational style between dialect communities, in the course of which he contrasts Cockney and neighbouring East Anglian styles.

16. Hughes and Trudgill, *English Accents*, pp. 44, 46.

17. For these and other slang terms, see Eric Partridge, abridged by Jacqueline Simpson, *A Dictionary of Historical Slang* (Harmondsworth: Penguin, 1977).

18. Wright, *Cockney Dialect*, pp. 61 and the beginning of ch. 5.

19. M. A. K. Halliday, 'Antilanguages,' in *Language as Social Semiotic* (London: Edward Arnold, 1978) pp. 164–82.

20. Reprinted in A. V. Judges (ed.) *The Elizabethan Underworld* (London: Routledge & Kegan Paul, 1930, repr. 1965) pp. 381, 382. Judges is a good source for vagabond literature, glossaries on the slang, etc. See also A. F. Kinney (ed.) *Rogues, Vagabonds, and Sturdy Beggars* (Amherst: University of Massachusetts Press, 1990).

21. Wright, *Cockney Dialect*, pp. 20–1, and chs. 4 and 5.

22. Hughes and Trudgill, *English Accents*, p. 20.

23. Ibid, pp. 16–17.
24. The 'Circe' episode in *Ulysses* in turn recalls the encounter of Ulysses and his companions with Circe in the *Odyssey*, in which she turns them into swine, and the Hades sequence in the *Odyssey*.

    Important literary critical discussions of *Ulysses* and 'Circe' include S. Gilbert, *James Joyce's 'Ulysses'* (Harmondsworth: Penguin, 1963 [1930]); S. L. Goldberg, *The Classical Temper* (London: Chatto & Windus, 1961); J. H. Maddox, Jr., *Joyce's 'Ulysses' and the Assault upon Character* (Brighton: Harvester Press, 1978); C. H. Peake, *James Joyce* (London: Edward Arnold, 1977); J. P. Riquelme, *Teller and Tale in Joyce's Fiction* (Baltimore: Johns Hopkins University Press, 1983).
25. James Joyce, *Ulysses* (London: The Bodley Head, 1958) pp. 410–12.
26. The square brackets [ ] in this extract are in Orwell's text and do not indicate my own editorial amendments.
27. See S. C. Levinson, *Pragmatics* (Cambridge: Cambridge University Press, 1983) especially ch. 6; G. Brown and G. Yule, *Discourse Analysis* (Cambridge: Cambridge University Press, 1983).
28. Cf. J. P. Riquelme, *Teller and Tale in Joyce's Fiction* (Baltimore: Johns Hopkins University Press, 1983) p. 140.

Chapter 7

1. For discussion see Bernard Crick, *George Orwell: A Life* (London: Secker & Warburg, 1980) pp. 112–123.
2. Crick, Orwell, pp. 118–19. The opening, 'My epitaph by John Flory', is printed in *CEJL*, I, p. 166.
3. Orwell gives his own, subjective, account of his period in Burma in *The Road to Wigan Pier*, pp. 123–30.
4. E.g. J. R. Hammond, *A George Orwell Companion* (London: Macmillan, 1982) pp. 90–1.
5. The idea of focalisation provides for the technique, common in modern fiction, whereby events in a fiction are experienced by a consciousness separate from the narrator; it was clearly established by Gérard Genette: see his *Narrative Discourse*, trans. Jane E. Lewin (Ithaca, NY: Cornell University Press, 1980); for a well-illustrated introductory account, see Steven Cohan and Linda M. Shires, *Telling Stories: A Theoretical Analysis of Narrative Fiction* (London: Routledge, 1988) pp. 94–104.
6. T. S. Eliot, 'Hamlet and his Problems' (1919), repr. H. Adams (ed.) *Critical Theory since Plato* (New York: Harcourt Brace Jovanovich, 1971) pp. 778–90. The concept is part of the commonplaces of critical thinking, but is often felt not to be philosophically sound. For an account and a critique, see A. Preminger and T. V. F. Brogan (eds) *The New Princeton Encyclopedia of Poetry and Poetics* (Princeton, N.J: Princeton University Press, 1993) p. 848.
7. Orwell seems drawn to the visual kaleidoscope, thronging and 'hullabaloo' of markets as objects of description: compare *Aspidistra*, p. 113, *Coming Up for Air*, pp. 41–2.
8. For 'defamiliarisation', see references in Chapter 5, note 14.

Chapter 8

1. For modern linguistic approaches to point of view see R. Fowler, *Linguistic Criticism* (Oxford: Oxford University Press, 1986) ch. 9; P. Simpson, *Language, Ideology and Point of View* (London: Routledge, 1993).
2. On internal and external perspective, see R. Fowler, *Linguistics and the Novel* (London: Methuen, 1983) 2nd edn.
3. See M. Bakhtin, trans. C. Emerson, *Problems of Dostoevsky's Poetics* (Manchester: Manchester University Press, 1984).
4. For an introduction to Joyce's techniques for representing consciousness, see Katie Wales, *The Language of James Joyce* (London: Macmillan, 1992) especially ch. 3.
5. For mind-style see my *Linguistics and the Novel* (London: Methuen, 1983), and G. Leech and M. Short, *Style in Fiction* (London: Longman, 1981).
6. See B. McHale, 'Free Indirect Discourse: A Survey of Recent Accounts,' *Poetics and the Theory of Literature*, 3 (1978) pp. 249–87; Leech and Short, *Style*; D. Cohn, *Transparent Minds: Narrative Modes for Presenting Consciousness in Fiction* (Princeton: Princeton University Press, 1978).
7. On the history and technique of stream of consciousness, and on Joyce's individual use of it, see Katie Wales, *The Language of James Joyce*, ch. 3 and references.
8. The first-person narrators of, respectively, Mark Twain's *Huckleberry Finn* (1884), F. Scott Fitzgerald's *The Great Gatsby* (1926) and J. D. Salinger's *The Catcher in the Rye* (1951).
9. On oral mode see R. Fowler, *Language in the News* (London: Routledge, 1991) pp. 59–65.
10. See R. Fowler, 'The Referential Code and Narrative Authority,' in *Literature as Social Discourse* (London: Batsford, 1981) ch. 6.
11. The original discussion of *skaz* is B. Eichenbaum, 'Kak sdelana "Shinel"', which first appeared in *Poetika* in 1919. There are two translations, 'The structure of Gogol's "The Overcoat"', trans. Beth Paul and Muriel Nesbitt, *Russian Review*, 22 (1963) pp. 377–99; 'How Gogol's "Overcoat" is made,' trans. Robert A. Maguire, in Maguire (ed.) *Gogol from the Twentieth Century* (Princeton, New Jersey, 1974: Princeton University Press). The idea is developed in M. Bakhtin, *Problems of Dostoevsky's Poetics*, pp. 185ff.

Chapter 9

1. Quoted in Crick, *George Orwell: A Life* (London: Secker & Warburg, 1980) pp. 262–3.
2. Ibid, pp. 262–3 and 273 'When he wrote *Animal Farm* and then *Nineteen Eighty-Four*, he must have assumed that people knew already where he stood politically, would recognise the assumptions behind his satires'.
3. The text is reproduced in the first edition of Crick, *Orwell*, pp. 407–9.

4. Windmills (arguably, grotesque objects in themselves) have popularly symbolised human delusion ever since Don Quixote jousted at one in Cervantes's tale *Don Quixote*, thinking it was a giant; hence the expression 'tilting at windmills' applied to someone who foolishly attacks a position which is a figment of his own imagination.

5. Aesop, *Fables*, trans. by S. A. Handford (Harmondsworth: Penguin, 1954).

6. See J. R. Hammond, *A George Orwell Companion* (London: Macmillan, 1982), pp. 160–2; Valerie Meyers, *George Orwell* (London: Macmillan, 1991) pp. 104–8.

7. Letter to Leonard Moore, quoted in Hammond, *Orwell Companion* p. 162.

8. Letter to Orwell quoted in Crick, *George Orwell: A Life*, p. 340. Empson's study of the essential plurality of meaning in literature is *Seven Types of Ambiguity* (London: Chatto & Windus, 1930).

9. G. Woodcock, *The Crystal Spirit* (London: Jonathan Cape, 1967) p. 156.

10. W. J. West suggests that the simple style and conciseness of *Animal Farm*, as well as the speed at which it was written, owe much to the work that Orwell was doing towards the end of his period at the BBC, namely, the adaptation of stories for broadcast. Clearly a concise and clear product was required; and Orwell apparently worked on these adaptations at great speed, under much pressure from administrative business, often having only one day to rewrite a story. One of the texts he adapted was Ignazio Silone's *The Fox*, according to West 'a political allegory set in a pig farm'. See W. J. West, *Orwell: The War Broadcasts* (London: Duckworth, 1985) pp. 60–61, and *The Larger Evils* (Edinburgh: Canongate Press, 1992) pp. 64–5.

11. Hammond, *Orwell Companion*, p. 164.

12. On 'we' and consensus in public discourse, see R. Fowler, *Language in the News* (London: Routledge, 1991); J. Hartley, *Understanding News* (London: Methuen, 1982).

13. On speech acts, see J. R. Searle, *Speech Acts* (Cambridge: Cambridge University Press, 1969); S. C. Levinson, *Pragmatics* (Cambridge: Cambridge University Press, 1983).

Chapter 10

1. Examples occur in the British 'broadsheet' newspapers every few days. For instance, on the day this note was written, 21 August 1994, *The Sunday Times* had a headline which quipped **'Help! Big-brother Clinton's telling lies on TV again'**; the President's over-exposure on television was referred to as 'an Orwellian plague', and the Clintons were 'the Orwellian Clintons'. Coincidentally, but testifying to the continuing importance of Orwell as an ideological point of reference, another section of the same newspaper that day had an article on popular British humour which discussed and quoted Orwell's essay

'The art of Donald McGill'. The *Independent* newspaper during the following week quoted Orwell on sport in a leader on the use of drugs in athletics, and headed a feature article on the animal liberation movement **'Four Legs Good, Two Legs Bad'**.

2. W. J. West, *The Larger Evils: 'Nineteen Eighty-Four', The Truth Behind the Satire* (Edinburgh: Canongate Press, 1992).

3. Press Release, 15 June 1949, replying to some reviews. Reprinted in B. Crick (ed.) *Nineteen Eighty-Four* (Oxford: Clarendon Press, 1984) pp. 152–3.

4. *CEJL*, IV, p. 564.

5. W. Steinhoff, *George Orwell and the Origins of 1984* (Ann Arbor: University of Michigan Press, 1975). There are also references in B. Crick (ed.) *Orwell: Nineteen Eighty-Four* (Oxford: Clarendon Press, 1984) and in the usual critical introductions, e.g. Valerie Meyers, George Orwell (London: Macmillan, 1991) pp. 116–19).

6. Meyers, *Orwell*, p. 132.

7. George Eliot, *Middlemarch* [1871–2] (Harmondsworth: Penguin, 1972) p. 29.

8. Cf. p. 138 'She was one of those people who can go to sleep at any hour and in any position': Winston, apparently, on Julia, but the ensuing comments could well be construed as authorial, exceptionally in this book. Another rare comment on Winston occurs earlier in the same scene, when Julia puts on make-up: 'It was not very skilfully done, but Winston's standards in such matters were not high' (p. 126).

9. See extracts in Irving Howe (ed.) *Orwell's 'Nineteen Eighty-Four'* (New York: Harcourt, Brace and World, 1963) pp. 163–8.

10. P. 137; cf. p. 73 'the solid world exists'. Orwell's respect for 'solid objects' is voiced in 'Why I Write': see Ch. 3, p. above.

11. 'Sanguine' is in fact used in the learned, old-fashioned sense derived from the medieval theory of the 'Humours', a particular kind of personality inferred from a red complexion.

12. The image is usually said to be borrowed from Jack London, *The Iron Heel* (1909); see Steinhoff, *Orwell and the Origins of 1984* pp. 10–13 and Crick, (ed.) *Nineteen Eighty Four*, note 96, p. 448.

13. On 'estrangement devices' including expressions like 'as though', 'seemed' which are classically associated with external perspective in English, see R. Fowler, *Linguistics and the Novel* (London: Methuen, 1983) 2nd edn.

14. There are other styles coming from within Winston that there has been no space to analyse, for example the hysterical, semi-literate style of his diary entries (pp. 12–13, 20, 21, 59, 62, 63, 65, 72, 73); his own selfish 'booming' and 'snivelling' tones as a boy (pp. 143–4).

15. B. Crick (ed.) *George Orwell: 'Nineteen Eighty-Four'* (Oxford: Clarendon Press, 1984), text p. 165 and note 22, p. 433; he claims that 'speech' is a misreading of the Orwell typescript.

16. In its context, the metaphor echoes Orwell's description of an incident which, he said, inspired the story of *Animal Farm:*

I saw a little boy, perhaps ten years old, driving a huge cart-horse along a narrow path, whipping it whenever it tried to turn. It struck me that if only such animals became aware of their strength we should have no power over them, and that men exploit animals in much the same way as the rich exploit the proletariat. (Preface to the Ukranian edition of *Animal Farm*, 1947, *CEJL*, III, 458–9.)

17. Usually cited in this connection is Eugene Lyons, *Assignment in Utopia* (New York: Harcourt Brace, 1937), which Orwell reviewed in 1938 (*CEJL*, I, pp. 368–71). Lyons was a correspondent in Russia for the United Press Agency 1928–34. His book gives an example of cablese, p. 338; samples are printed in Steinhoff, *Orwell and the Origins of 'Nineteen Eighty-Four'* p. 169, and Crick, ed. p. 430. To confirm the influence of *Assignment in Utopia* on *Nineteen Eighty-Four*, note that Lyons quotes and discusses the formula '2 + 2 = 5' used by the Soviets to sloganise 'The Five-Year Plan in Four Years': see Crick, ed. *Orwell: Nineteen Eighty Four* p. 440 and, for more detail and a quotation from *Assignment*, Steinhoff, *Origins of Nineteen Eighty Four*, pp. 172–3.

18. On the peculiar and reality-changing features of news discourse, see A. Bell, *The Language of News Media* (Oxford: Blackwell, 1991); R. Fowler, *Language in the News* (London: Routledge, 1991).

19. See B. L. Whorf, *Language, Thought and Reality* ed. by J. B. Carroll (Cambridge, Mass.: MIT Press, 1956); R. Brown, *Words and Things* (New York: Free Press, 1958); H. H. Clark and E. V. Clark, *Psychology and Language* (New York: Harcourt Brace Jovanovich, 1977), chs. 13 and 14; R. Fowler, *Language in the News*, ch. 3.

20. A handy synopsis of Basic, together with a reproduction of the original 850-word vocabulary, is contained in D. Crystal, *The Cambridge Encyclopedia of Language* (Cambridge: Cambridge University Press, 1987) p. 356.

21. Jonathan Swift, *Gulliver's Travels* ed. by Robert A. Greenberg, (New York: W. W. Norton, 1961).

22. Beyond these three comparisons of class-division, lack of creativity, and fixity of 'meaning', the analogy breaks down, of course, and it would be misleading to pursue it.

23. See R. Fowler, R. Hodge, G. Kress and T. Trew, *Language and Control* (London: Routledge & Kegan Paul, 1979); N. Fairclough, *Language and Power* (London: Longman, 1989).

24. On the jargon of CB radio as 'antilanguage,' see M. Montgomery, *An Introduction to Language and Society* (London: Routledge, 1986) pp. 93–101.

Bibliography

ADAMS, H. (ed.) *Critical Theory since Plato* (New York: Harcourt, Brace, Jovanovich, 1971).

AESOP, *Fables* trans. by S. A. Handford (Harmondsworth: Penguin, 1954).

BAKHTIN, M., *Problems of Dostoevsky's Poetics* trans. by C. Emerson, *[1929]* (Manchester: Manchester University Press, 1984).

BAKHTIN, M., *Rabelais and his World* trans. by H. Iswolsky (Bloomington: Indiana University Press, 1986).

BAUGH, A. C. and CABLE, T., *A History of the English Language* (London: Routledge, 1993) 4th edn.

BEAUGRANDE, R. de and DRESSLER, W., *Introduction to Text Linguistics* (London: Longman, 1981).

BELL, A., *The Language of News Media* (Oxford: Blackwell, 1991).

BENNETT, T., *Formalism and Marxism* (London: Methuen, 1979).

BIRCH, D., *Language, Literature and Critical Practice* (London: Routledge, 1989).

BIRCH, D. and O'TOOLE, M., *Functions of Style* (London: Pinter, 1988).

BROOK, G. L., *The Language of Dickens* (London: Deutsch, 1970).

BROWN, G. and YULE, G., *Discourse Analysis* (Cambridge: Cambridge University Press, 1983).

BROWN, R., *Words and Things* (New York: Free Press, 1958).

BUDDICOM, J., *Eric and Us: A Remembrance of George Orwell* (London: Frewin, 1974).

CARTER, R. (ed.) *Language and Literature: An Introductory Reader in Stylistics* (London: Allen & Unwin, 1982).

CARTER, R. and SIMPSON, P. (eds) *Language, Discourse and Literature: An Introductory Reader in Discourse Stylistics* (London: Unwin Hyman, 1989).

CLARK, H. H. and CLARK, E. V., *Psychology and Language* (New York: Harcourt, Brace, Jovanovich, 1977).

CLUYSENAAR, A., *Introduction to Literary Stylistics* (London: Batsford, 1976).

COHAN, S. and SHIRES, L.M., *Telling Stories: A Theoretical Analysis of Narrative Fiction* (London: Routledge, 1988).

COHN, D., *Transparent Minds: Narrative Modes for Presenting Consciousness in Fiction* (Princeton: Princeton University Press, 1978).

CRICK, B., *George Orwell: A life* (London: Secker & Warburg, 1980, 2nd edn, 1992).

CRICK, B. (ed.) *George Orwell: Nineteen Eighty-Four* (Oxford: Clarendon Press, 1984).

CRYSTAL, D., *The Cambridge Encyclopedia of Language* (Cambridge: Cambridge University Press, 1987).

CULLER, J., *Structuralist Poetics* (London: Routledge & Kegan Paul, 1975).

DICKENS, C., *Hard Times* ed. by D. Craig (London: Penguin, 1985).

EHRMANN, J. (ed.) *Structuralism* (New York: Doubleday-Anchor, 1970).

EICHENBAUM, B., 'How Gogol's 'Overcoat' is made', trans. by R. A. Maguire, in Maguire (ed.) *Gogol from the Twentieth Century* (Princeton: Princeton University Press, 1974).

ELIOT, G., *Middlemarch* [1871–2] (Harmondsworth: Penguin, 1972).

ELIOT, T. S., 'Hamlet and his Problems,' [1919], repr. H. Adams (ed.) *Critical Theory since Plato* (New York: Harcourt, Brace, Jovanovich, 1971) pp. 788–90.

EMPSON, W., *Seven Types of Ambiguity* (London: Chatto & Windus, 1930).

ERLICH, V., *Russian Formalism: History, Doctrine* (The Hague: Mouton, 1965).

FAIRCLOUGH, N., *Language and Power* (London: Longman, 1989).

FOWLER, R., *Language in the News* (London: Routledge, 1991).

FOWLER, R., *Linguistic Criticism* (Oxford: Oxford University Press, 1986).

FOWLER, R., *Linguistics and the Novel* (London: Methuen, 1983) 2nd edn.

FOWLER, R., *Literature as Social Discourse* (London: Batsford Academic, 1981).

FOWLER, R., 'Oral Models in the Press,' in M. Maclure, T. Phillips and A.Wilkinson (eds) *Oracy Matters* (Milton Keynes: Open University Press, 1988) pp. 135–46.

FOWLER, R., HODGE, R., KRESS, G., and TREW, T., *Language and Control* (London: Routledge & Kegan Paul, 1979).

FREEMAN, D. C. (ed.) *Linguistics and Literary Style* (New York: Holt, Rinehart & Winston, 1970).

GENETTE, G., *Narrative Discourse* trans. by J. E. Lewin, (Ithaca, New York: Cornell University Press, 1980).

GILBERT, S., *James Joyce's 'Ulysses' [1930]* (Harmondsworth: Penguin, 1963).

GOLDBERG, S.L., *The Classical Temper* (London: Chatto & Windus, 1961).

GRAMLEY, S., and PÄTZOLD, K-M., *A Survey of Modern English* (London: Routledge, 1992).

HALLIDAY, M. A. K., 'Antilanguages,' in *Language as Social Semiotic* (London: Edward Arnold, 1978) pp. 164–82.

HALLIDAY, M. A. K., *An Introduction to Functional Grammar* (London: Edward Arnold, 1985).

HALLIDAY, M. A. K., *Language as Social Semiotic* (London: Edward Arnold, 1978).

HALLIDAY, M. A. K., 'Language Structure and Language Function', in J. Lyons (ed.) *New Horizons in Linguistics* (Harmondsworth: Penguin, 1970).

HALLIDAY, M. A. K., 'Linguistic Function and Literary Style: An Inquiry into the Language of William Golding's *The Inheritors*', in S. Chatman (ed.) *Literary Style: A Symposium* (New York and Oxford: Oxford University Press, 1971) pp. 330–64.

HALLIDAY, M. A. K., 'The Linguistic Study of Literary Texts', reprinted in S. Chatman and S. R. Levin (eds) *Essays on the Language of Literature* (Boston: Houghton Mifflin, 1967).

HALLIDAY, M. A. K., *Spoken and Written Language* (Oxford: Oxford University Press, 1989).

HALLIDAY, M. A. K., 'Spoken and Written Modes of Meaning', in R. Horowitz and S. Jay Samuels (eds) *Comprehending Oral and Written Language* (San Diego: Academic Press, 1987) pp. 55–82.

HALLIDAY, M. A. K., McINTOSH, A. and STREVENS, P., *The Linguistic Sciences and Language Teaching* (London: Longman, 1964).

HAMMOND, J. R., *A George Orwell Companion* (London: Macmillan, 1982).

HARTLEY, J., *Understanding News* (London: Methuen, 1982).

HAWKES, T., *Structuralism and Semiotics* (London: Methuen, 1979).

HODGE, R., and KRESS, G., *Language as Ideology* ([*1979*]; (London: Routledge, 1993) 2nd edn.

HOLQUIST, M., *Dialogism: Bakhtin and his World* (London: Routledge, 1990).

HOWE, I. (ed.) *Orwell's 'Nineteen Eighty-Four'* (New York: Harcourt, Brace & World, 1963).

HUGHES, A., and TRUDGILL, P., *English Accents and Dialects* (London: Edward Arnold, 1987) 2nd edn.

JAKOBSON, R., 'Closing Statement: Linguistics and Poetics,' in T. A. Sebeok (ed.) *Style in Language* (Cambridge, Massachusetts: MIT Press, 1960) pp. 350–77.

JOYCE, J., *Ulysses* (London: The Bodley Head, 1958).

JUDGES, A. V. (ed.) *The Elizabethan Underworld* (London: Routledge & Kegan Paul, 1930, repr. 1965).

KEATING, P. J., *The Working Classes in Victorian Fiction* (London: Routledge & Kegan Paul, 1971).

'KINGMAN REPORT': *Report of the Committee of Enquiry into the Teaching of English Language* (London: Her Majesty's Stationery Office, 1988).

KINNEY, A. F. (ed.) *Rogues, Vagabonds, and Sturdy Beggars* (Amherst: University of Massachusetts Press, 1990).

LEE, R. A., *Orwell's Fiction* (Notre Dame: University of Notre Dame Press, 1969).

LEECH, G. N., *A Linguistic Guide to English Poetry* (London: Longman, 1969).

LEECH, G. N. and SHORT, M. H., *Style in Fiction* (London: Longman, 1981).

LEMON, L. T. and REIS, M. J., *Russian Formalist Criticism* (Lincoln: University of Nebraska Press, 1965).

LEVINSON, S. C., *Pragmatics* (Cambridge: Cambridge University Press, 1983).

LYONS, E., *Assignment in Utopia* (New York: Harcourt Brace, 1937).

McHALE, B., 'Free Indirect Discourse: A Survey of Recent Accounts,' *Poetics and the Theory of Literature*, 3 (1978) pp. 249–87.

MACLURE, M., PHILLIPS, T. and WILKINSON, A. (eds) *Oracy Matters* (Milton Keynes: Open University Press, 1988).

MADDOX, J. H., Jr., *Joyce's 'Ulysses' and the Assault upon Character* (Brighton: Harvester, 1978).

MARSHALL, T., 'Dialogism', in R. E. Asher (ed.) *The Encyclopedia of Language and Linguistics* (Oxford: Pergamon Press, 1994), IV pp. 908–14.

MEYERS, J. (ed.) *George Orwell: The Critical Heritage* (London: Routledge & Kegan Paul, 1975).

MEYERS, V., *George Orwell* (London: Macmillan, 1991).

MILROY, L. and MILROY, J., *Authority in Language* (London: Routledge & Kegan Paul, 1985).

MONTGOMERY, M., *An Introduction to Language and Society* (London: Routledge, 1986).

PAGE, N., *Speech in the English Novel* (London: Longman, 1973).

PARTRIDGE, E., abridged J. Simpson, *A Dictionary of Historical Slang* (Harmondsworth: Penguin, 1977).

PEAKE, C. H., *James Joyce* (London: Edward Arnold, 1977).

PREMINGER, A. and BROGAN, T. V. F. (eds) *The New Princeton Encyclopedia of Poetry and Poetics* (Princeton, New Jersey: Princeton University Press, 1993).

RINGBOM, H., *George Orwell as Essayist: A Stylistic Study* ((Åbo: Åbo Akademi, 1973)

RIQUELME, J. P., *Teller and Tale in Joyce's Fiction* (Baltimore: Johns Hopkins University Press, 1983).

SAUSSURE, F. de, *Course in General Linguistics* [1916] tráns. by W. Baskin, reprinted with an introduction by J. Culler (Glasgow: Fontana, 1974).

SEARLE, J. R., *Speech Acts* (Cambridge: Cambridge University Press, 1969).

SHELDON, M., *Orwell: The Authorised Biography* (London: Heinemann, 1991).

SIMPSON, P., *Language, Ideology and Point of View* (London: Routledge, 1993).

STANSKY, P. and ABRAHAMS, W., *The Unknown Orwell* (London: Constable, 1972).

STANSKY, P. and ABRAHAMS, W., *Orwell: The Transformation* (London: Constable, 1979).

STEINHOFF, W., *George Orwell and the Origins of '1984'* (Ann Arbor: University of Michigan Press, 1975).

SVARTVIK, J. and QUIRK, R. (eds) *A Corpus of English Conversation* (Lund: C. W. K. Gleerup, 1980).

SWIFT, J., *Gulliver's Travels* [1726] ed. by R. A. Greenberg (New York: W. W. Norton, 1961).

TANNEN, D. (ed.) *Spoken and Written Language: Exploring Orality and Literacy* (Norwood, New Jersey: Ablex, 1982).

TOOLAN, M., *Narrative: A Critical Linguistic Introduction* (London: Routledge, 1988).

TOOLAN, M. (ed.) *Language, Text and Context: Essays in Stylistics* (London: Routledge, 1992).

TRUDGILL, P., *The Dialects of England* (Oxford: Blackwell, 1990).

WALES, K., *A Dictionary of Stylistics* (London: Longman, 1989).

WALES, K., *The Language of James Joyce* (London: Macmillan, 1992).

WELLS, J. C., *Accents of English* (Cambridge: Cambridge University Press, 1982).

WEST, W. J., *The Larger Evils*: Nineteen Eighty-Four: *The Truth Behind the Satire* (Edinburgh: Canongate Press, 1992).

WEST, W. J. (ed.) *Orwell: The War Broadcasts* (London: Duckworth, 1985).

WHORF, B. L., *Language, Thought and Reality* ed. by J. B. Carroll (Cambridge, Massachusetts: MIT Press, 1956).

WIDDOWSON, H. G., *Stylistics and the Teaching of Literature* (London: Longman, 1975).

WILLIAMS, R., *Orwell* (Glasgow: Fontana, 1971).

WILLIAMS, R. (ed.) *George Orwell: A Collection of Critical Essays* (Englewood Cliffs, New Jersey: Prentice-Hall, 1974).

WOODCOCK, G., *The Crystal Spirit* (London: Jonathan Cape, 1967).

WRIGHT, P., *Cockney Dialect and Slang* (London: Batsford, 1981).

Index

Notes: the index covers the main text and substantial points mentioned in the Notes; names in the Notes and Bibliography are not indexed; page numbers which refer to the definition or first discussion of technical terms are printed in **bold type**.

accent 93–109
Aesop 161
Amis, Kingsley, *Lucky Jim* 141
animal imagery 57
antihero 141
antilanguage 96, **105–6**, 207
archaism **29**, 212

Bacon, Francis 49
Bakhtin, Mikhail viii, 89, 137, 155, 232 note 7, 234 note 3
Basic English 220–1, 226
Blair, Eileen (O'Shaughnessey) 3, 4, 5, 159
Blair, Richard 5
borrowings **29**, 212
Brontë, Emily 92
Burgess, Anthony 62
Burnham, James, *The Managerial Revolution* 184

cablese 215–16
carnival 46, 232 note 8
Chaucer, Geoffrey 87
Cockney 17, 21, 22, 89, 95–106, 129, 133, 207–11
Common, Jack 25–6, 27, 89
conversation 114–15
Crick, Bernard 35–6, 120
cue **39–40**, 63, 131, 196, 232 note 5

Day Lewis, C. 71
dead metaphors **29**, 212

defamiliarisation 79, 129, **234** note 14
Dekker, Thomas, 'The Canting Song' 105–6
demotic speech **24–5**, 34, 35, 41, 43, 87, 92, 150, 153, 169, 197
descriptive realism 61, **63–4**, 65, 142
dialect 37, 38, 92–3, 93–109, 116
dialogism **45**, 54, 150, 153–5, 175–6, 232 note 7
Dickens, Charles 11, 50, 65, 92, 96–9, 137
  Bleak House 96, 97, 98
  Hard Times 21, 85–6
  Oliver Twist 96, 98
  The Pickwick Papers 96
Dostoevsky, F. 89
  Notes from Underground 141
dual voice *see* free indirect discourse
duckspeak 214–15, 219

East Anglian dialect 108–9
Eichenbaum, Boris 155
Eliot, George 50, 137
  Middlemarch 138, 187
  The Mill on the Floss 138
Eliot, T. S. 7, 122
Empson, William 163
external perspective *see* internal and external perspective

246

Faulkner, William
  As I Lay Dying 139
  The Sound and the Fury 139
Fielding, Henry 92
first-person narration 149–58
Fitzgerald, F. Scott, *The Great
  Gatsby* 149
focalisation viii, 121, **139**, 140,
  143–8, 164, 170–4, 184–91,
  236 note 5
Forster, E. M., *A Passage to
  India* 62
free direct discourse 146–8
free indirect discourse 139, 143–8
  (**143–4**), 190
functional grammar **15**
Fyvel, Tosco 159

Gaskell, Elizabeth 92
generalisation 47, 187
Genette, Gérard 139
Gollancz, Victor 82
Gorer, Geoffrey 159
grotesque 170–1, 203–5

Halliday, M. A. K. 12–13, 15,
  18, 27, 38, 105
Hammond, J.R. 65, 171
Hardy, Thomas 50, 92
Henson, Francis A. 183
heteroglossia 63, **88–90**, 107,
  109–110, 119, 129–35, 137,
  142–3, 158, 182, 203–11
Huxley, Aldous, *Brave New
  World* 184
hyperbole 45, 53, 54
hyperrealism *see* surrealism
hypotaxis and parataxis **43**, 48,
  54, 91, 152, 167

idiolect 9, 37, **39**, 53–4, 93–4,
  116–17, 130–5
information units in speech 26,
  152–3
interior monologue 139
internal and external
  perspective **138**, 170–1, 201
Irish English 107–8

Jakobson, Roman 12
jargon **29**, 212
Joyce, James vii, 139, 160
  *A Portrait of the Artist as a
  Young Man* 139, 140
  Ulysses 3, 7, 36, 110–12, 118,
  138, 140, 146–7
judgement 81–3

Kipling, Rudyard 62

language and class 20–2
language and thought 31–4
Larkin, Philip 87
Lawrence, D. H. vii, 7, 92, 139,
  160
  Lady Chatterley's Lover 22
  Sons and Lovers 138, 140
Leech, Geoffrey 91, 92
Lewis, Wyndham 22
linguistic criticism viii, **11–18**,
  229–30 note 10
linguistic determinism 218–19
linguistic varieties 37–41
linguistics 13–14
literary competence 14, 229 note 9

marked and unmarked **91–2**
meaningless words **29**, 212
Meyers, Valerie 187
Miller, Henry 120, 121
Milroy, James, and Milroy,
  Lesley 28
mind-style **140**, 149, 185, 189
modality **49–52**, 168
mode 26, **37–8**
  oral mode 54, 150, **151–3**
monologism **137**, 138

Nabokov, Vladimir, *Lolita* 140
naturalism 61, **64**, 65, 70–9,
  79–80, 142, 195–9
negativity 45, 53, 54, 57
Newspeak 31, 33, 181, 182, 184,
  207, 211–27
nominalism and realism **31–3**

objective correlative **122**, 139

official English ('stripe-trouser') 27

Ogden, C. K. 220

omniscient author 49–50, 138, 187

oral mode *see* mode

Orwell, George: general
life and career Ch. 1
personal voice 17, Ch. 4, 143, 157
styles 7–11, 15–18, 119, 141–3
views on language Ch. 3, 164–5

Orwell, George: writings
Animal Farm vii, 5, 7, 9, 11, 20, 36, 57, 60, 61, 63, 90, 119, 138, 141, Ch. 9, 181, 182, 183, 238 note 10
'The Art of Donald McGill' 44–6, 54
'As I Please' 4, 41, 119
Burmese Days 2, 3, 10, 15, 36, 40, 61, 64, 68–70, 88, 90, 93, 110, 119, Ch. 7, 138, 139–40, 184, 203
A Clergyman's Daughter 2, 4, 10, 15, 21, 61, 64, 88, 89, 93, 95, 101–6, 107, 109–118, 129, 138, 140, 207
Collected Essays, Journalism and Letters 7, 41
Coming Up for Air 3, 4, 7, 35, 61, 62, 65–8, 87, 93, 136, 138, 139, 140, 148–58, 159, 160, 175, 184, 187, 190, 193, 196, 214
Down and Out in Paris and London 2, 7, 10, 21, 39, 40, 61, 62, 63, 70–9, 81, 88, 89, 90, 93–5, 98, 99–101, 102, 103, 107, 109, 129, 136, 137, 169, 203, 207
'The English People' 22, 24, 26, 27–8, 30, 41, 217
'A Farthing Newspaper' 8, 35
'A Hanging' 8, 41, 126–7
Homage to Catalonia 3, 10, 11, 40–1, 54, 61, 62, 63, 64, 79–80, 81, 127, 136, 141

'Hop-picking' 20
Inside the Whale 4, 159
'John Flory' 120, 121
Keep the Aspidistra Flying 3, 4, 10, 61, 74, 87, 88, 93, 110, 136, 138, 139, 140–8, 160, 184, 190, 195, 196, 206, 207
The Lion and the Unicorn 3, 159
'London Letters' 41
'The Moon under Water' 41
'New Words' 31–2
Nineteen Eighty-Four 4, 5, 6, 7, 10, 11, 16, 20, 21, 31, 33, 38, 57, 60, 61, 63, 65, 74, 87, 88, 89, 90, 103, 136, 138, 141, 158, 160, 175, 178, 179, Ch. 10
'Politics and the English Language' 8, 15, 19, 20, 30, 33, 38, 127, 169, 175, 180, 212, 213, 217
'The Prevention of Literature' 41, 46–8, 52
'Propaganda and Demotic Speech' 22, 24, 26
'The Question of the Pound Award' 8–9
Review of Winston Churchill, *Their Finest Hour* 6
The Road to Wigan Pier 3, 22, 55–9, 61, 62, 63, 70, 71, 74, 78, 81–6, 136, 141, 157, 169, 198
'Shooting an Elephant' 41, 42–4, 51
'Some Thoughts on the Common Toad' 41
'Why I Write' 19, 25, 36, 120, 122, 163, 182

Page, Norman 90–1, 93, 96
parataxis *see* hypotaxis and parataxis
parody 10, 17, 217–18
pastoral **64–5**, 142, 156–7, 193–5
persona **87**
picturesque **64**, 119–29

point of view in fiction Ch. 8
  (**136**)
polyphony 109–18 (**114**)
Prague Linguistic Circle 11–12
Priestley, J. B. 22, 25
Proust, Marcel 138

ready-made phrases **30**, 212
realism Ch. 5
realism and nominalism 31
Received Pronunciation
  ('RP') 22, 107
register 37, **38–9**, 45–6, 54, 173
rhetoric 174–80
Russian Formalism 11–12

Salinger, J. D., *The Catcher in the
  Rye* 140, 149
Sapir, Edward 218
Saussure, F. de 33
Scott, Sir Walter 92
semiotics 15
series **54**, 58–9
Short, Mick 91, 92
simile 126–7
skaz **155**, 157, 158
sociolect 37, 38, **39**, 93, 116,
  133
sordid realism *see* naturalism
speech and writing **25–8**, 230–1
  note 6
speech acts 177
speech representation 90–3
standard English 25–30, 90, 91,
  231 note 7
Steinhoff, William 184
stereotype 131, 155

stream of consciousness 139,
  146–8
stripe-trouser *see* official English
style **37**
stylistics 12–14
surrealism 61, **64**, 65, 70–9
swearing 100, 117
Swift, Jonathan 160, 211, 225
  Gulliver's Travels 161, 162,
    184, 219, 221–3
symbolism 84–6

Thackeray, W. M. 87
Thomas, Dylan, *Under Milk
  Wood* 117
Twain, Mark, *Huckleberry
  Finn* 149

Watson, Susan 5
Wells, H. G. 183
  When the Sleeper Awakes 184
Wells, J. C. 103, 108
West, W. J. 183
Whorf, Benjamin Lee 218
Williams, Raymond 55
Woodcock, George 55, 164
Woolf, Virginia vii, 7, 139
  To the Lighthouse 138
  Mrs Dalloway 140
Wordsworth, William 87
  'Preface to *Lyrical Ballads*' 24
Wright, P. 97, 98, 100

Yeats, W. B. 87

Zamyatin, Yevgeny, *We* 184, 191
Zola, Emile 72, 233 note 4